Penguin Books
GREEN ARMOUR

Osmar White (1909–91) was born in New Zealand
and educated in Sydney. As a young journalist he
roamed the Pacific islands and Asia for several years,
writing of his adventures in 'wildcat' mountaineering
and in exploration. At the outbreak of the Second
World War he went to New Guinea as a war correspondent: invalided out of New Guinea he was accredited to the US Pacific Fleet and later to the US Army
for the invasion of the Solomon Islands, where he was
wounded during a Japanese bomber attack. On
resuming active duty he transferred to the European
front, where he remained for the duration of the war
and represented all Australian newspapers at the official surrender by Germany. In the 1960s he became
a fulltime writer, his many successful publications
including children's books, travel guides and wine
books.

Sir Edward Dunlop, AC, CMG, OBE, KCSJ, MS, FRCS,
FRACS, FACS, LLD (Hon.), DSc. Punjabi (Hon.),
was born in 1907 near Shepparton in rural Victoria.
'Weary', as he was known, graduated in medicine and
surgery just before the outbreak of the Second World
War. He served with the AIF in the Middle East,
Europe and the Pacific during the war. Captured in
Java by the Japanese in 1942, he survived more than
three and a half years in some of the most notorious
Japanese prison camps; his devotion to his men and
his inspirational leadership are legendary. After his
return to Melbourne in 1945 Sir Edward continued to
practise as a surgeon and was actively involved in
community service in Australia and abroad. He was
knighted in 1969. *The War Diaries of Weary Dunlop*, his
bestselling account of prison-camp life, was published
in 1986. Sir Edward died in July 1993.

AUSTRALIAN 🐧 WAR CLASSICS

GREEN ARMOUR

OSMAR WHITE

Foreword by E.E. (Weary) Dunlop

PENGUIN BOOKS

PENGUIN BOOKS

Published by the Penguin Group
Penguin Group (Australia)
250 Camberwell Road, Camberwell, Victoria 3124, Australia
(a division of Pearson Australia Group Pty Ltd)
Penguin Group (USA) Inc.
375 Hudson Street, New York, New York 10014, USA
Penguin Group (Canada)
10 Alcorn Avenue, Toronto, Ontario, Canada M4V 3B2
(a division of Pearson Penguin Canada Inc.)
Penguin Books Ltd
80 Strand, London WC2R 0RL, England
Penguin Ireland
25 St Stephen's Green, Dublin 2, Ireland
(a division of Penguin Books Ltd)
Penguin Books India Pvt Ltd
11 Community Centre, Panchsheel Park, New Delhi – 110 017, India
Penguin Group (NZ)
Cnr Airborne and Rosedale Roads, Albany, Auckland, New Zealand
(a division of Pearson New Zealand Ltd)
Penguin Books (South Africa) (Pty) Ltd
24 Sturdee Avenue, Rosebank, Johannesburg 2196, South Africa

Penguin Books Ltd, Registered Offices: 80 Strand, London, WC2R 0RL, England

First published in Australia by Angus & Robertson, 1945
New edition published by Wren, 1972
First published by Penguin Books Australia Ltd, 1987

10 9 8 7 6

Text copyright © Osmar White 1945

Cover design by Adam Laszczuk © Penguin Group (Australia)
Cover photographs by Australian War Memorial Negative Numbers 069248 and REL29538
Printed in Australia by Mcpherson's Printing Pty Ltd

National Library of Australia
Cataloguing-in-Publication data:

White, Osmar, 1909–1991.
Green armour.
ISBN 0 140 147063.

I. –White, Osmar, 1909–1991. 2. World war, 1939–1945 – Campaigns – New Guinea.
3. World War, 1939 – 1945 – Personal narratives, New Zealand. I. Title. (Series: Australian war classics).

950.5426

www.penguin.com.au

FOREWORD

FIRST published in 1945, *Green Armour* has an extraordinary immediacy that conjures up only too well the grim days of fighting in the swamps, mountains and jungles of New Guinea and the Pacific islands in 1942 and 1943.

The early part of 1942 was a time of great peril for Australia. In only four months Japanese forces had occupied Malaya, Singapore, Burma, the Dutch East Indies, the Philippines, New Britain and the northern Solomon Islands. Australia, whose main fighting force was still in the Middle East, was now gravely threatened. Following the Allied victory in the Battle of the Coral Sea in May 1942, the battle moved to the jungle-covered mountainous terrain of New Guinea – the 'green armour' of Osmar White's title – that shielded Port Moresby and northern Australia.

The Japanese landing at Buna in northern Papua marked the beginning of a drawn-out conflict. Port Moresby, under constant air attack from February 1942, remained precariously in Australian hands; sparsely manned and equipped, it was often called 'the Tobruk of the Pacific'. Much was owed to the heroism of Australian airmen who defended the city in outgunned and outpaced aircraft. In the north, the pilots of commercial planes also rendered magnificent service, evacuating civilians from exposed coastal settlements as they fell to the Japanese.

Osmar White pays special tribute to 'Kanga Force', a guerilla group drawn from the New Guinea Volunteer Rifles and later assisted by a commando unit, which waged an 'invisible war' against the Japanese around Lae and Salamaua.

He records the awesome difficulties posed by the terrain in which they battled, and the physical realities of exhaustion, isolation and disease. The New Guinea Volunteer Rifles, at best only half-trained, performed heroically as scouts and in resistance activities: their ability to exploit the inhospitable landscape so successfully was to become a model for jungle warfare. White also describes the fortitude and devotion of the 'fuzzy wuzzy angels', the natives who acted as servants, guides, porters and stretcher-bearers, leaving Australian soldiers forever in their debt.

In the bloody and exhausting fighting across the Owen Stanley Range, the Allied troops not only did battle with an elusive enemy but also had to contend with formidable mountains, dense jungle, oppressive heat, pouring rain, dank mud, and disease. Even the battle-hardened Australian forces recalled from the Middle East suffered serious reverses in such hostile conditions. Osmar White depicts in vivid anecdotal style the sufferings experienced on the Kokoda Trail where the Japanese troops, seasoned experts in the art of jungle fighting, were finally repelled at great cost to the Allies.

In *Green Armour* I recognise leaders I knew in the Middle East, such as the commander of the New Guinea forces, General Rowell. To his cost Rowell clashed with General Blamey, who in 1942 was sent to New Guinea by General MacArthur to demand an offensive to retake Papua. Memories are also rekindled of that great soldier, George Vasey, who led the distinguished 7th Division in New Guinea. With New Guinea secured the struggle moved to the Solomon Islands, where the counter-offensive gathered strength with the build-up of US forces.

As Osmar White notes, *Green Armour* was written 'from the viewpoint of a man looking from the inside out, rather than from the outside looking in'. Few authors have shared the exertions and dangers that he writes about with such penetrating insight and controlled, unsentimental prose.

E. E. Dunlop

CONTENTS

AUTHOR'S FOREWORD

THIS is a story of fighting men in the swamps and jungles of New Guinea, in the islands and atolls and tangled waterways of the Solomon Islands. Its sources are four dog-eared notebooks marked *New Guinea, February-October, 1942,* a diary *With the U. S. Pacific Fleet, April-July, 1943,* a file of dispatches to Australian newspapers, and a recollection of certain places, things, men, and events which need no annotation to remain forever in memory.

There was a phase in the Pacific war when, because of unpreparedness, the Allied strategy was one of near-static defense, but in those days of patience strained to the breaking point, we learned how to beat the Japanese. That is what *Green Armour* is about.

The enemy's intensive study of climate and terrain in relation to a war in Southeast Asia and the Pacific islands was one of the prime reasons why the Japanese scored early and spectacular successes. The great problem in planning a counteroffensive was provided not by the intrinsic quality of the Japanese military machine, of its equipment and generalship, but by the apparent impenetrability of the equatorial wilderness in which the enemy was entrenched by reason of his early conquests.

When human history was beginning, New Guinea and the islands and seas surrounding it were already a barrier between two worlds. To the north and west were the animals and plants of Asia, and to the south and east were the animals and plants of Australia. There was little interpenetration.

9

The barrier stood through history, and today still stands. On New Guinea's narrow beaches the teeming east ends. Its mountains and jungles and rivers are the green armour guarding the empty south.

When World War II spread to New Guinea in 1942, very few people knew much about the region in which the first real trial of strength between Japan and the Western democracies was to take place. That terrain, which had through the ages remained a neutral division between two great areas of the earth's surface, was still largely terra incognita to the twentieth century. To most of the men destined to fight in and for them, those dark, fiercely inhospitable islands were as remote as the mountains of the moon.

Though nations had squabbled over possession of New Guinea, core of a great archipelago, it had resisted all but the most tenacious empire builders since its discovery by the Portuguese in the sixteenth century. The reason for its being one of the least explored and least exploited territories on earth lay in its physical nature.

The main island, shaped like a rearing dragon and lying just under the equator, has a spine of mountains 1,000 miles long. At the western end, snowcapped peaks rise to more than 16,000 feet. At the eastern end, the tallest soar between 13,000 and 14,000 feet, and are clothed almost to their summits in dense rain forests. From this mighty backbone of ranges, row upon row of razorbacks extend like herringbone, with roaring torrents in every canyon between them and everlasting rainclouds on every crest.

The drainage of the highlands flows through a multiplicity of streams into five major river systems – the Mamberamo, the Digoel, the Fly, the Sepik, and the Ramu.

Even as the mountains are an almost insuperable barrier between north and south, the great rivers, their tributaries and scores of lesser but still considerable streams bar free movement between east and west.

In any latitude a land so violently fashioned would resist settlement and civilization, but in addition, all of New Guinea lies within 11 degrees of the equator. It is drenched with flooding rains all the year round, except in the scattered 'dry belts' of the east. Its soil is fertile, and even the mountain precipices sprout forest. Wherever, by some caprice of nature, trees have not blanketed the face of the land, the grass grows 10 feet high. In the kunai grass country of the Ramu and the Markham rivers, it is recorded that some American paratroopers who landed for the airborne attack on Lae in September, 1943, collapsed within an hour from the effects of the tremendous heat and humidity.

In New Guinea lowlands, men may rot with malaria, typhus, leprosy, hookworm, yaws, and skin diseases of unimaginable variety. There, night and day, the moisture in the air condenses on every surface and trickles back to earth.

In the highlands, travellers may shiver in frost and hail or be drenched in downpours so violent that an inch of rain has been known to fall in five minutes. The only inhabitants are the small, dark, frizzy-haired peoples who still seek human heads for trophies and who live by primitive horticulture or by hunting the scarce game with blowpipes, darts and poisoned arrows.

Even though the existence of such a country be known to white men for more than 400 years and its potential wealth in minerals, oil and forest products suspected for half a century, it is not surprising that tens of thousands of square miles should still be unexplored. With the single exception of the goldfields in the Bulolo valley, white colonization has been limited to coastal strips where the sea offers lanes of communication denied by the jungle-smothered mountains and ravines.

Its discoverer was probably Antonio d'Abreuva, a Portuguese navigator who visited the island in 1511. One of his countrymen, Jorge de Menezes, named it in 1527, but in 1606 Torres annexed it to Spain. After 150 years that doubtful title lapsed, and in 1793 Britain assumed possession of it through the East India Company.

'Assuming possession' and effective occupation were, however, totally different things. In those days there were easier worlds to conquer, closer to home, and there is no record of British protest when in 1828 the Dutch, who had now firmly established their East Indian Empire, annexed all of the island

11

that lay west of the 141st meridian. The eastern half remained a no man's land for half a century longer, until competiton sharpened between German and British imperial expansion in the Pacific.

The great trading house of Godeffroy and Sons of Hamburg, building an empire within an empire in the Central Pacific, pressed the German government to make secure their increasing interests in the Bismark Archipelago. The Australian states, anxiously watching the uncertain currents of imperial politics in the Pacific, became aware for the first time of the no man's land just outside their northern gateway, and moved fast. At the orders of the Queensland government, the union jack was hoisted on the eastern end of the New Guinea mainland.

However, the British secretary of state for the Colonies did not want to provoke the Germans. He promptly repudiated the action of the Queensland government. Ownership of eastern New Guinea became the subject of diplomatic negotiation, with the Australian states worried over the prospect of 'rapidly becoming surrounded by French and German island possessions'.

In 1884 Germany took over the northern half of eastern New Guinea, together with the big islands of New Britain, New Ireland, Buka and Bougainville in the Solomon, the Marshall, the Caroline and the Pellew groups, and Nauru. The British set up a protectorate in the southern half of eastern New Guinea and over adjacent small islands. This final staking of claims, however, did not mean a great deal.

In the next 30 years, the only visible sign of development was the establishment of small European towns in Rabaul in New Britain and at Port Moresby in Papua. A number of plantations and missions sprang up at intervals around the coasts – in such places as Lae, Salamaua, Buna, Samarai, Finschafen and Wewak, made familiar to the world only since 1941 – but it was not until the gold discoveries of the middle twenties that these settlements grew to the proportion even of villages. Copra, pearls, bird of paradise skins, trochus shell and *bêche-de-mer* remained the region's chief products.

The Germans, operating under the aegis of the New Guinea Company until 1901, and thereafter under a regular colonial administration, developed their plantation holdings with comparative energy but did little to bring the hinterland under control, or even to explore it. They were content if their recruiters of native labour could carry on in the coast villages without molestation by head-hunters. Few of the white overseers ever penetrated the hills beyond the plantations for more than three or four miles.

The British in Papua, as the southeastern division of the territory was called, were less enterprising profit seekers, but made some effort to explore the area and to bring the native population under control. In the more accessible regions around Port Moresby and the southeastern tip of the island they succeeded, but the extensive swamps and mountains to the west defied even cursory exploration, let alone civilization.

Even in the east, the government officers and their native policemen, who made contact with the savage tribes, had to travel on foot through the complicated series of narrow and often precipitous jungle trails that still are the only means of communication between inland villages. In the early days, these patrol journeys often took six or nine months.

Commercial and administrative ventures barely scratched the skin of savagery. Missionaries were perhaps a more potent civilizing influence, but even they rarely enlarged their sphere beyond the immediate neighbourhood of the mission stations.

If Antonio d'Abreuva could have revisited his island when the great war broke out in 1941, he would have noticed no difference in the scenery at all, except an occasional glimpse along the coast of iron-roofed, wooden buildings menaced by the jungle or mountains that pressed in upon them from every side.

World War 1, however, induced another of Australia's rare flashes of consciousness concerning her northern approaches. At the request of the Imperial Government, the Commonwealth dispatched a small force to occupy Rabaul, the administrative centre of the German colony.

The troops left by transport from Sydney on August 18, 1914, and were 'trained' for tropical warfare for 10 days on an island off the Queensland coast. On September 11 they landed at Kokopo, a village near Rabaul, and after a brisk skirmish in which two men were killed, they destroyed the German radio station and re-embarked. The transport then steamed up to Rabaul wharf and discharged the expeditionary force, which chased the tougher German settlers into the hills, rounded up the rest, told them to behave themselves and sent them back to work their plantations.

Until 1921 New Guinea remained under military administration, and the military administration was not slow to realize that the Germans had developed a very profitable small business in that area.

Apart from that, certain things were observed about the country which might usefully have been recalled in later years. S. S. McKenzie in the *Official History of Australia in the Great War* (vol. X) states:

Two facts have been clearly demonstrated during the military occupation of German New Guinea – that the country is one for men between 25 and 40 years of age, and that the insidious climate fastens relentlessly on any physical weakness.

Only seasoned men of robust bodily fitness could be depended on to endure the rigours of even a few days marching and fighting in these latitudes, where the moist heat hangs like an oppressive curtain and makes strenuous exertion for more than a few hours intolerable to a white man.

Japan made a first entrance on the New Guinea stage when the spoils of the war were being divided. In return for her nominal participation in the war against the Central Powers, she received at Versailles as her chief rewards a mandate over all islands in the former German New Guinea protectorate lying north of the equator, including the Marshall, the Caroline, the Marianas and the Pellew groups. Though these Central Pacific islands were separated from New Guinea by many hundreds of miles of sea, their acquisition turned out to be of immense strategic importance. Japan blandly ignored a condition of the mandate that the territories were not to be militarized and set about developing them as a screen of naval and air bases.

14

By one neatly unobtrusive grab, the little men of the east had outflanked the Philippines, extended their sphere of military influence some thousands of miles farther into the Central Pacific, and were now camped permanently on the doorstep of the South Pacific. Nevertheless, interest in this remote part of the world again faded – except possibly in Japan.

Australia was satisfied with her own territorial reward at Versailles. She received all of what was formerly New Guinea south of the equator, expropriated German property, deported most of the Germans and settled a handful of her own returned soldiers on their plantations. An Australian administration responsible to the League of Nations was set up in what then became known at the Mandated Territory.

The Territory might have lapsed into a tropical backwater if Australian prospectors in the Morobe district had not made sensational gold discoveries 70 miles inland from the tiny settlement of Salamaua in 1926. Even then the field might still have remained unexploited, despite its rich promise, if the progress of air transport had not offered a new means of entry. Air transport – and air transport alone – was capable of breaking down New Guinea's geographical defences.

The Morobe mining settlements were built and maintained entirely with materials brought in by air. Even to reach a goldfield that yielded more than £25,000,000 in ten years, it was found impracticable to lay down 70 miles of road through New Guinea mountains and jungles.

The gold discoveries drew attention to New Guinea as nothing yet had done. They led to an era of development and exploration which increased the 'foreign' population of the island sixfold in 15 years.

Then oil prospectors located fields in country near the northern end of the Dutch-British border, and on the upper reaches of the Sepik River. International oil companies began to take notice. Even the Dutch, who had succeeded in keeping their half of the island almost unexplored and wholly undeveloped for more than a century, adopted a more active policy toward the 19th Province of the Netherlands Indies. After 1935 they admitted a number of approved mineral prospectors and granted large development concessions.

By the eve of World War II, it seemed likely that New Guinea – long unconquered barrier of wilderness between east and south – was at last to yield its solitude and secrets to the probing fingers of civilization. Yet when war came the white population in 500,000 square miles was still only about 7,000 people, nearly all of whom lived in the administrative 'capitals' of Rabaul and Port Moresby, or in the goldfield settlements around Huon Gulf. Seven tenths of the island was still completely unknown, and the rest known only to the hardiest tropical administrators and pioneers.

This was the country to which the tide of Japanese conquest rolled in 1942 – and this was the country that contained and held the tide.

I have given a great deal of thought to the problem of why the Japanese drive southward stopped where it did in the early months of 1942. It probably stopped for very much the same reason that the German drive stopped where it did late in 1940. The Japanese high command, like the Germans, refused at the crucial moment to take the ultimate risk of hurdling a great geographical barrier without an accidentproof preparation for the venture.

The Germans baulked at the hazard of invading Britain in the fall of 1940 because (1) France collapsed so quickly they were not organized to make the next move immediately, and (2) they were unwilling to commit an extempore invasion force to so technically difficult a project as crossing the English Channel without unchallenged air superiority.

The Japanese baulked at the hazard of invading Australia, New Caledonia and New Zealand in the winter of 1942 because (1) their successes in the Far East had come so quickly they were not organized to make the next move immediately, and (2) they were unwilling to commit extempore invasion forces to so technically difficult a project as leap-frogging the Arafura Sea and New Guinea without the insurance of cover by land-based aircraft for their invasion fleets.

In both cases, the delay enabled the opposition to rally its defences. Ultimately it denied Germany and Japan territorial gains which would have placed them in an unassailable position, despite the great strength of Russia and the United States.

There, however, the analogy ends. The Luftwaffe was defeated and temporarily crippled by the Royal Air Force in the Battle of Britain, but the Japanese suffered no such defeat. They were foiled because they could not solve the terrain problems of New Guinea and the Pacific Islands quickly enough to seize the airfields they needed before opposition solidified.

In the first four months of the Pacific war – December, 1941, to April, 1942 – the Japanese occupied Malaya, Singapore Island, Burma, Sumatra, Java, the 19 provinces of the Netherlands Indies, the Philippines, New Britain and the northern Solomons. A Japanese Churchill might have coined himself a phrase and said: 'Never before in the field of human conflict has one nation acquired so vast an empire in so short a time – and at so small a cost.' In April, 1942, one task, and one task only remained to be done before Japan could claim a complete and permanent consolidation of her gains. That task was the elimination of Australia.

To eliminate Australia, the Japanese had first to cut it off from help, and second to destroy or capture its industrial centres and occupy regions from which the country could be kept in subjugation. The first necessity, isolation, required the seizure of sea and air bases as far south as New Caledonia, from which the shipping lifeline to the United States could be severed. The second necessity, subjugation, required the capture of strategic points on the northeastern Australian mainland, from which an orderly advance could be made against the industrialized southeast.

The only alternative approach was an attack on the southeast *across* the continent, after landings in the central north, northwest or west. This project would have involved the use of immense forces, and even if it were virtually unopposed would have been infinitely slower and more costly. Probably the only operations the Japanese contemplated against western or northern Australia were landings at Wyndham, Broome and perhaps

Fremantle to secure additional bases on the Indian Ocean. The occupation of these places would not have been directly related to their main thrust against the industrialized heart of the continent in the southeast.

When Singapore and the Netherlands Indies fell, the Japanese could have launched a direct attack on Australia in one of two ways. They could have hurdled the sea and land barriers protecting the continent by sending invasion forces with limited carrier-based air cover to occupy New Caledonia and the New Hebrides and to attack Port Moresby, Port Darwin, and strategic points on the coast of north Queensland; or they could have elected to push through the barriers by seizing outlying bases and building requisite airfields as they went.

The Japanese decision to employ the second and slower method – gambling on the speed of their advance outdistancing the speed of American aid to Australia – may have been taken because they did not have adequate shipping, materiel or organized forces available at the time. But it is more likely that the decision was taken because they did not know what resistance to expect and were willing to violate what then appeared to be a new law of strategy – that amphibious task forces had to have adequate land-based air cover if they were to succeed without disproportionate loss against land-based air opposition.

In any case, whatever the reasons for the Japanese decision to push through New Guinea and the islands instead of hurdling them, it now seems almost certain that had they chosen the latter course, they would have won their war.

The Japanese attacked Rabaul on January 23, 1942. Their landing was opposed by approximately 1,400 Australian soldiers with inadequate artillery and seven obsolete 'fighter' aircraft. Four hundred and fifty miles away at Port Moresby, one brigade of semitrained militia had just been 'deployed' to meet an attack against that equally important base. Air support for this force was one flight of Hudson reconnaissance bombers and one squadron of Catalina flying boats, with reinforcements at Townsville in north Queensland. On the main-

18

land, one division of semitrained militia were at battle stations to resist invasion.

I do not know what total of aircraft could have been mustered in all Australia to attack any Japanese convoy menacing the coast in January, 1942, but I do know that not one would have been a first-line bomber and not one a first-line fighter. The most modern bomber was the Hudson – carrying four .303 machine guns and a 1,000-pound bomb load. The only 'pursuit' type aircraft in service was the Wirraway – an under-powered, undergunned plane designed originally as an advanced trainer and built in Australian factories. The slowest and least heavily gunned Japanese carrier-based fighter could outmatch either machine.

As for exactly what naval forces could have been assembled to intercept an invasion force, it is extremely unlikely that a single full cruiser squadron with screen could have been gathered for service in eastern Australian waters in February and March.

On land, at sea and in the air, the forces available for the defence of Australia were desperately weak.

To support the war against the Germans and Italians in the Middle East, three out of Australia's four fully trained and equipped volunteer divisions had been sent overseas. The fourth had been lost in Malaya. Even the modest stocks of munitions which might have been accumulated in Australian arsenals for home production were depleted to vanishing point by exports to the Middle East. It has been publicly admitted by Australian politicians that at this time there were not enough rifles to arm the forces drafted for home defence, not enough bullets to fill their ammunition pouches, and only enough shells to keep field artillery in action for 36 hours.

It is difficult to imagine a nation more completely open to even the most hastily prepared invasion than Australia was in the first three months of 1942. All that stood between her and the Japanese were a few hundred miles of unguarded sea, a few hundred miles of uninhabited jungle, a few groups of palm-fringed, roadless islands and her own shellback of desert - the inert armour of a neglected and undeveloped north.

19

Yet that armour served.

While the Japanese were struggling to disjoint it by capturing airfields and airfield sites in northern New Guinea and the Solomon Islands, Australia made a supreme effort to mobilize and supplement what few defences she possessed. The United States rushed modern aircraft, weapons, ships and troops to the only bases left to the Allies on Japan's southern flank.

By May that aid had not reached very great proportions, but it was enough to assure more than token defence. The Japanese now really needed airfields before launching an attack. It was too late to hurdle the wilderness. Both sides were committed to a full-scale campaign to contest its ownership.

Geography is impartial. When the Japanese were in a position to maintain an overwhelming offensive, a barrier of unpeopled sea and jungle saved Australia. But when Australia was ready to meet the Japanese on relatively even terms, the very factor that had upset the enemy's plan of complete conquest was now a potent factor in enabling him to hold what he had gained.

As the campaign went on, various uncertainties became apparent. At first the time factor was uppermost. Could Japan move fast enough to take advantage of Australia's helplessness and America's surprise at being precipitated into a global war before the nation was prepared for it? Then the paramount question altered. Could Japan continue to push, at the same time matching increasing opposition? Finally, the emphasis upon terrain grew heavier. Which combatant could best deal with the geographical entanglements that separated the two forces and engage the enemy – one belatedly to secure his position, and the other to dislodge the invader from territories he had already occupied?

Eventful 1942 quickly decided the first two uncertainties. Japan failed to overcome logistic and geographic obstacles quickly enough to strike either at Australia or Australia's lifeline, before possession of air bases in the islands became an actual rather than an imaginary necessity.

The arrival of American heavy and medium bomber squadrons in North Australia, New Guinea and New Caledonia during March, April and May, and the transfer to the South Pacific of substantial American naval forces, threatened Japan's golden opportunity of winning half a world without fighting one real battle. She finally lost the opportunity in the Battle of the Coral Sea.

By the end of October the second question – whether Japan could continue to push on – had been answered. Though still operating against forces inferior in numbers and equipment, the Japanese failed to make any substantial gains and suffered disproportionate losses of ships, aircraft and materiel in the attempt. A Japanese landing force was defeated at Milne Bay on the southeastern tip of New Guinea. Another force landed at Buna and pushed across the Owen-Stanley range but could not be maintained at the end of the trail. When United States forces reoccupied Guadalcanal with its immensely valuable airfield, the Japanese were unable to dislodge them, despite intensive efforts on land and a series of bitter air-sea battles.

The answer to the third major uncertainty had still to be given. The Japanese had failed to engage the enemy successfully on the Allied side of the barrier. Could the Allies now engage the Japanese successfully on the other side of it?

The recapture of Buna proved little. Failure of supply, and not Allied pressure, was the prime cause of the enemy's withdrawal across the Owen-Stanleys. The conclusion was not reached until the Americans successfully attacked Munda in July, 1943, and Allied forces recaptured Lae, Salamaua and Finschafen in September and October of that year, and in the next few months landed on Bougainville Island and New Britain, and pushed west to Hollandia and Schouten Island.

These victories showed that an effective formula had been found for getting to grips with the Japanese behind their breastworks of island and jungle. Its basic elements were reduction to an irreducible minimum of the development of large number of white troops in the jungle and in strategy of seizing key supply point in an area by the use of overwhelmingly superior war machines. The elements from which this plan were evolved are both interesting and significant.

In their conquest of Malaya and the Indies, the Japanese enjoyed the advantage of surprise. The surprise did not lie in the fact that they attacked Malaya, the Philippines and the Indies – there surely had been ample warning of that – but in the methods by which their attacks were carried out.

For many years Japanese strategists had closely studied the problems of a campaign in Southeast Asia. They created an aeroamphibious striking force especially trained and equipped to fight it. In this force, the role of the army was predominant. It was an army in all ways composed and balanced differently from a European army. The basic human material was different, for it was an army of Orientals. It consumed less food, and in a less diversified form, than a European army. It required fewer clothes and accoutrements. It demanded less in the way of shelter, transport and creature comforts. Because of the innate characteristics of its soldiers, it was less susceptible to the enervating effects of hard physical labour and travel in the tropics. For the same reason, conditions being equal, it was less quickly affected by disease.

In such an army the all-important supply integer was much smaller than it could be in a European army created for service in similar conditions.

Moreover, the soldiers of this Oriental army had been indoctrinated over a period of many years with the belief that death in battle is the finest destiny to which men can aspire. In its best units fear of death as a factor of battle morale was largely eliminated.

New and unorthodox tactical principles were evolved for the employment of this army in specific terrain – the heavily wooded, broken, comparatively roadless countries of Malaya, southern China, Burma and the Netherlands Indies. The army was taught to operate where necessary in small, self-sufficient units. Sections of it were trained until they reached a high degree of efficiency in the art of silent and concealed movement in the jungle. Officers learned to direct infiltration and confusion tactics; men were schooled in stalking, sniping and bush reconnaissance, and taught to supplement their standard rations (rice) with foodstuffs locally available. Military leaders closely studied the organization and balance of forces required for island landings. In brief, the Japanese high command said: 'We want Malaya and the Philippines and the Netherlands Indies. How can we get what we want with what we have?

When the present war was brewing, Japan was still a nation of severely limited industrial strength, despite her recent grabs on the mainland of Asia. She could not hope to compete with Britain or America in an outright arms race. Her only chance of realising an ambition to control all East Asia lay in her ability to wage a type of war that did not impose an intolerable strain upon her economic weaknesses, and to begin it at a time of her own choosing so that she need not meet her enemies at full strength until geography had been added to her defensive armament.

The first point – avoidance of unsupportable economic strain – was achieved by creating the specialized force for seizing the territories of Southeast Asia. Highly mechanized and armoured units could not be employed in such heavy terrain. The industrial effort needed to build an army on the western European pattern could therefore be diverted by Japan to other corollaries of conquest – greater naval strength, more merchant shipping, and more air power.

The military decline of Britain in the era of the Fool's Peace took care of the second point – opportunity. Japan made her bid to dominate Asia at the ideal moment, when it seemed that her 'have-not' partners, Germany and Italy, must inevitably overthrow Britain and Russia.

How carefully Japan had weighed her chances and how fully she had prepared to take advantage of them was dramatically illustrated in the first four months of 1942. In spite of the fact that the terrain of Southeast Asia greatly favoured defence, the Japanese specialist striking force disproved every enemy assessment of its capabilities. It passed with magical rapidity through 'impassable' mountains and jungles, made a tragic jest of the fortress of Singapore, mauled the Philippines into submission, and swarmed over the Netherlands Indies. Its progress was halted only by open ocean and beyond it by a terrain so difficult that even its superb specialization was momentarily inadequate.

In so much the Japanese had succeeded. In just how much had they failed? I have already expressed the belief that their prime and fatal omission was the failure to add Australia to the list of conquered territories before the Allies could use Australasian bases to bring pressure against the Japanese weaknesses – air inferiority, shortage of merchant shipping, limited reserves, and a production potential insufficient to sustain large mechanized forces in combat for prolonged periods.

Yet while the Japanese fell short of unassailability, they nevertheless achieved a position in which geography immensely strengthened their defences. If the Allies were to hope for the ultimate defeat of Japan, they now had to consider ways of overcoming the geographical factor. As the Japanese themselves had so painfully shown, a 'continental' concept of war for Southeast Asia was impractical. New methods of warfare had to be devised.

One method was to train an army to fight as the Japanese army had been trained to fight, and trust in its higher common denominator of intelligence and its superior mechanical support and equipment.

An alternative was to work out some strategic formula for bringing to bear against the enemy superior machines and more machines, in the hope that conquered territories would be made untenable for him – in other words, to carry on a war of attrition mainly by mechanical means. Neither method in itself seemed to promise the complete answer – victory soon enough and at a low enough price to be politically acceptable to the democracies – so Allied strategy took ingredients from both methods and mixed them. Results were at first slow in coming.

The ingredient of training men for jungle warfare was used too sparingly. The gargantuan battlefields that encircle the Japanese islands today were not built or equipped or manned overnight.

In two years of war the Allies recaptured from the Japanese only half a dozen small islands in the Solomons and three or four settlements with airfield sites on the northeast coast of

New Guinea. MacArthur's colourful personality shed upon these gains a lustre utterly disproportionate to their war-winning value, though it is true that in contesting them, the enemy suffered losses of aircraft, ships and material which he could ill afford. The important thing is that the Allies discovered and tested a basic formula for getting at the Japanese behind their defences and beating them.

It was a formula evolved out of the debacle of Malaya, the agony of Bataan, in the bloody groves of Guadalcanal, and in New Guinea where white men slipped and slithered, panted, plodded, sweated, bled, sickened, dropped and died in a sodden and crinkled hell of mountain and forest and swamp.

It is not in the province of this book to examine the formula in any detail. *Green Armour* aims only to describe parts of the strange and sometimes terrible laboratory in which it was developed – and to record some of the reactions of the men who took part in it.

If at times the story seems to lack continuity and direction, the only excuse is that it is written from the viewpoint of a man looking from the inside out, rather than from the outside in – a viewpoint that lends itself easily to distortion of perspective. If it puts no great store by dates or tactical details, if it ignores the names of units and individuals almost entirely, that is because I believe that dates and tactical details and names would contribute little to the story as I want to tell it. If much of its space is devoted to observations on the nature of the country in which battles were fought and comparatively little to the descriptions of battles themselves, then that is because the war on the margins of Southeast Asia is, in terms of human experience, proportioned that way. The mountains, the swamps, the rivers, the storms and the beating sun were and will forever be a greater and more merciless enemy of man than men.

O.W.
New York
1945

To Susan and Sue

Part One
LAST BASTION

ON JANUARY 23, 1942, the battle for Australia began. Bypassing the doomed fortresses of Singapore and Corregidor, the Japanese swept south to the island of New Britain and landed strong forces to seize the key harbor of Rabaul. Outnumbered twenty to one, a garrison of 1,400 Australian troops at first fought desperately. Then they fled west through the jungles. Four hundred and fifty miles to the southwest, Port Moresby, defended by another handful of Australians with obsolete planes and guns, was now the last major island base remaining in Allied hands in the Central-western Pacific. Protected on three sides by trailless wilderness and on the fourth by what was left of the United States Pacific fleet, this last bastion was held . . .

CHAPTER 1

THE LITTLE SINGAPORE

THE FIVE men were very thin. That was the first thing one noticed. Their new drill hung on their bodies in stiff folds. Their temples were hollow, with delicate blue veins showing through the skin. Their faces were quiet and pallid. The pallor had a greenish tinge.

They had been flown into Port Moresby from the islands of Samarai where Catalina flying boats were rescuing survivors of the Rabaul garrison.

I well remember the afternoon they came. The New Guinea campaign was 37 days old. It was raining gently out of a leaden sky. The wet season was having a final fling, with the thunderstorms sweeping down the river valley from the hills, the rainclouds advancing like an army of dark giants through a barrage of thunder.

It was an important occasion. We sharpened pencils and began new notebooks. We pushed the typewriters back and arranged cane chairs in a half circle, and put bottles of beer and a carton of cigarettes on the table.

The censor, a rotund little patriot, came in a minute or two before the five men and said officiously: 'Now take it steady, will you, boys? Intelligence has given these lads a grilling already, and they're deathly tired.'

But they didn't look tired – unless very bright eyes with puffed, reddish lids, and a network of fine wrinkles radiating from them were signs of tiredness. When they sat, they sat alertly and seemed to be listening for something.

We shook hands all round, passed the cigarettes, opened the beer. Being first survivors out of Rabaul rated a beer, didn't it?

They smiled frostily at the little joke. They agreed that maybe it did. Yes, maybe it did. They said 'Good luck!' or 'Mud in your eye!' and swallowed, heads tilted back, the chapped skin moving on their throats.

The silence was uneasy. Someone said: 'I suppose it's right about you fellows being the first out. That is, the first out after the actual fighting?'

As far as they knew, yes, they were the first men out. The first overland, anyway. They looked a little proud, and at the same time a little shamefaced.

A tough trip?

They smiled again. Yes, you might call it that. Tough enough.

Were there many more to come?

The five faces went bleak. Everybody asked that. They didn't know how many more were to come. They wished they did. They were silent again, thinking.

The censor cleared his throat. 'It's all right to tell the story,' he said. Any articles written for the newspapers would be subject to censorship. The best idea was to begin at the beginning. That was the simplest. Begin at the beginning.

The beginning. Well . . . that would be the eighteenth, the eighteenth of January.

No, the nineteenth, Rocky . . . the nineteenth. The nineteenth was the Monday. The eighteenth was the day the plane came in with the report. Yes. On the Sunday a plane came in with a report that a Jap fleet was coming off the tip of New Ireland. Sunday was the day the troops went to battle stations.

The boys in the reconnaissance plane said there were 25 to 30 ships, with a battleship and two aircraft carriers . . . cruisers, destroyers, minesweepers, tankers and transports. A regular invasion fleet. The weather was thick, and the plane spotted them through a gap in the clouds and headed for home. The Japs didn't do anything about it.

Sunday was a busy day. The last of the civilians were getting out along the Kokopo road and the troops were hard at work putting out the last of the wire and digging machine-gun pits.

How many? Well, a battalion of the 2nd Australian Imperial

Force, the 2nd/22nd, the signalers, the engineers, the artillery . . .

Fourteen hundred men, Jim. Fourteen hundred in all. The major said that.

Prepared positions? Sure. There were two six-inch naval guns on Praed Point, the antiaircraft, the wire between the tidemarks at Talilli Bay and Raluana Point, and off Vulcan. Vulcan was the volcano. It stank of sulphur . . .

The troops took up positions at company strength. One company was left on the upper airfield. Some of the officers thought the Japs might try a parachute landing. But the shooting didn't start until the Monday morning. Monday morning, the nineteenth, was when the Jap bombers first came over.

Just at dawn. It was a queer sound, hearing them come. They made a noise like millions of bees. They came straight in from the sea – a hundred of them, with fighters on top. The sky was full of planes. The big bombers zoomed straight across the airfield in fives and got a lot of gasoline dumps. Then the dive bombers and fighters gave hell to hangars and the grounded aircraft and the machine-gun pits.

Yes, we had planes. A Hudson or two and nine Wirraways. But they got the Wirras on the ground.

No, only four of them. The fellows at Raluana airfield saw five Wirraways get off while the bombs were dropping. The bursts followed them down the runway. The machine gunners stood up and cheered them. They mixed it with the first fighters and clawed down two of them. But there were so many Japs three of the Wirras got shot to pieces inside of five minutes. They came through the sky like streaks of flame. You could hear them winding up – *whee-whee-whee*. Faster and faster. There'd be a puff of black smoke in the bush where they crashed. The other two belly-landed among the bomb craters, and the pilots got away.

The antiaircraft got five Japs. Dive bombers. Anyway, they claimed five Japs. Then the business was over for the day.

Yes, the rest of Monday was quiet. That afternoon the word went round that the Jap fleet was sheltering behind Watom Island. The sea was a bit rough outside and it was raining. The

Japs disembarked troops at Watom, so the natives said. The next morning was quiet, too. And the next.

On the twenty-second, 70 bombers came over and finished the guns on Praed Point. For the gunners, it was the worst day. The Japs came over at about 200 feet and lobbed 500-pound bombs right into the top emplacement.

Blasted everything in sight. You couldn't see anything for dust and smoke. Columns of yellow dust and smoke. The top emplacement collapsed on the lower emplacement and buried the gun crews. Hardly a man got out. Yes, it was a bad day all right. The shorings must have collapsed. The rock was crumbly. After the first wave had gone over, some men from the nearby positions ran over and tried to dig their mates out, but the Jap fighters gave everything hell.

Those Jap fighters sure could dive. In – and away again like a bat out of hell.

The antiaircraft was knocked out, too.

Nobody had much hope, really. Everybody knew an attack was coming, but what chance did you have? With the guns knocked out, and only four companies to look after about 60 miles of coast and two airfields.

But everybody was in it – even the cooks and the headquarters clerks. The officers said a landing was expected that night. It was a dark night and rained a bit.

You could see the glare of the dumps burning at the airfields. The town was on fire. There were demolition parties out dynamiting the storehouses and setting wooden buildings afire. You could hear the thump of the dynamite exploding. But the town didn't burn so good. The fires didn't seem to catch, everything was so damp . . .

'A' company was on Vulcan. They had taken up new positions there that day. God, but it was nervous business waiting! You only heard the rain pattering, the clink of entrenching tools, men moving about in the pits, waiting.

Some got a bit of sleep under their ground sheets. They were pretty tired. The sentries stayed awake, lying on their bellies looking out into the dark, rifles cocked. An officer made the rounds. He crashed through the undergrowth like a bloody rhinoceros. You could see him flashing his torch under his hand and hear him saying, 'No smoking, men!'

All up and down the coast, nothing to be seen but palm trees leaning over the water. The beaches were dark and the water was slopping . . . nothing to be heard.

It started at 0235 hours, Friday. The sentries on Vulcan heard something. It was machine-gun breaches clicking. A funny, oily noise. Then out to sea, the voices. Someone laughed – a sort of giggle. The Japs were smoking. They were cheeky. You could see their cigarette ends. Maybe they didn't expect to see anybody on Vulcan.

Then somebody fired a Verey pistol – three flares that made a green light on the sea. The light showed a cluster of square-nosed barges inshore. You could hardly hear their engines.

The Japs wore black shorts and shirts, and had blackened their faces.

When the lights went up, one machine gun started to slap in short bursts, then another and another. A mortar fired and the shell went whizzing overhead and burst among the barges.

The Japs started to yell and shriek. All along the beach you could see the flash of firing from the gun muzzles. Everybody let them have it. The Japs replied with tommy guns but their shooting was rotten and the barges hauled off.

But some landed . . .

Yes, they must have landed – on the flank. They always look for the flank. Some must have crept through just before dawn, because a sentry high up on the side of Vulcan saw the shape of a man rear up and show against the sky. What a crazy little swine he was! He was a bugler. He had a bugle and he started to blow it. He got just two sour notes out – '*Tara tara.*' Then a Vickers gun slapped him and he went bounding and rattling down the ash, dead as mutton.

Everyone knew what would happen. It was only a matter of time till the Japs flanked us and landed. At dawn the word came to get out. There had been landings at Talilli Bay and Matupi Island and Raluana Beach as well.

The Raluana show was best. That was where the mixed company was – odds and ends, cooks and clerks.

That mob was really shrewd. They waited till the barges were only about 20 yards from shore and hung up on the wire that had been laid in the sea. Then let them have it, everything, including the kitchen sink. It must have been good. They said the Japs shrieked and squealed and bubbled and howled banzai!

They came on in spite of it. When they jumped overboard they got tangled in the wire. Hundreds and hundreds died that way, but they kept coming on. Those in the rear seized the bodies of their dead comrades and laid them across the wire to make bridges.

Once they set foot ashore the company didn't have a chance. The Japs went yelling through the bush in all directions, so the mixed company gave up and ran with them. There was no shooting, because you couldn't tell whether it was Japs or your own people.

The difference was that our fellows knew where they'd parked their motor transport and the Japs didn't. They got down to the road and lit out for the hills.

There were too many Japs. Two divisions, the major said. Between the first landing and the middle of the morning, about 25,000 men.

Against our fourteen hundred.

At dawn it was all over.

Not quite. There was a lot of firing until midmorning. No one knew what was happening at the upper airfield. There was firing until half-past ten. Some said the 'B' company fought to the last man. Anyway, there weren't any of them on the trail out of town.

The Jap transport came into the bay with the minesweepers in front of them and steamed up to the wharves. Some officers were angry about the wharves not being blown. The Japs were discharging men and cargo at the wharves by midafternoon. It didn't make much difference. The boys didn't have a chance of stopping the Japs anyway. Not so many of them.

It was hard to say just what happened next. Every man for

himself. The word had got round to make for Rabata, a little village inland. There was a fair road up there and for a while it was jammed with trucks, the men hanging on like flies.

But later in the morning the Jap fighters came over and started strafing. The fighters would come down to treetop level and let a truck have it. The men would fall off and bolt into the ditch like rabbits. A fighter chased one poor chap on a motorcycle – made five passes at him and missed every time. He gave up and took to the ditch when the Jap came back a sixth time.

Sporadic action till midday? Yes, you could put it that way. Four or five hundred men escaped to Rabata. There were reports that the colonel was captured. The officer said to retreat down the coast or into the hills.

A few thought the sensible thing was to surrender, but most were against that. A lot talked big and said they were going back in the hills to fight. It wouldn't have been a bad idea, if a man could fight without food or ammunition.

If there were any dumps in the hills, the men didn't know about them. There'd been no talk about a retreat into the hills. If there had been, the major would know about it.

Everybody had his own idea. But the ideas all added up to the same thing – make for home.

Some reckoned reinforcements were bound to be landed down the coast. The signalers tried to get the radio set operating but couldn't raise anything. Some reckoned the navy would turn up.

A man stuck to his mate or to his section. Parties built up. Not too big. The order was to scatter. Some went over the hills and some cut back on to the coast.

There weren't many maps, but the idea was to travel west. West, you had a chance of being picked up or meeting the reinforcements.

The trails got worse and worse. Some parties took one route, and some another. Some traveled fast and some traveled slow. The smart ones traveled slow. They'd doped it out that it was going to be a long walk. It was funny how you'd be overtaken at first by party after party, traveling like hell. But a day or two later you always caught up with them, pooped out, sitting by the trail, heads between their hands, boots off and their feet red-raw and maggoty.

It was easy enough to follow the coast trails, but every now and then you had to cut back a long way inland to avoid the swamps at the mouths of rivers, or places where the hills ran right into the sea. . .

It was tough going all right. You didn't see much. Most of the chaps had grabbed a can or two of beef, but you couldn't carry anything even if you'd been able to get it. The going was too tough. You got hungry.

There were plenty of native villages for a start. You got kau-kau and yams and boiled them up with a bit of beef in your tin hat. Wonderful how well you could cook in a tin hat when the taste of paint burned off.

But after the first few days, a man didn't feel so hungry. He got weak in the guts and hadn't any fight left in him. He just kept walking.

You'd see big strong fellows sitting by the side of the trail crying like kids.

It all depended on how tough a man was. It wasn't always the big ones who made out best.

Before long a man learned things that made the going easier. Things like where to look for a native canoes to cross rivers. Like persuading the natives to carry your pack and rifle for you from one village to another. The ones who could persuade the natives got on best.

God, were some of the villages filthy! Too filthy for a man to stop in if he could possibly face another night in the rain. The natives were pot black and covered with grille (a kind of ringworm) and yaws. Some of the villages were lousy with typhus.

No wonder. They did their latrine business right on the edge of the village clearing. You could smell them a mile down-wind.

You didn't stay in a village if you could help it, but some-times you had to, to dry out.

The rain was the worst thing. Not the heat, the rain. You

never dried out. You were never even half dry. Your clothes and boots rotted. Your feet got spongy and bled.

Jesus, the mosquitoes!

And sandflies. A man could use his willpower against mosquitoes but not sandflies. You *had* to scratch. See the sores on Rocky's legs!

Crossing the rivers was bad, too.

News kept coming of men who were attacked by crocodiles and sharks when they tried to swim the estuaries. You saw the crocs drifting like logs, waiting. A man was crazy to swim. You cut inland until the river narrowed down, if you couldn't find a canoe or make a raft.

One or two men were smashed up trying to swing from one edge of a gully to the other on hanging lawyer vines. But it was the only way in some places. A man had to risk it.

Yes. Just kept traveling west. Not many knew where they were going. They just kept going and hoped something would turn up.

There was a bit of fighting. The Japs landed patrols down the coast to try to round up the biggest parties. At an early stage there was one scrap in the bush at Tol plantation. Some of the men were wounded and sick. There was a story that they surrendered and that the Japs gave them cigarettes and food and then took them out into the coconut groves and bayoneted them to death.[1] After that a fellow was pretty careful how he approached any new clearing in the bush.

It was toughest on a man who had a sick or wounded friend to worry about. There were always Japs on your heels. Often the sound men ended up as bad as their mates.

A lot got malaria. They had to travel with it until they were raving. Then they'd lie up in a native village or an abandoned plantation house until they could walk. The Japs overtook plenty of them that way.

If you didn't like the idea, you could always rig up a string

[1] One hundred and twenty-three men were bayoneted to death by the Japanese at Tol. Three men survived the bayoneting and were rescued by other parties. At Port Moresby in April, they gave a circumstantial and entirely credible account of the massacre.

between the trigger of your rifle and your big toe. One or two went out that way, poor devils. They reckoned they were only a drag on their friends.

They may have done the right thing at that. A man didn't blame them. You had to be tough.

The second week was hell. It was hard to judge miles because of going off course to cross the rivers.

Estimate the walk at 300 miles and it wouldn't be far wrong. That took 22 days. After the second week you didn't do much remembering or thinking ahead. You just kept going.

Our party was pretty pooped out when we struck a couple of civilian old-timers hiding in a cave down the coast. They were scared to move but they knew where a launch was laid up.

We persuaded them to have a try at getting to the mainland. Jesus, did that launch look good! She was a 24-footer, had been out of the water too long and her beams had opened up, but that was easily fixed. The engine was harder. It took three days to get it going, and when it was going, nobody dared to stop it.

A man spent his days and nights bailing and praying over the engine, but it kept going. The launch rolled so much you couldn't go to sleep, but it was better than walking.

The sun was good at first, after walking in the jungle, but it soon scorched you. It was the reflection off the water. Red eyes, see? A man went half blind staring for reefs and for the first sign of mountains across Vitiaz Strait.

A few planes passed over. Japs, of course. Never saw any of ours. But the Japs didn't come down. Maybe one small gasoline launch wasn't worthwhile.

In three or four days we struck the mainland. One of the civilians picked up a landmark and coasted through the islands to Samaria. There wasn't anything to tell after that. We got picked up by a Catalina flying boat.

How long altogether? Thirty-seven days. Ticked off in a notebook. Exactly 37 days since Rabaul fell.

A long time, all right. A long time and most of it tough. Still, a man couldn't complain about his luck. It was over.

Tomorrow we'd be going for a medical examination and maybe we'd get home for a spell.

That was all there was to it, really.

The story of the beginning . . .

The five men answered us patiently, distantly. To question them seemed a stupidity. What they did not tell was obviously so unimportant. Their minds, like their bodies, were lean and stripped of unessential details.

They shuffled their new thick-soled shoes and got up one by one and shook hands. They said thanks for the beer, it was good stuff, and walked out in single file into the rain, and did not notice it soaking the shoulders of their shirts. They hadn't started yet to be conscious of such trivial things as wet shirts. They had told their story exactly as one might relate a dream. For them it bore no relation to real life and one could expect no logic of it.

If the story they told needed interpretation, it could be put down that the battle for Australia began on January 23, 1942, when 1,400 soldiers, ordered to defend the most important harbour and airfields in the Central-western Pacific, were overwhelmed by 25,000 Japanese; that their 'coast defences' had been two rejected naval guns; that their 'air support' had been nine obsolescent planes; that their plan of action had never envisaged retreat.

It could be put down that in all the annals of human suffering, there are few records of journeys more terrible than the journey made by those 400-odd men who escaped and fled from Rabaul along the coasts of New Britain, westward, toward home.

CHAPTER 2

TOBRUK OF THE PACIFIC

AT TWO o'clock on the afternoon of February 13, 1942, a Lockheed Electra airliner landed at the Seven Mile airfield, Port Moresby, with 14 passengers. It was the last civil airplane to cross the Coral Sea from Australia.

I climbed down from the cabin and stood blinking. It was savagely hot. Twenty or thirty natives and Europeans under the direction of an officer were industriously rolling gasoline drums and moving sacks and packing cases.

I looked around. Since then it has often struck me that in one glance I saw the few acres of New Guinea soil, the possession of which was to determine the fate of Australia in the Pacific war, and not improbably affect the result of the war itself.

It was a raw, metaled landing strip scooped out of a valley surrounded by low hills. The only aircraft on it were the Lockheed, an old Junkers transport pockmarked by bullets, and a single Hudson bomber. Bright kurukuru grass, four to seven feet high, grew down to the runway. Near the strip of road that served the field, the grass was powdered with grayish-white dust. Low gum trees with broad, soft leaves were growing out on the rolling hills as far as the eye could see. Away to the north a high, inky-blue range of mountains, the Owen-Stanleys, was topped by the cumulus cloud that will always, for me, be the epitome of the New Guinea scene. In that land, whenever the sun shines and whenever one looks at mountains, there are always battlements of cloud tipped by light and shadowed in purple.

The airfield had not yet been bombed. It looked what it was —a lonely, sun-scorched clearing in the bush. Yet in this leveled

40

hollow on New Guinea's hide of crinkled green a great campaign was to be conceived and gestated and delivered.

In the months to come, cities of drab, dappled tents and mountainous dumps were to spring up in the valleys about it. The hilltops and ridges were to be scarred with gun emplacements and earthworks. From the dusty ribbon of road a network of military highways was to spread slowly through gum and grass-clad savannah into the jungles and mountains.

For nearly a year the establishment of an effective defensive front against the Japanese in the Southwest Pacific was to hinge upon Allied control of the Moresby airfield. For nearly two years the hope of one day developing effective counterattacks was to depend on its maintenance.

From it, the first American heavy and medium bombers took off to hamper Japanese development of their newly seized base at Rabaul, and to harry their shipping. Over it, the first modern fighters employed by the Allies south of the equator contested the enemy's early control of the air.

Possession of the Moresby airfield tipped the balance in the Battle of the Coral Sea. Under the protection of bombers and fighters based upon it, the tenuous shipping lifeline to Australia was kept intact. The first airborne supplies for embattled troops over the mountains were loaded into planes on its runways. The first airborne troops for Buna and Sanananda filed into their transport from revetments concealed in its dusty bush.

But in February, 1942, it was just a bush clearing. The town was seven miles away. Neither I nor many others knew enough to realize that the shape of the Pacific war was primarily to be a struggle for airfields. Towns and even harbors would be secondary in Pacific strategy.

I left the airfield and set off for town, down a strip of road twisting through gum-clad gullies until I came within sight of the sea – along Ela Beach with its sad casuarinas and the reef waters a singing green in the sun.

It was asleep – a little, heat-smothered bush town subdued by hills on the margins of its calm bay. A stick of bombs had fallen along the waterfront. A few houses and a store or two had

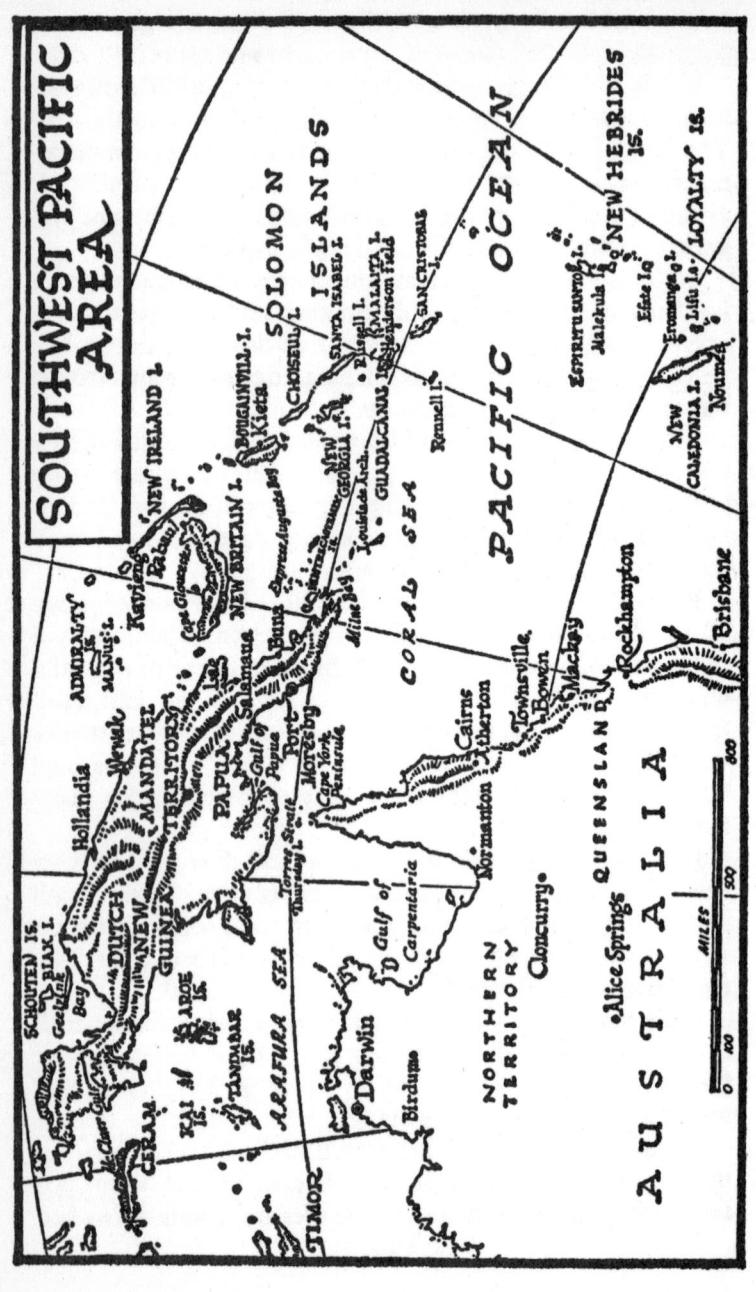

been gutted by fire, their windows staring like blinded eyes. The air was still and golden. Several men in rumpled drill and tussore were standing in the shade of trade-store doorways talking. One caught snatches of their conversation.

'*Last boat out, they say . . . so I said to him, "Well, what the hell else is there to do?"* '

'*The bloody military . . . nice state of affairs. They said if he didn't come in, they'd send out a picket and arrest him.*'

'*Damn them to hell is what I say! This would have broken the old man's heart.[1] Thank God he never lived to see the day!*'

The group I approached looked me over curiously. One man, a thin, tall fellow with angry black eyes, squinted at my correspondent tabs and said: 'Headquarters you want? Out in the bush somewhere. I don't know where. Haven't you heard? – the town's evacuated.'

I said there must be a military post somewhere. He put a butt of a cigarette back between his lips and replied:

'Sure. Try the guard at the Burns, Philp store. There's a guard on B.P. store. A newspaperman, eh?'

'Thanks,' I said. 'Yes, I'm a newspaperman.'

He took the butt out again and the angry black eyes went over me slowly.

'Bet you something,' he said.

'What's that?'

His hand jerked – a wide, all-embracing gesture. 'That you don't write the story of *this*.'

I walked slowly, looking. A bomb had blown in the front of a frame building. Glass and splintered wood were strewn across the street. Two flying boats were settled on the water off the jetty resting lightly. A steamer with a gray-daubed hull lay alongside, a wavy pencil line of smoke streaming up from her stack.

Natives were asleep in the shade of the struggling tamarind trees. A camouflaged truck, laden with arrow-branded cases, roared down the waterfront and took the turning out of town.

[1] A reference to Sir Hubert Murray, lieutenant governor of Papua from the turn of the century until his death a few years before the war.

The houses were built in tiers on the hillsides. For the most part they were shabby little affairs of four or five rooms, built in sun-scorched weatherboard or fibroplaster, with iron roofs. They had been abandoned in haste, and later looted. The doors stood open. One could see smashed furniture, crockery, papers scattered on the floor, draggled clothing, torn photographs.

These were once homes. How long ago? A week, a fortnight? They had been built through the years, and panic had destroyed them in a night. Panic is an honest mount – but not its rider. There is nothing honest about pictures wantonly defaced or a child's toy cupboard used as a latrine...

There were guards on the stores – militiamen dozing in the sweaty shade, with rifles and bayonets fixed. But guards had been set too late. Through the chinks in boarded-up windows one glimpsed floors covered ankle deep in ruined merchandise. Piles of canned food had been swept from the shelves and picked over for delicacies. Bales had been ripped open, their contents bulging from the gashes.

One store still defiantly did business. While I passed, a white man opened the doors and a crowd of waiting natives filed in, their eyes rolling from side to side curiously. They lined up at the food counter and pointed to things. The white man passed them down and took the shillings they had been holding in their hands like children.

I passed the offices of the resident magistrate. The garden was still bright with tended flowers, but the windows were broken and the shutters hung loose. Here was the epitome of the story that the man with angry eyes had dared me to write – menace, then panic; panic, then flight; flight and despair; despair and lawless desolation. It was a story as old as war itself.

Two days later Singapore fell. The five war correspondents then in Port Moresby, the first batch accredited by the Australian government, called upon the military administrator and general officer commanding New Guinea Force, Major General Basil Moorehouse Morris. He had taken up quarters in a bungalow some miles out of town. A small union jack hung limply from the flagpole in the front garden. Two very black police boys in blue-serge singlets and loincloths edged with scarlet presented arms smartly as we marched up the garden path.

The general was a tall, imposing man with a brown mustache and sharp, small eyes. When abroad he wore an expensive sun helmet and carried a horsetail flywhisk, elegantly mounted. By its oscillations junior officers learned to gauge very accurately the state of his temper.

He received us with courtesy and offered us a drink. He said he had nothing to say.

Singapore?

His only comment was 'Ah, bad!'

Would he care to comment on the defense position in New Guinea?

He flicked expressive and pronounced eyebrows.

Was he convinced that Moresby should be defended if the Japanese attacked it?

Certainly.

At all costs?

At all costs.

'In fact.' someone suggested, 'if necessary, Moresby should become a Tobruk of the Pacific?'

'If necessary, Port Moresby must become a Tobruk of the Pacific,' he said gravely.

Now that Singapore had fallen, the significance of New Guinea to Australia had increased?

It had.

Would it be true to say that if the Japanese captured Port Moresby it would provide them with an excellent base for attacks on Australia?

That would be true.

Would it also be true that, so long as Port Moresby remained an Australian stronghold, it would be a direct threat to any Japanese advance southward?

It would.

'Do you believe that you have sufficient forces to defend Port Moresby, if the Japanese attack it?'

'We shall see,' he said.

'We may quote you, General?'

He considered. Yes, we might quote him – except any reference to the forces at his disposal for the defense of Port Moresby. The interview was concluded.

War correspondents were quartered at administrative headquarters 17 miles inland from town in an old plantation house. Once it must have been a pleasant enough home. The doctor to whom it belonged had conducted small-scale experiments with tropical crops, but the rank kurukuru grass had closed in on the tillage. After six weeks of neglect in such a climate, a garden reverts almost to jungle.

The house, its white fibrocement walls now daubed with green paint, in a grotesque attempt at camouflage, was set in a shallow valley near the Laloki River, here a broad, briskly flowing stream speckled with small rapids and volcanic boulders. The site was hot and unhealthy. To the north, the 1,500-foot mass of Hombrun Bluff and Vetura Peak blocked the winds of the northwest monsoon, and the sea breezes of the southeast trade wind rarely penetrated so far inland.

Yet however hot and unhealthy, the site had this advantage – it was 17 miles away from the nearest point at which the Japanese could land. As privileged investigators it did not take us long to appreciate the potential advantage of a 17-mile start on the Japanese.

For an office, we were assigned a small, grass-thatched, woven-cane hut behind the main building. We furnished it with issue cots and mosquito nets and – in the manner of every other establishment for 30 miles around – with furniture 'borrowed' in town. Cheap maps pinned on the walls gave the place a properly professional atmosphere. From here, punctually at six o'clock every morning, we issued forth to chronicle the heroism of the Pacific Tobruk.

The daily round involved three, sometimes four or five, trips in a commandeered truck up and down the appalling road to town. The command posts of the Pacific Tobruk were strung out at intervals along the only 30 miles of hard public road then existing in the territory of Papua.

In the crucial weeks following the fall of Singapore, the defenders numbered fewer than 3,000 combat troops. Most of these men were militia draftees who had received only perfunctory training before being sent to battle stations. Their employment was, at best, a gesture of defiance. Many had been called up only a few weeks before from stores, factories and farms. Clad in ill-fitting khaki, issued with weapons they hardly knew how to fire, 2,000 of them had poured from the decks of a single transport onto Moresby's solitary T jetty one day late in January. They were charged with the defense of a base vitally important to the fate of their homeland.

Their arrival gave the *coup de grâce* to a civil administration already weakened by panic. A small permanent garrison had for many months been quartered in the town, but whatever arrangements it may have made to receive, quarter and ration reinforcements proved inadequate – to say the least.

No one believed the force could resist a landing on the Rabaul scale. Nevertheless, defensive elements were deployed, and a few strips of wire set in the water off the foreshores. It was planned to make the chief effort a fighting retreat up the road, which ended 30 miles inland in a narrow pass through the Hombrun cliffs. What troops survived could disperse in the hills to wage guerrilla war.

On February 3, Japanese long-range flying boats bombed the town and inflicted some casualties. Further raids were certain, and it seemed probable that the enemy would mount a full-scale amphibious attack within a matter of weeks.

The newly arrived troops looted the town savagely. Confused, unequipped, inadequately rationed, they were immediately moved into open country. For weeks after the evacuation, hundreds of men were without shelter or camp equipment in the open bush or grasslands. It was well into the wet season and they were drenched nightly with heavy rains.

Clad only in shorts and shirts, they were tortured night and day by swarms of mosquitoes and flies. Many could not obtain mosquito bars. Their faces and arms and bare legs became grotesquely swollen and infected. An officer commanding one infantry unit told me that for more than a week the only food he could get on issue was five pounds of rice and a one-pound tin of beef per section (11 men) per day. Two hundred men drew drinking and washing water from a single three-quarter-inch standpipe. Within a month of the arrival, dengue fever, malaria, bacillary dysentery and tropical ulcers had reduced the effective strength by a quarter.

By the time I visited Moresby's 'battle stations' in February, the more spectacular aspects of this confusion had been corrected, but the physical condition of the men as a result of it was tragically evident.

Most of them were youngsters between 19 and 23. They had lost an average of 20 pounds in weight. They were scrawny, yellow, wild eyed, and listless in their movements. Their skins were pocked by infected insect bites. I shall never forget one boy who thumbed a ride from the airfield to town. His face was so badly bitten he had been unable to shave for a week. His knees and lower legs were encased in scabs that oozed serum and pus.

Someone said: 'You must have been scratching yourself, son.'

His miserable eyes accused the speaker. 'I don't when I'm awake,' he muttered. 'But a man can't help himself when he's asleep.'

About the middle of February the Japanese began raiding every day. The weather was fine, but the raids were not heavy and did surprisingly little damage. Formations of 9, 11, 15 or 18 bombers – Mitsubishi 97's – would come over the mountains in the morning. There was always ample warning from the watchers stationed out in the mountains. The planes would approach the airfield or the town from the north, beginning their run at 23,000 feet and bombing from 18,000 feet.

Their bombing was execrably bad. When they attacked the harbor area the bombs usually fell in the water and stunned enough fish to provide a meal for the units stationed on the

48

foreshores. When they attacked the airfield, they usually plastered the bush at the western end, to the great disgust of the defense company that manned machine-gun posts there.

Casualties hardly averaged one man killed or wounded per raid, but after a few weeks the raid morale of the troops began to drop. A single battery of 3.7-inch antiaircraft guns was emplaced and went into action on Turaguba Hill near the town. The gunners scored a kill or two but, like all antiaircraft, had to pay off their luck in long, lean periods. To make things more difficult, the Japs began to stay above 23,000 feet, beyond our effective range.

At first the daily visit by the Japanese was exciting and stimulating. We used to travel considerable distances to reach high ground overlooking a probable target area and watch for the fun. More than once a week we were pasted with overshots for our pains. The troops would poke their heads out of slit trenches and cheer or jeer at the gunners, according to the accuracy of the modest barrage.

But the one-sidedness of the business worried the men. Like other Allied soldiers at battle stations all over the world at this time, they started to ask: 'Where the hell are *our* planes?'

It became habitual to take shelter at the first sound of the siren and to stay there until it was well over, regardless of where the enemy was bombing. There is nothing more dangerous to morale than the leisure to think over an unsatisfactory military situation in the bottom of a muddy slit trench.

Most of the troops were now employed on work that would have been done by labor units if the establishment of the Pacific Tobruk had run to such specialization. Side by side with any native laborers who could be persuaded to return from the bush, they worked from dawn to dark extending the runways of the airfield, forming supply trails to positions on the Bootless Inlet or Gallery Reach flanks of the harbor, clearing camp and dump sites, or unloading ships at the single vital pier which the Japanese bombers consistently failed to hit.

This work of scraping the crude foundations of a war base out of the stony soil received priority over all other kinds. It continued to do so until, months later, colored engineering units of the United States army moved in. Only then did the Moresby garrison have time to undertake even the most formal training exercises. Their main recreation in the first two or three months was gossiping in the slit trenches as they watched small formations of enemy bombers make leisurely runs over the targets.

This was the era of the 'Daru Derby.'

The Australian soldier is, above everything else, a realist. He has too much horse sense to make good cannon fodder. The 'death or glory' idea fails to move him. He believes wholeheartedly that it is much better to be a live dog with the will to bite – and a bite or two left – than a dead lion with no will or bite at all. He can see no virtue in stubbornness for the sake of stubbornness, nor in discipline for the sake of discipline. Give him a logical objective and competent leadership and he is one of the most dangerous and resourceful fighters in the world. But employ him on a task or in a manner beyond the limits of intelligent patience, and he makes a poor defender of last ditches.

It did not take the Moresby garrison long to realize that it lacked the organization, equipment, leadership and numbers to resist effectively any large-scale landing attempt by the Japanese. The men were aware of their position. If and when the time came, they intended to take it out of the Jap's hide to the utmost – yes. But die to the last man? – certainly not! They were going home. They agreed that home was going to need live men, not dead ones.

Every group of friends, every section, had its own private plan of escape and made its own private preparations. As a rule, the plan was to retreat into the hills and by various routes make for Daru. Daru was a small government station 400 miles west along the coast. It was chosen, I think, simply because it was the New Guinea settlement nearest to the Australian mainland. Between Moresby and Daru lay some of the deepest coastal swamp and wildest jungle on the whole of the island. Between Moresby and Daru were the great deltas of the Kikori and Fly rivers. But these obstacles were considered incidental.

'Have you picked your team for the Daru Derby yet, Digger?' was the frequent facetious greeting when the bombers were overhead.

But the Daru Derby was nevertheless a deadly serious concept. Many men had their Daru Derby haversacks – their 'whizz through bags' – always on hand. They contained the minimum emergency gear and trade tobacco with which they believed they could go into the hills and stand a chance of survival. Months later I saw a little of the western delta swamps and have never ceased to thank God that the western Daru Derby was never more than a plan for escape, a grim joke among dispirited and disillusioned men.

It was a hard life. It was a hard life even with quarters in the comparative luxury of administrative headquarters, after the first confusion had been straightened out. Until acclimatization was achieved, the continual sweating was the worst discomfort. At half-past five in the morning I would begin the day by putting on a dry shirt. Half an hour later, it was sticking to my back in dark patches. The physical exertion of walking 30 yards to breakfast under the plantation house drenched me.

All day – bumping my behind raw in the back of a utility truck over that 30 miles of unmentionable road – I continued to sweat. I sweated while questioning tired officers at G1, or tired troops shoveling mud in the water tables and gravel on the runways, or tired bomber pilots sitting in Royal Australian Air Force headquarters. I sweated leaning on the parapet of trenches, staring through glasses at the pattern of flak bursts. I sweated through interminable evenings playing poker or writing dispatches. Then I crawled under a mosquito bar and sweated afresh, lying naked, itching and stifled. When I was asleep the sweat would soak through a doubly folded blanket and leave a wet patch on the canvas cot.

Every afternoon and every night it rained. Every night hordes of black, voracious mosquitoes came singing hungrily out of the grass. Every dawn hordes of black, voracious flies came in buzzing thirstily. They slept in clots and festoons on the rafters of the mess. Assaults on them with insecticide at night would bring down a squirming carpet that covered the packed earth floor, but it never appreciably diminished their numbers.

If one had been able to take an interest in food, the food would have been unendurable. It was baked beans, canned corned beef, rice, soggy bread, canned butter – rancid and oily with long standing in the sun – and occasionally jam which became crusted with ants between meal and meal. There was no variation in these staples.

But there were things harder to endure than the diet. One was the A.H.Q. latrine. Until troops could be spared to expand it, men with delicate stomachs and noses had to wear gas masks when they paid it a visit.

Late in February the Japanese began to send over fighter sweeps. They did more damage than pattern bombing. The Zeros, usually operating in flights of five, would swoop in impertinently from the sea at 50 feet, drop their belly tanks and roar up and down the road or across the airfield and harbor, strafing. They destroyed a few of our grounded aircraft and flying boats that way, and set gasoline dumps on fire. They would have destroyed more if there had been more to destroy.

After the Zeros started to make regular calls, life in the camps beside the field and in town became edgy. The bombers approached over the mountains and one could see them coming a great distance away. The fighters were unpredictable. Often truck drivers and their passengers had to dive for the ditch with no more warning than the roar of a motor pulling an airplane out of a dive, and the spatter of tracer burning the grass at the side of the road.

Machine gunners soon scored a Zero or two. Then the Japs located the gun positions and became more prudent. But the gunners' success encouraged the more combative and optimistic souls to spend their time off duty sitting on the tops of the little hills with which the area is liberally dotted, hugging tommy guns and praying for a Jap to fly within range.

Early in March there was a rumor that Australian fighter squadrons with P-40 Kittyhawks were due to arrive any time. Troops were detailed to build revetments for them near the airfield. Morale rose sharply. But as the weeks passed and the

Kittyhawks did not come, it began to sag again. Sometimes it pulsated under stimulus of a series of stories that the Kittyhawks were due to arrive tomorrow. In time the mythical fighters were known as Tomorrow-hawks, eventually as Neverhawks.

Now and then little flutters of panic followed in the wake of other rumors that *the* Jap convoy was on the way. Traffic accelerated through the Rouna Pass at the head of the 30-mile road. It was a precipitous defile giving entrance to the foothills of the Owen-Stanley's. Trucks that stalled on the one-way bottleneck were enthusiastically manhandled over the cliffs.

The general officer commanding then held a sunset conference of all the officers in a field near his house. Switching the horsetail savagely, he informed them that the morale of both officers and men in the garrison left a great deal to be desired. He was fully aware of certain unsatisfactory aspects of the defense position, but nevertheless the prime duty of each Australian serving here was to kill at least three Japanese. Possibly four. He was putting the ratio so low on account of the garrison's obviously poor quality. Henceforward, officers would be responsible for keeping their men at whatever job they were doing until bombs began to fall not more than 200 yards away. When bomb bursts were observed at not more than 200 yards, officers would be permitted to order their men to take shelter. At the conclusion of this so-called conference, the officers dismissed pensively.

My memory of that meeting would have been somewhat different if it had not been for an incident that occurred three days later. The general officer commanding was in session with G1 when the press called for its daily-situation report. We were invited to wait in the outer office.

Suddenly came the unmistakable roar of Zeros strafing the road. There was a prolonged burst of machine-gun fire. Large, ominous punctures appeared high up on the wall opposite me.

I took cover smartly in a big refrigerator that stood in one corner of the room. The strafing continued for about two minutes, then the planes zoomed away. With caution I disentangled myself from a heap of soda-water bottles and poked my head into the room. It was very empty, but through the open door of the inner sanctum I saw a strange tableau.

The general officer commanding was still seated imperturbably at his table, studying a sheaf of aerial reconnaissance maps. Opposite him sat the G1, his hands clenched and his forearms stiffly extended before him on the table. His eyes were glassy. The general officer commanding looked up from his maps and frowned. *'What was that noise,* Douggie?' he inquired.

Quickly, surely, Japan closed her fingers and gathered in the Indies and the Islands: January 23, Rabaul and Kieta; February 15, Singapore; February 20, Timor; March 7, Rangoon and Batavia; March 8, Lae and Salamaua; March 10, Buka and Bougainville; April 11, Bataan.

In the hollow of the Japanese palm but yet uncrushed, 2,000 mosquito-bitten youths continued apathetically to spread gravel on Moresby's bush-clearing airfield, dig ditches and latrines, and manhandle packing cases. On three sides, hundreds of miles of rolling forest and mountain insulated them from any reality of conflict more grim than bombing from the air. The sea at their rear was the danger. So to the sea they turned their eyes.

CHAPTER 3

JAPAN 'E COME!

AFTER the first sensational torrent of Japanese conquest in the early months of 1942, the stream of war stagnated. Yet uneventful Moresby graduated as a subject for martial headlines – within well-nigh limitless limits of military security. We made what we could of little news. We dubbed the defenders 'The Mice of Moresby.' Those who served sheets of a deeper dye even went so far as to call them 'The Miracle Men of Moresby,' in black letters an inch high.

This latter epithet was too much. They resented it and the author was chided. He was taking a shower in the front garden of the press hut one evening when a truckload of filthy, sunscorched, unshaven gravel shovelers from the airfield pulled up.

'Are you B—— Y——, the war correspondent?' they called.

'Yes, sure,' he called back.

'Well, we're the goddamn Miracle Men of Moresby. Take a good look at us!' they replied, and drove off without further comment into the twilight.

We could not write: *The strength, equipment, training and leadership of the New Guinea Force is inadequate for the task it has been briefed to do. It is enervated by tropical diseases and it is badly fed, overworked, discouraged and very nearly hopeless. It is without reserves or air support. If the Japanese come, organized defense will last not more than 48 hours.*

All we could do was tell of the exasperated antiaircraft gunner who, when the bombers dropped their eggs at the emplacement from 23,000 feet, leapt out of his pit, brandished his fists and yelled: 'Why don't you come down, you dirty little yellow bastards, and let us have a crack at you?' This served the

55

double purpose of symbolizing the Australian Digger's unquenchable spirit and of delicately underlining the absence of fighters.

All we could do was relate the funny story of a power grader crew caught on a hill near the airfield in a raid. They took shelter under the machine but forgot to leave it in gear. Just as the bombs were dropped, the machine began to move off downhill. The shelterers industriously crawled with it, noses in the dust. The accelerating grader outpaced them, but unconscious of this, they continued to crawl, noses down, while ribald spirits in a nearby slit trench whistled 'Get along, little dogie.' This served to emphasize the fact that although the Australian fighting man maintained his irrepressible sense of humor, he was human enough to take cover when the occasion demanded it!

For the most part, however, light relief was provided by the natives assigned to officers as batmen or mess servants. As we were neither fish, flesh nor good red herring – only war correspondents who confound honest soldiers in every combat area with their utterly indefinable status, or lack of it – we were at first assigned some remarkable characters for shirt washing, bed making and boot cleaning.

Probably the most remarkable was a willowy, copper-colored youth who limed his hair to a delicate henna, wore a lavender loincloth and a hibiscus blossom behind each ear, and was forever admiring himself in a splinter of discarded shaving mirror. He made us self-conscious, so we gave him to a sergeant who lived down the hill.

His immediate successor was an 'old soldier' of the worst type, Jack-With-No-Toes, a black, aged villain who had accompanied a previous master on a voyage to Scotland, and was therefore much too knowledgeable to demean himself with work. He received all orders with an enthusiatic 'Okey-doke-by-God-okay-yes, taubada' (master) and thereafter ignored them. Jack-With-No-Toes had a small, potbellied, ringworm-afflicted assistant whom we named Wellington for some now-forgotten reason. Wellington affected to have no English. It was difficult to do the proper thing and kick his behind for sins of omission, because he was impervious to any expression of anger we could assume. He took the whole business of serving white men as a rich joke, and when threatened with physical violence would giggle shrilly and imitate Joe Louis shaping up.

The servant problem was not solved until we were allotted half a dozen mission-trained boys from eastern Papua. To alien eyes they were indistinguishable, so we played poker for the order of choice. I chose Gibson Duluvina simply because he looked the cleanest, but as time wore on, he achieved the status of a personality in his own right.

My interest in him began, so to speak, with a pair of sky-blue shorts that were, and probably still are, the most prized and precious item of his wardrobe – and it worked up. He appeared to be about 16 years old. He was a medium-brown color, and unhandsome above the neck. He clipped his woolly hair short, and had protruding, negroid lips; a sullen, puzzled, crinkled forehead like a thoughtful ape; remarkably clear, large, sharp eyes. He had a stout, delicately rounded body and tapering legs ending in immense, calloused, noble feet.

For a time, he was an indifferent servant. He was not lazy, but he loved leisure so much that for all practical purposes it amounted to the same thing. For instance, he would sit all the afternoon on the boy-house steps when he should have been ironing my shirts, singing a song woven on five semitones that went: *Hi-dee, hi-dee-hi-dee, hi, de-de ho!* Thus when at nightfall I should have had a fresh shirt, he would explain quite truthfully that the jets of the gasoline iron were blocked.

This state of affairs, I realized, was my own fault. So one evening at mosquito-bar time – six o'clock – I sat down on the lowest available chair, called Gibson Duluvina, motioned him to stand directly in front of me, and then pretended assiduously to read a month-old newspaper. At the end of two minutes, I folded the newspaper and asked the now wriggling boy if he still wished to work for me.

Io, taubada – with great anxiety – he wished to work for me.

Very good. Then, in future, whatever happens to the jets of the gasoline iron, I must have a clean shirt, one pair of clean socks, and appropriate underclothing every night – come hell, rain, hail, fire, earthquake, or even air raid. Understood?

Kamonai.

The mosquito bar must be tucked in, with no mosquitoes under it. *Kamonai?*

Kamonai.

My glass, shaving mug, razor and soap holder must be washed and dried. The mud must be removed even from the crevices between the uppers and soles of my shoes. *Kamonai?*

Good. Since everything was so perfectly *kamonai,* the pay would be exactly what it had been before – ten shillings on the first of each month. Gibson Duluvina wished to work for me, but there would be serious bottom kicking – possibly even a new job working in the quarry – if these things were not done.

Henceforward these things were done. Gibson of the blue pants was outshone as a personal servant only by one Nasubah Namo, long since forced into a habitual near perfection by an evacuated spinster from Samaria. I began to notice things about Gibson – that occasionally he went about his work dolefully whistling hymn tunes or *The Prisoner's Song,* that he was personally very clean, that on Sundays he wore a spotless white *rami* (loincloth) and went to church when a service was held, that he became excited as a suburban vesteryman when the Anglican bishop of New Guinea, Dr P. N. W. Strong, arrived. He had learned to read and write English in the mission school at Wedau.

Sometimes he would creep up noiselessly at night and try to overhear news broadcasts on the mess radio set. One Sunday morning when no one else was around, he asked very diffidently what the news had been. I told him as simply as possible. Next Sunday he arrived with his great friend – and fellow slave of the press – Cyril Aradne, and asked again what the news had been. Eventually the Sunday-morning audience for my weekly news digest in very basic English rose to eight, and was becoming embarrassing when a change of quarters put an end to it.

Sometimes I would catch the thirster after knowledge furtively reading an old newspaper on the veranda, when he believed nobody was looking. And I noticed, with a vague, disturbing sense of personal guilt, how utterly, hopelessly baffled were those simian crinkles on his forehead, how profoundly melancholy the shadows under his large, remarkable eyes.

I was to owe a very great deal to Gibson. Through a little understanding of him, I was to progress to a little understanding of his people. Out beyond the hills of Moresby, they were no background figures. They were the living land itself – the dark-skinned people from the delta of the Fly who worked the luggers and the launches and their cargoes, pouring with sweat, singing under the burden of the sun; the coffee-colored people who poled long, laden canoes up stubborn rivers; the teeming toilers of the sago forest; the people who stank in their villages yet greeted a white man as a king, proudly and solemnly with a procession, who hung upon his slightest gesture or word, eager for the honor of serving him, down to the smallest child. They were the carrier people with corded legs, who were soon to rub their shoulders to the bone, lugging the white man's sacred war over mountains and through torrents; and soon to lug the human salvage of it back again, tending the wounded gently as women, weeping for them when they were beyond aid. These were Gibson Duluvina's people.

There *was* a war in New Guinea beyond Moresby. By hearsay we patiently plotted its present shape and history, as the last drops of civilian life were squeezed out through the jungle.

The London Mission Society had a station along the water-front road beyond Hanuabada village, northwest of the port. It was a cluster of ugly, ocher-painted buildings around a bare compound shaded by straggling mango trees. Civilian refugees were housed there while passages were arranged for them on southbound ships.

A visit to this dismal barracks was always certain to produce some new tale of terror, escape and endurance. There we obtained the first eyewitness stories of the Japanese landings at Lae and Salamaua, of the savage bombings of the goldfield towns, of the surrender of Kieta to the crew of a single Japanese seaplane; stories of epic journeys through trailless hills, wild voyages of flight in little ships; stories of fortitude, heroism, cowardice, bungling, cunning, fire, explosion, looting, murder, wealth lost, and lifework destroyed.

Japan'e come. White man'e go bush.

The compound was a fascinating place. It was the setting for the last scene of a tragedy, where the players awaited their exit lines. Their eyes betrayed them. That was the most pitiable thing in their secret brokenness. The shadow of the fear that had broken them was in their eyes.

I remember an old, old man with a placid, gentle face. His skin was clear and almost transparent. His hair, thin on a blue-veined skull, was as long as a woman's, as yellow as cream. He tied it in a knot at the back of his neck with a string of plaited flax, in the fashion of a little girl's hair ribbon. He wore mud-stained dungarees that hung with scarecrow looseness on his bones. He was one of the original gold miners on Edie Creek – one of the unlucky ones. He had escaped from Salamaua after the first Japanese bombing and had walked out across the island hundreds of miles through the jungle. He was exhausted almost to death.

The old man was very anxious to tell the story of the evacuation of Salamaua accurately and circumstantially, but he was long winded and his voice was monotonous. The others with him were irate, malaria-ridden men who contradicted him repeatedly. They ended up by snatching the story from his lips and finishing it, rapidly and pithily. But whenever they paused, he would resume his own version exactly where he had been cut short. We heard him out to the end, and he summarized it all in a mild, faraway, unresentful tone.

'It was a terrible thing, however it happened,' he said. 'A terrible thing. Oh my, the fires! The fires! I shall always see them in my dreams.'

I remember a woman, too. Three or four weeks after the last regular evacuee ship had sailed she walked in one morning from the bush. I saw her sitting by the roadside outside administrative headquarters, waiting for papers to sail on the ship leaving for Australia that night. She had refused a chair on the veranda and sat among the native boys. She was about 35 years old. Her hair was cut short like a man's. Her face was yellow brown and her eyes hard, a bright china blue. Her teeth – I saw them when she smiled at one of the squatting natives and spoke to him in rapid pidgin – were short and square and white as porcelain. I never learned her story. There was something in that resolute, bitter face that forbade questioning.

It does not take many bombers to wreck a little wooden town. It doesn't take many bombers to uproot an order so shallowly founded as the European colonization of New Guinea. The blows were struck at Lae, Salamaua, Samarai, Wua, Bulolo, Madang, Wewak, Lorengau. For all these settlements there was a fatal morning when the Japanese planes came droning in over the sea, circled, dived, bombed, sprayed bullets as they climbed, and droned away again.

The story of one place was the story of all. Panic ran like fire through dry forest. The old and the sick, the women and the children, crowded to the airfields clamoring for escape. Stores were abandoned, homes fled at an hour's notice, native laborers turned loose to roam at will. It was an ugly story, a story of hopeless, leaderless confusion, relieved only by a few shining examples of individual heroism.

The small communities had never had much permanence or stability in their own right. Most of the residents were the type of colonists who regarded their jobs merely as a means of livelihood lucrative enough to earn early retirement, either on substantial profits or pensions. Or they were people who had suffered in the unsettled economy after World War I. They had gravitated to the outskirts of civilization, where they enjoyed higher status and greater privileges than their talents would have demanded at home. The society they built was a precariously rooted growth on the skin of a great wilderness.

Like the British in Malaya or the Dutch in the Netherlands Indies, they had been uncomfortably aware of the growing pressure of 'color' on the thin-walled vacuum of the white boss's world. But unlike the British in Malaya or the Dutch in the Indies, all of them lived so close to their administration that they had little respect for it and little confidence in its capacity to meet crises.

So it happened that in the crisis they failed their administration, and their administration failed them.

Only a slight framework of military organization survived the crash of civil institutions. A small volunteer militia, which had existed for many years, had been active since the outbreak of the European war. After the first Japanese air attack, the steadier types of men of military age obeyed their call-up orders. (The less steady types were caught in Moresby and enlisted, anyway.) About 1,000 men were thus mobilized. Of these, three or four hundred had received some military training with the New Guinea Volunteer Rifles, or were soldiers of World War I.

The men were loosely organized, armed with Lee-Enfield .303 rifles and a few antiquated machine guns. They had reserves of food in inland settlements and were provided with small-arms ammunition from local stocks or by air. They were instructed not to resist large-scale Japanese landings but to retire to the hills and act as scouts and guerrillas, reporting by radio to headquarters New Guinea Force. This they did. How heroically and how well they did it was not known for many months.

The record of the New Guinea Volunteer Rifles, the steadiness of Christian missions, and the performance of the civil pilots employed by airlines operating in New Guinea did much to compensate for the unhappy disintegration of European administrative and commercial institutions in the face of the Japanese threat.

There is no chapter in the history of civil aviation in the Pacific prouder than that written by New Guinea pilots during the weeks of the north-coast evacuation. They were a band of men with a magnificent record of skill and enterprise in peacetime. They had contributed more than any other professional group to the development of this tropical frontier. They earned their daily bread flying some of the most difficult and hazardous air routes in the world.

When war came, they measured up. After the first bombings, every aircraft that could be coaxed into the air was mobilized to get women and children and invalids out of the menaced settlements before the invasion. Every aircraft was flown to the uttermost limits of its structural endurance, day and night, in all weather.

The enemy bombed the terminal airfields heavily, but the pilots carried on, taking off and landing among the bomb craters. Some were killed and wounded by strafing fighters. In the clumsy, slow transport craft some evaded pursuing Zeros by flying at treetop level through the winding canyons in the mountains. At least two lost their lives in the crashes of planes that had been flown until they literally fell to pieces in the air. Yet not one civilian evacuee was killed or injured by accident to commercial aircraft during the evacuation of New Guinea towns.

The courage of the men who flew them to safety was not surpassed even by the pilots of the R.A.A.F. – the deathless few who used their riddled Catalinas and Hudsons to stab again and again at the enemy's gathering strength in Rabaul and – who knows? – may have delayed and hurt the enemy just enough to make the difference between defeat and victory when the trial came.

Salamaua, March 7, 1942 – There had been a last, furious burst of bombing, In the evening, watchers on the hilltops behind the town saw a long line of gray ships in the sea. '*Japan 'e come! Japan 'e come!*' The natives ran, chanting the final fear, eyes staring, lips slack.

Panic had only ashes to burn now. The demolition squads trotted from store to store, house to house. The fires flowered, one by one. Flame licked through the cracks in roof and thatch, crept from lintel to eaves, crawled over window frames. Old, fever-stringy beachcombers reeled from drinking what they could of the whisky, buried the rest under the floorboards, staggered singing off into the night, followed by retinues of natives bent double under loads of loot.

A civilian nurse, Esther Stock, had refused evacuation by air and remained to tend patients in the European hospital. When the invasion fleet was sighted, she gathered her sick together and led them into the jungle. It was raining. They traveled by the light of a muffled hurricane lantern. Natives carried on litters those who were too infirm to walk.

The way to Komiatum Hill, rendezvous for the last of the stragglers, led through a swamp. Knee-deep mud sucked the boots from their feet. Hunting crocodiles barked in the shallows.

The little town burned luridly at the edge of the sea. They saw it through the drenching rain. A few shells whistled in, and burst amid the ruins. They heard the dull crashing. Rear guards in the town were led by an Australian officer who had escaped from Rabaul and arrived only a few days before. Homemade mines were laid on the runway of the airfield. Demolition squads waited until the Japanese advance parties from the landing barges had approached within a few yards of them, then rammed home the plunger. The mines exploded, throwing up fountains of earth. One Australian pistoled a Japanese officer point-blank, then bounded off in the long grass like a kangaroo, bullets spattering round him.

The jungle sweeps almost on to Salamaua airfield. From a densely wooded hilltop, scouts peered down at daybreak. They saw wisps of ground fog rising from the drenched lalang grass. They saw a Japanese battalion parade among the craters in the tarmac – ranks of small yellow men in khaki drab and jungle green. They saw battle standards of white and crimson silk stirring from the ruins of the Mandated Airlines hangar – bringing the New Order in East Asia to half a dozen natives who had refused to say where their masters had gone. Then they saw the sun, the rising sun, a blood-red ball over Komiatum Hill.

At a rendezvous in the bush 132 refugees gathered. They divided themselves into two parties, the sick and the well. The 100 men who were well decided to walk to Wau, 60 miles over the mountains, and there to plan further. Group by group, they drifted off into the bush.

Thirty-two were sick. They did not believe they could endure the hardships of an attempt to cross the unexplored central mountains. They decided the only chance of escape was to voyage by canoe down the coast to Buna, 100 miles away, where they might receive the help of missionaries and any officers of the administration who might still be at their posts. A latecomer brought news of a small launch concealed in the estuary of a creek. Esther Stock stayed with the sick. Seven of them were on litters. They crept cautiously down to the coast and gathered together dugout canoes, which they lashed together in a clumsy string for the launch to tow. When the boat and the canoes had been loaded with provisions, there was not enough room for all to ride. The stronger walked on the faintly defined trail that skirted the coast, trying to keep the launch in sight.

It was a journey of heartbreaking slowness, heart-chilling perils and hardships. The northwest wind was blowing and the sea was rough. The small craft pitched violently. The sick men raved with fever, retched with seasickness, groaned in a misery of restlessness. Sometimes the sea rose so high it threatened to overturn the canoes and they had to run in through the surf and wait for the storm to abate. The walkers stumbled through sand and mud and mangrove roots, clambered over rocky headlands.

By night the voyagers gathered together on beaches, huddled over little fires in the rain. By day the sun scorched them mercilessly. They cowered at the sound of aircraft in the sky. The men who told the tale said Esther Stock was more than the nurse upon whom they depended to keep life in their bodies. She was their silent leader. She did not complain; and the men, however old and sick and weak, were ashamed to complain. She showed no fear; and they were ashamed to be afraid. She admitted no doubt that by God's mercy they would be saved; and they were ashamed of their doubt.

Twenty-one days after the Japanese landing, Esther Stock led her party into Buna, whence by devious routes they were brought to safety. All lived.

At Wau, the last men from the outposts of the jungle came together. Each had his tale of terror. In the more remote districts, in the valley of the Sepik and along the Aitape coast, the natives were not even a single generation removed from cannibalism and head-hunting.

65

Japan 'e come. White man 'e go bush.

The news ran from village to village. The drums beat it out in the hills. Plantation houses were looted and burned by roving bands of masterless laborers. Even the nails were wrenched from the timbers and thrust triumphantly for adornment into the ear lobes and distended septa of the raiders. Lonely prospectors, several of them Chinese, were speared or shot to death with arrows. Their heads were taken to the man houses and their entrails ceremonially eaten.

Two hundred men, too old or too ill to serve with the guerrillas, at last found their way to Wau. They determined to walk through the mountains to Moresby, a feat previously attempted only by one or two of the territory's hardiest patrol officers. The route lay through passes 10,000 feet above sea level, through forests ranged by hostile tribes. Its traverse involved the passage of great razor-backs and roaring mountain streams. They passed them. Only a few died, and they were buried in the hills.

We saw the men who had made the journey sitting under the mango trees in the mission compound. Some had even brought gold from their mines with them. Others had tried to bring too much and had been forced to hide it in the jungle. One old man complained that he had lost 300 ounces of dust when his canoe overturned in a river, but he did not seem very downcast. Some of the hidden gold was recovered later. Months afterwards an officer of one of the big mining companies that operated in the Bulolo valley went back and brought out dust valued at more than £100,000. It lay unguarded, bundles roughly wrapped in burlap, in the gutter outside headquarters while the salvager paid his respects to the general.

From the mountains and the seas, day after day, tales came of lost frontiers – from Bougainville to Humbolt Bay, Manus to Merauke; tales even from those remote specks of habitable land in the ocean one occasionally sees from the decks of passing ships but can never find on a map; tales told by wind-weathered people with lonely eyes.

One looked at them and could image the homes they fled, the shadowed copra sheds under the groves. One could image the houses and the sheds falling to ruin; the sand drifting against the bleached bones of whaleboats drawn up on forgotten beaches; the never-ending trade wind sighing on the empty verandas where unfastened, sun-warped shutters banged, unmarked.

Japan came – and the wind and the sand and the sea. Only Moresby, looted and bomb blasted, remained as a remnant of the world that once was.

CHAPTER 4

ONE EYE COCKED

IN JUNE a gag went the rounds – that you could always tell the mice of Moresby because they were cockeyed. They got that way watching for planes and trying to dig slit trenches at the same time.

The author of the creaky little joke was observant. People *did* go about with one eye habitually cocked. The cause of that was more than a fear of surprise raids. It was the realization that the crisis of Australian defense, of which Moresby garrison was so much part, was now being decided in the air.

Whatever the reason, a full-scale Japanese attack on Moresby did not follow fast upon the occupation of Rabaul in January and of the base sites on the north coast of New Guinea two months later. Several hundreds of miles of mountain and jungle kept land forces effectively apart; and reefs, narrow channels and confined waters made the deployment of naval forces perilous and difficult except under a leakproof air umbrella. So land and sea warfare stagnated until an issue was fought in the air.

A race was on – a race between the ability of the Japanese to accumulate sufficient all-round strength to resume their advance through obstructive terrain and of the Allies to accumulate sufficient air strength to block an amphibious punch. The men of Moresby were at a vantage point from which they could watch the race from start to finish. They were never bored by watching, for they not only had their shirts staked on the result but their hides as well. No plane, in those early days, flew across New Guinea skies unnoticed by the toilers below.

There was little encouragement in watching – but there was at least pride. Britain is fiercely and rightly proud of her few fliers, and Australia has the right to be equally proud of *her* few. Britain's few flew Hurricanes and Spitfires against Heinkels and Messerschmitts. Australia's few flew Hudsons and Catalinas against Zeros.

In March the arrival at Moresby airfield of a single squadron of P.40 fighters manned by Australian pilots marked the beginning of a new phase in the air war, but for two months previously the task of checking constantly increasing Japanese pressure had been borne by a handful of Hudson and Catalina crews of the R.A.A.F., whose endurance and heroism were prodigious.

Day after day, night after night, one heard their machines droning over the mountains singly or in fours or fives – never more – to bomb Rabaul and Gasmata, to harry the Japanese shipping that was slowly gathering, to spy out thousands of square miles of island-dotted ocean. Pitifully few though they were, they hit with all they had – and their blows hurt.

Often in those days we went down to the Moresby waterfront to watch the Catalinas come home. They would lumber out of the haze and flop on the water as though metal, as well as men, were weary with strain. Flak and cannon shells had scarred their hulls. Sometimes limp, bloodied men were eased out of the hatches into the tender. Sometimes the ships themselves were wounded to death and settled quietly down at their moorings, or were dragged up the slipway and scrapped for spare parts.

The youngster who led the Catalina squadron was a tall, white-skinned, dark-haired Jew. His brown eyes were reflective and gentle, but his specialty was using his big aircraft as a dive bomber against ships in Rabaul Harbor, putting its nose down at 6,000 or 7,000 feet and pulling out at 400. After bombing he would keel-scrape over the hills, and thus confound the Japanese antiaircraft.

The squadron leader and his men not infrequently flew reconnaissance missions lasting 20 hours at a stretch, returned to base, slept while the fitters and riggers swarmed over their ship and did what they could to make it airworthy again, then took off on a bombing mission to New Britain. When there were not enough bombs for a full load, they took cases of empty beer bottles and spoiled butter cans. They would return from these strikes so exhausted they could hardly stand, eyes like raw beef from glare, and bodies palsied by snapping nerves. Many did not bother to go ashore except for briefing. They fitted the hull space of the flying boats with bunks and spirit stoves, and 'lived in' between strike and strike. Then after an hour or two of sleep in the humid heat of the cabin, they were restored enough to set out again.

One by one their numbers dropped. The dwindling was a breathless, terrible thing. Few were shot down in combat, for their skill at evasion was great and the Catalina is one of the most robust aircraft ever designed. But they dwindled from forced landings at sea, from wounds, and from the deterioration of their ships to a point where they could no longer be coaxed into the air.

Strafing Zeros caught a few on the water. I saw one crew die in a blazing hull that shot smoke and flames 400 feet above the placid harbor. The men had been asleep when seven Zeros came suddenly round the headland. They rolled and turned and looped with the skittish exuberance of Japanese fighter pilots who see no fighters to oppose them, then they blasted the bay shipping and the foreshores with cannon shells and incendiary bullets.

The Hudson crews worked at the same inhuman tension as the Catalina men, striking by night, spying by day. They did not complain because they had to run the gauntlet of Japanese fighters with a speed of 100 miles an hour faster than their own aircraft; nor that the machines they flew to the limit of range were worn out; nor that for days on end they would spend more time in the air than on the ground; nor that they were outnumbered, and haggard with living in dirty little bush camps pestered by flies and mosquitoes. Their sole complaint was that their .303-caliber guns were useless against the enemy in a clear sky. With .50-caliber guns the Japanese could keep

70

out of range and methodically shoot the Australian planes apart. The only way a Hudson or Catalina pilot could get a Jap was to outthink him in cloud so that he made an attack within range, or else to have the luck to run into one who was overcocky and careless.

The nadir of the 'Never-hawk' period was reached toward the middle of March. One day I saw seven Zeros jump a Hudson just preparing to land after a long reconnaissance flight. Happily for the Australian there was cloud cover fairly low down. He skipped so agilely in and out of it, blasted away so valiantly with his pathetic turret guns, defied every rule of aerodynamics and ignored the limitations of his aircraft so successfully that after 20 minutes the Zeros gave up and buzzed angrily home.

This visual evidence of superiority over the enemy brought the most confirmed slit-trench addicts out of their holes, cheering and yelling. But it did not alter the fact that friendly planes had by now almost disappeared from the sky.

We knew that American help was coming, that the first squadrons of B-17's and B-26's and P-40's were assembling in Australia, but we prayed that the help would arrive in time. Hope leaped particularly high at the end of the second week in March. Word went round that the chimerical P-40 squadron was due to arrive – not merely tomorrow but at nine o'clock in the morning.

Precisely at nine o'clock the roar of aircraft was heard. They approached the airfield from the direction of Bootless Inlet. All along the road troops poured out of their camps, cheering, waving towels, tossing hats, yelling 'Christ, look at 'em! Good old Never-hawks!'

The fighters passed overhead at about 1,000 feet and swooped down on the airfield. They weren't P-40's! They were only an unusually large gang of Zeros paying an unannounced call. I have often wondered what the Japanese pilots thought of our demonstration.

Upon us, the moral of the disappointment was profound. It was so profound that when the first five friendly fighters did arrive on the field a few days later, liaison between the army

71

and the air force had broken down, and our machine gunners put so many holes in the P-40's that three of them were unserviceable for weeks. Only by a miracle did the pilots escape death or wounding.

Fortunately, a diversion distracted the airmen's attention from their rough reception. A few minutes after they landed, a snooping Mitsubishi 97 was reported approaching over the mountains. One of the perforated P-40's flown by a youngster who had just won his wings, took off to intercept.

When the fighter was up about 12,000 feet, the Jap spotted opposition and turned away. But it was too late. The Australian made two passes abeam. To me – and to hundreds of other onlookers seeing the employment of fighter cover for the first time – his tactics looked perfect. The waspish P-40 shaved the bomber so closely that collision seemed inevitable. I could not understand why the squadron leader standing beside me groaned aloud and said: 'Jesus, there's no future in that, you bloody young fool!'

But whatever its shortcomings in finesse, the attack succeeded. The bomber faltered, fell away on one wing, and began a glide that grew steeper until it was screaming straight down the sky with a ribbon of white smoke behind it. It crashed with a mighty explosion far out to sea.

We onlookers fell on one another's necks, howling hysterically with joy. For miles around, men found that they had business at the airfield. They came roaring up the road in lorries, cheering and laughing. They stopped, poured out of the vehicles, and stood staring with a mixture of awe and disbelief at the fighters on the ground. For my own part, I had a sneaking feeling it was all much too good to be true. Something was bound to happen. No one had told me the rest of the squadron was due. When more planes came in suddenly, low over the hills, shepherded by two Hudsons, habit asserted itself. I dived far and fast for the cover of the nearest solid object, which happened to be a full drum of aviation gasoline.

It was, perhaps, a clue to the general feeling that neither the dive nor the extraordinary cover brought as much as a smile to the faces of the onlookers. They merely called after me sympathetically, 'It's okay, son. They're *ours*.'

The arrival of this first fighter squadron in New Guinea was really an event of immense importance. It did not spare the Moresby mice much bombing, but it helped their morale. It showed that American aid had reached Australia. If the Japanese now decided to push on, there would be some sort of fight instead of a hopeless, bloody walkover. True, it was no indication of how much American aid was reaching Australia, or if that aid would prove sufficient when the trial came. But any aid was cause for jubilation.

As the weeks passed however, it became painfully apparent that a score or so fighter aircraft could not solve all problems. Contrary to expectations, the sky did not rain riddled Japanese bombers. The Japanese bombers merely came with quadrupled fighter cover. They raided more heavily as the first small groups of American-manned B-25 and B-26 bombers, with some assurance of forward airfield protection, crossed the Coral Sea from Townsville and began to hit at concentrations of enemy ships and material thickening on the far side of the jungle barrier.

At Moresby, the Australian fighter pilots assumed a burden as heavy as that just relinquished by their comrades of the Hudsons and 'Cats' to the new bomber groups of the United States Army Air Force. Their period of ordeal was shorter, but it was long enough for those who survived to look back and say in their own laconic argot, 'We've *had* it.'

Though the P-40 as then powered and designed was a good army co-operation and low altitude fighter, it was no match for the Japanese Zero, particularly when employed as an interceptor. For one thing, the P-40's rate of climb was not high enough. It was heavily armored and ruggedly built, and could take punishment that would disintegrate a Zero into a bundle of blazing scrap, but its weight made it sluggish and unmaneuverable above 12,000 feet. Above 20,000 feet it was practically useless. The Japanese bombers continued to come over at 20,000 feet, and their escort would sit up at 25,000 or 26,000 feet.

Even at that, the P-40's did better than break even –

although seldom were there enough serviceable machines for them to fight in formation as they should have fought, declining individual combat. Dogfighting Zeros with P-40's – or trying to dogfight – cost the life of many an excellent pilot. Operational losses – crashes on rough fields, forced landings, other accidents – kept the squadron strength at an irreducible minimum, and finally came near extinguishing it. Almost unhampered, Japanese pattern bombing went on, while Zeros mixed it with the would-be interceptors.

The situation was serious – desperately serious. A shallow pool of precious fighters was being rapidly drained of machines that would have been needed to counter a possible Japanese thrust against the mainland. Yet whatever human courage, tenacity and enterprise could do, the P-40 pilots did. They even found 'leisure' for excursions the Japanese no longer dared to undertake: strafing sweeps on airfields, which did more damage than high-level bombing. Even so, the unpleasant truth could not be concealed. When a fighter came spinning out of the brazen morning sky above Moresby, writing its own brief epitaph in a thin line of flame and smoke, the chances were even on it being a Zero or one of ours. And there were so many more Zeros.

The men who lived an hour or a night or a week removed from death were in tent camps near the field. They conformed to no physical type, only to a standard of courage. Some were big fellows with stubbly beards on their cheeks; others were small, delicately made boys with pimples and hardly any beard at all. Off duty they lay on their cots, sleeping or reading in the steambath atmosphere under the tent tops, or talking in the 'mess' – a tent with trestle tables where unappetizing meals of oily canned meat and off-color bread were perpetually laid out for latecomers. On duty call, they lounged in a tiny tent at the far end of the landing strip. The tent was ragged with shrapnel holes, and behind it was a string of deep bomb craters which no one had bothered to fill in. Some pilots preferred the meager shade under the wings of their aircraft, and sprawled there looking dreamily at the sky. They wore shorts and shirts mostly, with blue-uniform caps and shiny black flying boots from which their scarred, bony knees protruded.

Morning after morning there were air battles that we earth-bound watchers craned our necks to see. The toneless drubbing of guns and the air-thinned whine of motors sounded overhead. Afterward there were never quite so many shark-nosed planes drawn up in a line at the head of the runway.

One who was not of them could never really know these men, or understand what transmutation of mind and soul let them laugh and eat and read and sleep and dream, disregarding the shadow that was upon them. I used to think that perhaps they had conquered time's illusion by giving themselves so wholly to the performance of a task and to the ideal of courage that seconds and years were all one to them. But they were very human. They almost worshiped the man who led them. He was a tall, clumsy-looking man with a brown, drooping mustache, a florid face and prominent eyes. He was older than the rest and had a paternal air with them. He had flown with a famous Australian fighter squadron in the Middle East.

The only time I ever saw depression or nervousness in the camp was the morning the commanding officer did not return from a lone strike against Lae airfield. He had just been awarded a D.F.C. for his work in the Middle East, and that evening was to have attended a dinner party given by the general in celebration. A fortnight or so before, I was in the mess when the news came that the squadron leader's brother, who served under him, had been shot down by Zeros in the sea. The big man's face was absolutely expressionless after he heard what had happened. There was a small table set aside which he had used as an 'office.' He sat down, finished some paper work very deliberately, rose and spoke to two other pilots at the trestle table. The three lounged off together, and we heard a station wagon start up.

Later that day we learned that they had staged an impromptu strafing raid on Salamaua and had killed many Japanese. About the same time, the squadron leader's brother was picked up by natives in a canoe and delivered, still dripping, to the jubilant mess. Twenty-four hours later he was flying again.

But the grudge strafes continued. The P-40's were well used in darting out of the mountain canyons upon the surprised enemy. They killed more Japanese and destroyed more Zeros that way than they could ever hope to do in air combat.

The morning the C.O. went missing, three Zeros surprised him. He knew better than to try to fight. He put the plane's nose straight down and leveled off at treetop height, looking for a valley mouth up which to fly and elude the pursuit. He found a valley, but in a few minutes was horrified to see that it ran out in a blank, precipitous wall of rock. There was nothing to do now but fight. He turned, caught a Zero in his sights and pressed the firing button. After one burst the guns jammed. The enemy fighters then shot the helpless P-40 to pieces, but by a miracle did not hit the pilot. He coaxed the riddled aircraft over the low range of hills seaward and belly-landed on the water, 1,200 yards from shore.

The plane floated just long enough for him to escape from the cockpit and inflate his life jacket. He lay limply in the water, feigning death. The Japanese repeatedly circled at 50 feet altitude but did not fire. When they were gone he began to swim. Natives in canoes sighted the swimmer but were afraid to help. The Japanese had already made savage reprisals on coastal villages that gave aid to crashed airmen. Two New Britain boys, however, waded out to help him through the surf. They said the villagers were debating whether to hand him over to a Japanese patrol that had left Lae in a launch. They offered to try to lead him to an Australian outpost, and the three plunged into the jungle while the villagers were still debating.

The pilot had kicked off his flying boots in the water and had to travel barefoot. After an hour or two of rough going he was in agony from cuts, scratches and bruises, but continued doggedly. The natives said an enemy patrol was close behind. They avoided trails, pushed into the densest thickets and swamps, and swam rivers, carefully smoothing footprints from the sand and mudbanks. At one crossing the white man was rushed by a crocodile. He was forced to use his revolver although the Japanese patrol was within earshot. The patrol caught up, but a torrential rainstorm broke and saved the fugitives.

76

That night they camped in an abandoned village. One of the natives produced from his *belum* (string bag) a small bottle of iodine, a roll of lint, and some adhesive tape. He tenderly dressed the pilot's tattered feet. Next morning they picked over the village garbage pile and found a pair of half-rotten beach-shoe soles, which they strapped on the sufferer with plaited grass thongs. They fashioned for him a crude pair of crutches and he was able to go on. Six days later the three reached the camp of a New Guinea Volunteer Rifles patrol, who obtained bearers and carried the crippled airman into Wau.

But the trial by ordeal was not yet finished. Radio sent news of the rescue to the rejoicing squadron at Moresby. They immediately approached the commanding officer of an American navy dive-bomber squadron, then staging on Moresby for a series of strikes against enemy shipping. He was rightly dubious about sending a machine to the bomb-scarred and continually menaced Wau field, but eventually agreed to try.

Thirteen days after the squadron leader had been shot down, he climbed into the rear seat of the first combat aircraft ever to alight on the tilted Wau field. He squinted through the rear gunsight and settled himself for a quiet ride home.

Just as the dive bomber was about to land on Seven Mile airfield, it was attacked by four Zeros. The Australian had already stowed the rear gun, and the American pilot was forced to take such violent evasive action that he was unable to get it out again. The defenseless Douglas roared up and down, skimming the runways and the timbered approaches to the airfield through a hail of lead aimed at the Japanese pursuers by wildly excited machine gunners. It got too hot for the Zeros, and they gave up and flew out of range. The Douglas landed with its fuselage and wings so full of holes that the ground crew said willpower alone must have kept it in the air. A Japanese bullet had neatly removed the end of the squadron leader's little finger.

The day after this affair of the dive bomber and the Zeros over Seven Mile, the war correspondents were invited to dine with the general for an informal discussion of the changed military

77

situation since the arrival of United States military aircraft.

The presence of a visiting group of American and English pressmen – at the head of whom strode the inimitable little Mr H. R. Knickerbocker, who could extract more literary color from distant machine-gun fire than any other four correspondents I ever met – lent the gathering an international flavor.

As we sat down to table, the rescued fighter commander arrived, limping slightly and with his hand in bandages.

'I owe you an apology, sir,' he told the general with a faint, dry smile. 'I'm exactly a fortnight late for dinner.'

He told his story willingly. One could see he was amused by it, and more than a little wondering. He did not mention his personal feelings. His body was thin, but his complexion was still ruddy. His hands and eyes were still rock steady. Yet – and this is not wisdom after the event – whoever looked at the man with friendly eyes that night saw one weary in soul. Too long in shadows had etiolated the strong stem of his resolution to live. I have never seen a man who needed more desperately some gentleness to make him feel again, as living men should, that the face of death is terrible and to be feared. He had done more than conquer fear – he had killed it.

About a week later the Japanese made a heavy raid. Accident, combat damage and loss, and delay in replacements had diminished the P-40 squadron to three machines. The squadron leader led them again. It was to be the last time.

There were 17 Zeros, so high that they looked like small translucent insects. The sun shone brilliantly on the silver wings of the bombers, running below them in two deep V's of seven and nine. The bombs came away. Over the crest of the hill, dust and smoke rose in massive, fluted columns. The valley shook and the mountains gave back the snarling rumble of explosions. The bombers turned and climbed away, followed by patterns of antiaircraft fire. Somewhere, at so great an altitude one could not see, there was fighting. The guns tapped plainly. A watcher beside me called: 'Look! Look there!'

A little dark cross was drawing a line of white straight down the sky. *He was one of ours.*

CHAPTER 5

OUT OF NEWSPAPERS, OUT OF MIND

As THE weeks passed into months and the observable Japanese peril was still limited to air raids, the nerves of Moresby's garrison steadied. Among the rank and file, out of sight was out of mind. Headquarters of New Guinea Force was not so sanguine. The war with Japan was now five months old but the strength and equipment of the garrison had not noticeably increased. Only enough shipping came into harbor to sustain supply and replacements. Rarely did more than one moderately sized vessel berth in a week. The knowledge that America and Australia were making immense efforts to arm and organize a defense was little solace. The betting was that too little would once again come too late.

In Moresby, work on the airstrips and roads progressed, although retarded by a paucity of proper mechanical equipment. A few months later, American construction machinery was to accomplish in hours what now took days or weeks for weary and ill-fed men with shovels.

What were the Japanese doing? Little effective liaison seemed to exist between headquarters, New Guinea Force, and the mainland. Possibly the general knew the Japanese movements – but he didn't say. War correspondents were not told the story until some six weeks later, after the crisis had passed. It was a justifiable precaution. Countermeasures were not the province of these tired and discouraged soldiers, this outnumbered handful of R.A.A.F. pilots. Countermeasures were the province of the United States Pacific fleet.

It was not until two months after the event, toward the end of March, that we learned that shore-based aircraft from

Townsville on the mainland had heavily attacked a concentration of Japanese shipping in the roadsteads of Lae and Salamaua. They sank or damaged 20 ships, and the remainder dispersed.

The Japanese had bungled. They had concentrated their shipping at the end of a tortuous and indirect route where they could not provide sufficient air protection. It was one of those elementary strategic blunders for which Australians and Americans fighting the Japanese had repeatedly to thank providence. The qualitative superiority of American bombers, resolutely handled, wrought damage out of all proportion to the size of their formations. Japanese organization recovered slowly from that blow. Either the enemy could not think quickly and improvise or else his disposition of reserves was hopelessly inelastic and ill balanced.

All through April, Allied reconnaissance planes reported a slow reconcentration of shipping – not, this time, in the enclosed waters of the Bismarck Sea but in the vicinity of New Ireland and New Britain. Eventually a formidable Japanese fleet was gathered near Tulagi in the Solomons. It was attacked by torpedo and dive bombers from the aircraft carriers of a powerful task force of the United States Pacific fleet. This task force was the only effective defensive weapon possessed by the Allies in the entire South Pacific Ocean at that time. It proved sufficient.

Three days after this Tulagi force had been scattered by the navy fliers' savage assault, the main body of the Japanese task force was sighted off the Louisiade Archipelago, steaming southwest.

The American commander immediately attacked with every aircraft he could muster, and small groups of heavy and medium bombers from General MacArthur's command participated in a nonstop series of offensive patrols in the Coral Sea.

On May 8, the Australian prime minister (Mr John Curtin) told his people: 'A battle of crucial importance to the whole conduct of the war in this theatre is going on.'

Two days later, it was announced that the Japanese forces had been defeated and dispersed. Much later, the enemy losses were revealed. In the air-sea fight of May 8, American planes sank the aircraft carrier *Rykoko*, one heavy cruiser, one destroyer and a tanker. Twenty-five enemy planes were destroyed for the loss of six American aircraft.

The following day, the American task force attacked the enemy carrier *Shokaku*, and left her ablaze. Several other ships were struck by bombs and torpedoes. The cohesion of the Japanese force was broken and it retired at full speed. The Battle of the Coral Sea was won.

The success, however, had not been gained without cost. The United States carrier *Lexington* was severely damaged in an attack by 108 torpedo and dive bombers. It later sank after a gasoline explosion. Other ships were hit. But the enforced retirement of the enemy was far more important than the balance of material loss to the sea-air fleets engaged.

What had been the purpose of the enemy concentration in the first place? Was it an attack upon Moresby? Possibly. Was it a move to occupy the strategically important eastern tip of Papua, or to advance down the island chain to the New Hebrides, or even across to New Caledonia? That is more probable, in view of the concentration at Tulagi on May 4. Until the war is over and some Japanese admiral tells the story, we cannot be sure.

One thing, however, can be stated. The force defeated in the Coral Sea was not an invasion convoy bound for Australia, as is popularly believed. Nor was it a force of great numerical strength, despite the presence of two aircraft carriers. Even the Japanese would not have been foolish enough to attempt invasion of the Australian mainland with fewer and less powerful ships than they sent through the Straits of Macassar to Java.

It is far more likely that their fleet in the Coral Sea was an opportunist task force, sent to occupy the New Hebrides and at the same time test the Allied naval strength in the South Pacific. Had it met no opposition, more ambitious moves would have followed. But the opposition it did meet was so waspish that the Japanese high command shelved its bold ideas and resolved thereafter to nibble cautiously and hope for the best. The Japanese blitzkrieg in the Pacific was finished.

None of this crucial struggle in the Coral Sea was seen, or much appreciated, at Moresby. It was only felt. The 'real' war was invisible over the edge of the sea or behind the mountains. At the end of April, however, there had been rumors of action at any moment. The Japanese were up to something.

An early sign of sensitivity was a savage flood of censorship directives and the insistence of MacArthur's general headquarters that field censorship was not competent to decide all matters of security. The use of the local radio station for press dispatches was forbidden. The slightest criticism or speculation meant the immediate 'canning' of a dispatch.

The correspondents were so dissatisfied and fractious that the sketchy public-relations system collapsed under the strain. No good purpose could be served by our remaining at Moresby any longer. We hadn't the faintest idea of what was really going on. If the enemy launched an attack on the base, no communications channel could be guaranteed us. Furiously prophesying another Singapore and cursing about incompetence and political censorship, we demanded our marching orders for the mainland.

By now the whole garrison believed that Moresby was 'in for it' at last. There was another rush to move supplies into the hills, a frantic coming and going to complete the pathetic little minefields and entanglements on the foreshores.

Badly shot-up American navy dive bombers began appearing on the airfield again. The pilots were not officially permitted to talk, but passed the word out of the corner of their mouths that there was 'one hell of a Jap fleet out in the Coral Sea.' Air Force headquarters shifted smartly inland. Pilots bitterly criticized 'the panic.'

I was not then hardened to the accepted correspondent technique of getting out while the getting is good, and went about miserably avoiding the eye of my service friends. One or two made me more uncomfortable by giving me messages to wives, mothers and sweethearts.

The general air of foreboding and gloom infected even the natives. When I told Gibson that I was going to Australia, he wept copiously. He asked to be taken too. He did not wish to work for the Japanese. I was his *taubada*. I said no. It was forbidden to take him to Australia, and I did not think the Japanese were coming. If however, they did come, they would not be allowed to stay long. He was to go to his village and explain to the others that they were not to help the Japanese. Otherwise they would be punished when the Australians and Americans came back.

The pep talk dried Gibson's tears, but it didn't do me any good at all. On the night of May 6, I sailed for Townsville by transport, in a mood of blackest resentment and depression. I was convinced that the Moresby garrison would not last a week if the Japanese attacked, and I doubted the value of a guerrilla campaign in the hills. I railed inwardly against the futility of making token resistances for purposes of morale. Memory of the five men who had brought back the first story of Rabaul was very vivid just then.

I stayed on the mainland a month, painfully adjusting my temper to the realization that an eyewitness is without honor in his own country and that no war correspondent can ever tell unpalatable truths soon enough to do any good. Once news sources are officially controlled by censorships, no individual writer can deflect by as much as a hair's breadth the impact upon the public mind of the tale wartime leadership wants to tell. But history may judge the relationship of dead facts.

Part Two
THE INVISIBLE WAR

ALTHOUGH the world heard little of it, there was already critically important land fighting against the Japanese in New Guinea before the landing at Buna Bay in August, 1942, precipitated the series of bloody battles in which Australian and American infantrymen reconquered the eastern half of the great island. The men who fought this invisible war against the enemy were a raggle-taggle army of miners, foresters and civil servants called to the colors on the day of Pearl Harbor. Though they were isolated from the nearest friendly base by more than 200 miles of savagely mountainous country, and were often threatened with starvation, with the help of a company of Australian commandos they immobilized two Japanese divisions based on Lae and Salamaua for nearly five months. The secret of their success was superb jungle craft. In their experience and performance was the genesis of the training and indoctrination which all Allied infantry units for service in the Pacific islands subsequently underwent . . .

CHAPTER 6

THE NEEDLE POINT

EARLY in June, I returned from Townsville, base of gathering American air strength, to Moresby. The scene had not changed very greatly, even if the atmosphere had. The significance of the Coral Sea battle had sunk in. Troops were almost cheerful. Rumor had reached them that the Australian Imperial Force, which had distinguished itself in the Middle East, was now re-grouping on the mainland after recall and would soon be thrown in against the Japanese. They wanted to know was it true that two divisions of the United States army were also training on the mainland, and that Queensland airfields were packed with B-17's and B-25's and fighters.

Major General Morris, still commanding New Guinea Force, removed his headquarters inland and bequeathed to the growing correspondent colony his bungalow three miles from town and his sergeant cook. Everybody was preparing to settle in for a few months of stagnation before the next trial of strength. It was apparent that sooner or later large scale land fighting must develop. Sooner or later either we would try to push through the jungle to contact the Japanese or the Japanese would try to push through the jungle to contact us. I wanted a preview of the conditions under which this campaign would be fought and started immediately to inquire about the chances of getting over the mountains and spending a few weeks with guerrilla patrols which, the 'grapevine' reported, were waging an increasingly active war against the Japanese in Lae and Salamaua on the Huon Gulf.

It was surprising how little authentic information could be gleaned about them, even from official quarters. To all intents and purposes their miniature campaign behind the mountains was a secret war. Yet they were experimenting with the realities of the land fighting which must eventually develop elsewhere from the existing set of circumstances. These few men were then the needlepoint of Allied resistance in the only area of conflict between ground forces in the South and Southwest Pacific areas.

The guerrilla force originally comprised elements of the New Guinea Volunteer Rifles, which had retired into the Bulolo valley after the Japanese landings along the north coast. They had only the most tenuous radio contact with Port Moresby. Yet for nearly four months they had carried on their private war, blocking all attempts by Japanese patrols to penetrate the hinterland. They depended for food and essentials chiefly upon accumulations salvaged from civilian stocks and stores in dumps at Wau and other goldfield towns. Only in recent weeks had any effort been made to supplement their supply by air.

Reinforcements had also been sent them – the bulk of the 5th Independent Company, commando-type troops especially trained for guerrilla warfare, and some small specialist units detached from the Australian Imperial Force. With the exception of one party sent overland as an experiment, the men had been flown into Wau airfield by transports and Hudson bombers during the last few weeks. The combined force of commandos and New Guinea Volunteer Rifles was then commanded by a 23-year-old lieutenant colonel, who had a brilliant record of service with the Australian Imperial Force in Greece and Crete.

Headquarters was extremely vague about the future. It hinted that if the Japanese obligingly remained quiet, the Bulolo valley force might eventually be built up sufficiently for serious attacks against Lae and Salamaua. In any case, its role was offensive – to strike at the enemy whenever and wherever the opportunity offered.

Supply was, admittedly, the difficulty. West of Moresby no route had ever been surveyed across the island – not even a foot trail, such as had been known for years to patrol officers and native postmen between Moresby and Buna. The miners who fled from Wau, however, had discovered practicable passes between Wau and the headwaters of the Lakekamu River, 120 miles west. Command posts had been established, and small quantities of supplies were staged in over the mountains from post to post by lines of native carriers. It was hoped to develop the route, and native labor was being recruited. Supplementary supply would be undertaken by air when enough planes were available.

I put in a formal application to headquarters for orders to join Kanga Force[1] as the guerrilla unit was called. In the interests of 'experience,' I stifled the temptation to wangle a transport plane ride to Wau and resolved to walk. My idea was to stay a few weeks with Kanga Force, then to return to Moresby via the Waria River valley and the Kokoda trail – a round trip of about 700 miles. The movement order to headquarters of Kanga Force soon came back, with all the correct endorsements. Next thing was to find out how to go there.

Maps? Headquarters looked blank. No, no maps. There weren't any. Better go by transport to Wau, they suggested. A plane was bound to be going in a month or six weeks – that is, if the Japs didn't move inland. Of course, there might not be room for me in the plane.

I remembered Major S., a veteran pilot officer and magistrate, now attached to the newly formed Australian-New Guinea Administration Unit. He greeted me enthusiastically. Walk over the Lakekamu? Splendid idea. I'd enjoy it.

But how to go? He frowned thoughtfully, then inspiration hit him. Walk, of course! He boomed with laughter at the suggestion that there could be any difficulty about walking anywhere in New Guinea. There couldn't possibly be trouble with natives, or any mishaps by the way. Why, he assured me, I would find shelter in native villages almost every night if I planned my route sensibly.

Planning the route? Ah, that was different. That would be up to me. A schooner would be carrying a few tons of stuff for Kanga towards the middle of the month. It was not yet

[1] Colloquial contraction of Kangaroo.

quite certain how the cargo was to go, but no doubt it would be transshipped into launches at Yule Island, thence taken to the mouth of the Lakekamu, landed through the surf, portered across one of the waterways, loaded on to paddle or pole canoes for Bulldog, and finally lifted by a line of carriers to Kudjiru across the mountains. Tag along with the cargo, that was the ticket! Just tag along with the cargo.

Under pressure, Major S. admitted that he had no first-hand knowledge of the district. It wasn't his country. But most of Papua was pretty much alike. I'd have no trouble. My personal boys could be interpreters. I couldn't get carriers for personal gear in Moresby, of course, but I could recruit them in the villages as I staged on. No trouble, no trouble at all, ha, ha! His rubicund face beamed at me.

He was so indefinite about the first 450 miles of the journey that I concentrated on the last lap – Kokoda to Moresby. Ah, he informed me with some pride, *there* was a stretch of country he *did* know. It was anywhere between 50 and 100 miles. Six days. More, maybe. Maybe as much at 10. It was hard to say. It depended on so much. It was a damned tough stretch, ho, ho, ho! Razorbacks. Razorbacks like nightmares. He distinctly remembered that on one day's march he had started climbing at six o'clock in the morning and was still climbing at three o'clock in the afternoon.

Finally I asked in a small, restrained voice about equipment. The major stroked his pink chin thoughtfully. Just the usual stuff, he said. Just the usual stuff – and plenty of it, because it was sure to be wet. A rifle was a good idea. Goura pigeon was good eating ...

I gave up and went to another Australian-New Guinea Administration Unit man, Major T., in hope that he could at least estimate traveling time between Wau and Kokoda. He had not been over the route himself, but knew patrol officers who had. It would be unsafe to calculate the stage at less than 18 days. The area was well populated, the natives friendly. They would probably be willing to supply carriers from village to village for one stick of trade tobacco per man per day.

T. was as grave as S. was merry – a lean, weary, harried-looking man with old eyes. He gave me an uneasy feeling that I was biting off much more than I could chew. But his information was mostly vague generalities.

One problem solved itself. Damien Parer, cameraman for the Australian Department of Information, promptly accepted an invitation to go with me. I was relieved at the prospect of congenial companionship. Parer had at that time seen more real action than probably any other war correspondant. He was – first, last and all the time – a front-line cameraman. Young, tough, keen and unshakably courageous, he had photographed the worst of the fighting in Greece, Crete, two desert campaigns and Syria. The more I saw of the man, the more I liked and admired him. He was long, stooped, black-headed, sallow-faced, smiling. He had great piston legs covered by a fuzz of black hair and ending in size 12 feet that looked as if they could crush the skull of a python.

In four months' close companionship with Parer, I never heard him speak critically of anyone – with the sole exception of a certain very famous and undoubtedly talented cameraman who salted his personal publicity with the fictions that are absorbed so eagerly by a gullible public. But for this one gloriously blind uncharity, Parer would be almost too kindly and good humored to be entirely human. No one, however crusty, could remain within earshot of the bubbling bass hoot that served him for a laugh without wanting to laugh too.

In the end, we obtained an approximate sailing date for the mysterious schooner and collected the last of the gear

I brought up the proposition of the big walkabout with Gibson, whom I coveted as my personal boy. He heard that the long patrol was to begin within a few days and stood tracing imaginary patterns with his immense great toe on the floorboards. A sullen-looking youngster at the best of times, his face assumed a deceptive expression of black, murderous villainy when he was worried. I asked if he was afraid of the Japanese catching him. A faint and reluctant grin acknowledged the jibe.

'It is not the Japanese, taubada,' he muttered. 'It is my friend Cyril!'

'Cyril will be able to come too, if he wishes,' I said. 'Mr Parer is going on the patrol and he will want a personal boy.'

The villainous brown face smiled widely. 'Oh *yes*, yes taubada! Cyril surely wishes to come. Oh yes, indeed.'

He retreated backward to the door, where the nicely enunciated English deserted him. He mumbled in his own dialect, blushed a dark chocolate, grinned, and coiled one leg around the other in an agony of gratitude. 'Oh, thank you, tabada, thank you for Cyril. One to go is good, perhaps. But both to go is, oh, how so much better!'

It seemed that in our adventure both Gibson and I were destined to be supported by friends.

CHAPTER 7

'OSSIKAR, OSSIKAR!'

LONG after adventures are dead or made commonplace by eclipse, the memory of setting out on them stays sharp and bright. Gibson woke me at six o'clock. The trade wind was blowing in the shutters. The dawn was yellow, and white dust rolled down the road before the wind. The boys brought tea, hot and rank, in a thick china cup. I took a shower from the kerosene tin suspended on its gallows in the front garden. It was chilly now, but there would be heat later.

Cyril woke Parer, blue with two days' growth of beard, wrinkles about the eyes, almost ill tempered. Cyril and Gibson also looked more sullen than usual. I wondered if they had been having a predeparture celebration on betel nut in the flapping gray tent down behind the latrines. There was very little to do – seal and stamp letters written belatedly, give final instructions about gear left behind, check over a few things to be carried personally. Breakfast was a flabby oatmeal porridge and canned beef fritters fried – specially to give us a last taste of civilisation – with dehydrated onions.

Everything was ready. The duffel filled the back of the truck. Combined, it tipped the scales at 290 pounds. We shook hands all around. I whistled to Cyril and Gibson and they came trotting, now rigged out in shirts and ragged shorts, grinning to the backs of the necks. By wearing shirts, they had promoted themselves to the status of 'boss boys.'

M., K., Parer and I piled in the front. Gibson and Cyril wormed themselves into the back with the dunnage. It was nearly eight o'clock and the heat was beginning to come. The sky was amber with it. Somebody said, 'Good day for an air

93

raid! The little bastards haven't been over for nearly a week. They're losing their punch.'

The house rolled away round the bend in the blue road, and the dusty gums and kurukuru sped by. Soon again there was that well-remembered vista of bay, its reef-green dimmed in the haze, splashes of scarlet and purple bougainvillaea, leaning palms where Gibson used to climb for coconuts every day until I got tired of them.

Weaving ribbon of road, and heat beating back. The heat of Moresby, little bush town under the menace of its far, shielding, purple hills . . .

Down in the trade store by the wharf it was cool and half dark. Elderly, barefooted 'boys' trundled casks about. There was a smell of candles and rat dirt and new rope and oil and tar. A yellow man in drill faded almost white shuffled forward and looked listlessly at the paper M. gave him.

'Caddy of Emu? Sure. Are you the fellows who're going over the Lakekamu?' He looked at us with mild curiosity, but no surprise. You can't surprise a man who has lived for 20 years in New Guinea.

There was at first some confusion about which ship was the one bound west. The navy was fanatically silent about such things. We located it lying on the western side of the pier among several other small craft, by spotting the last of a hundred or more shapeless canvas sacks and casks marked in black stencil KANGA, the code name of the guerrilla force. They were being loaded into the forehold.

She was a schooner typical of the island trade, the *Royal Endeavor*: 64 tons displacement; asthmatic oil auxiliary; stained, warped, wretched with sun. Fifty yards to windward of her, one could catch the reek of copra and trepang. She was heavily laden with stores for down-coast settlements and her deck level was well below the staging of the pier. A pair of muscular Kiwai boys fell with reckless abandon on the equipment passed to them from the truck by Gibson and Cyril.

The skipper, Bill W., came aboard – a lean, keen Scot in early middle age, with a mop of faded red hair and a pair of dreamy yet piercing blue eyes. He shook hands with us and jerked a thumb at two broken-down deck chairs under the awning aft. 'You'll be bunking in the big cabin,' he said. 'I'll show you later.'

The mooring lines were cast off. I kept looking at the heavy heat haze on the water and cocking an eye at the sky. Poor devils, I thought. It's a moral certainty they'll get a raid before the day's out. I dwelt on the probability of the raid to tone down the awareness of departure.

The *Royal Endeavor* thrust Moresby back into the haze. Twisting and turning she ran down past Daugo, the barren island of the reef. The skipper stood by Wusuru, the Kiwai helmsman, making a faint flick with his hand now and then to indicate a change of course. The sea was flat calm, as shiny and smooth as gray-green silk. All the reef waters were heavily mined. That is why Bill kept staring out at the broken water and back at the shore and flicking his hand. He was steering a course through the complicated channels by shore and reef marks. The task required concentration, and his sea-blue eyes never flickered. He said nothing.

Parer and I sat on under the awning for a couple of hours, watching familiar landmarks grow smaller and vanish. The mountains, which stand up clear behind Moresby and sweep down to within 15 or 20 miles of the coast, started to recede as we traveled west. The deserted villages of Boera and Porebada slid by – bleached, gray-brown thatches and walls, picturesque and still under a dado of palms – and gave way to flattening hillocks of gray-green gum and then mangrove swamp. All was a satiny monotony of tropic sea and penciled, forebidding coast on its margin. Sometimes, to port, a clump of palms would shoot up out of the ocean itself, rooted in a cay of coral, standing not five feet above the tide.

The mist closed in to within a half mile and hid the sun, but the heat increased steadily. Sweat stood out on Wusuru's crinkled forehead and coursed down the runnels of his cheeks. Three hours out we heard Japanese aircraft passing. They were either on reconnaissance or bound for Thursday Island, 500 miles southwest. A little later a flight of P-40's could be heard worrying in pursuit. Nothing could be seen.

Then, suddenly, an R.A.A.F. 'mercy ship' tore up the silk of the sea with two sparkling bow waves, cut above us in a curve at 20 knots and disappeared behind the tawny curtains. That launch would surely have poor hunting for any unhappy pilot forced down on the sea on so thick a morning.

At noon Bill dived into the little cabin forward of the wheel, rummaged out a can of beef, a can of butter, a loaf of stale, grayish bread, and set out 'lunch' on a newspaper spread on a three-legged table. Parer came back, after clambering about forward looking for camera angles, and swore he could eat a horse. Bill looked at us doubtfully. Had we made no arrangements for rationing? We said we understood that we were to be rationed along the route, according to the movement order. He shook his head. The army was mean about food, he said. If we wouldn't mind giving him a paper to say we had been supplied with the meals we had eaten during the course of the voyage, it would make things easier when it came to restocking the lazaret.

Bill was resentful of the miserliness of his rationing, apologetic for the poorness of his hospitality. He brewed tea for us on a small primus stove on which he did all his 'cooking,' and found a newspaper full of cold, flabby, sweet-potato chips.

'Ach, they're good!' he exclaimed broadly, cheeks bulging.

The heat in the 'big cabin' was weighty, sticky and dead. Gibson spread the bedrolls on the wire bunks and pulled off my boots and shirt. Parer fell asleep almost immediately, tossing every now and then and groaning. The sweat trickled into the hollows between his ribs and splashed down on the gray blanket. I lay, half conscious, thinking about Nauta, the hook-nosed engine-room boy below, nursing his decrepit machinery in a temperature of 130 degrees, testing the heat of the cylinders with his palms against the sizzling metal. Gibson, in his blue pants, and Cyril were sprawled like corpses in the flickering shadow of the sail. Seven crew boys, the cargo stowed, were squatted on the foredeck, solemnly delousing their lime-gingered hair. Only Wusuru was awake, vigilant. His knotted hands caressed lovingly the spokes of the old, old wheel . . .

Yule Island – or Kairuku, as the govenment and Catholic Mission settlement is known – was the first and only intermediate port of call on the voyage to Kukepe. After a day of monotonous rolling, the *Royal Endeavor* stood inshore just before sunset. In fading light Bill had a few anxious moments negotiating the reef entrances.

I had heard a good deal in Moresby about the beauty of Yule Island. It is small, arrogantly mountainous, fringed by noble palms. A handful of native huts is scattered by the anchorage beach. High on the hillside behind them is a little white church surmounted by a cross – strangely out of character, but for all that, a baroque gem in a setting of natural loveliness.

On the landward side is the delta of the St Joseph River, snaking through crocodile-infested swamps of sago and nipa palm. The dusk this day was mealy and grained, as the schooner stood inshore. Against it, a distant mightiness, was 11,000-foot Mount Yule, clothed to the crown in dripping forest.

All afternoon the sea had been flecked with the white sails of fishing canoes. As the ship came up to anchorage, a canoe slid past, homeward bound. The light dyed its crescent sail blood-red. A man with hair done in a high topknot, wearing a bright loincloth, stood at the steering paddle in the stern. A smoky fire built on a stone on the outrigger glimmered amidship. The grass-skirted woman with rounded legs and bare, retroussé breasts tended it, grilling steaks of red mullet and barracuda for her master's supper.

Darkness was as tonic as a plunge bath. The anchor chain clanked and the silence that followed was broken by the squeak of rowlocks. Onshore a light or two flowered yellow against the gloom of the hillside.

A voice hailed us: 'Hi, you, Bill!'

The skipper muttered in the dark: 'Och, it's the madman! It's the madman, sure enough! As mad as a cut snake, that one! Three months more and they'll carry him off the island.'

But when he came aboard, singing loudly about nothing in particular, it was only a redheaded 20-year-old with sergeant's stripes. His madness took the form of enjoying life and everything about it. He laughed happily in reply to practically anything you could say to him. No iniquity, no disaster, could quell his fixed conviction that all was well with the world.

We went ashore, rowed by four muscular Yule islanders to whom Gibson and Cyril chattered hysterically in Motuan. The darkness was scented with aromatic wood smoke and frangipani. The beach, crunchy coral fragments, gleamed luminously underfoot.

The redheaded sergeant gave us a great deal of information in a short time. The old man – the resident magistrate in charge here – was, he said, a bit of a tartar, an ex-Guardsman, and aggressively English. He had deeply offended the Australians by saying that Australian troops weren't worth a cracker unless they had an English regiment on either side of them! He was very regimental and insisted on a parade at seven o'clock every morning. The parade included the prisoners – 72 convicted native murderers and rapists who were having the time of their lives, living on the fat of the land in the compound, eating three hearty government meals every day and doing very little work in return for them. The personnel of the 'garrison' had not been changed for six months. They didn't mind.

When we got ashore, it turned out we were not going to the resident magistrate's bungalow for dinner but to a communal mess and quarters about half a mile away. The redheaded sergeant blandly and hospitably resisted or side-stepped every suggestion that we spend at least part of the evening on a courtesy call on the magistrate. It would be enough, he declared, if we attended the parade at 7.00 a.m. I pointed out that we were scheduled to sail at five, but that, according to him, made no odds at all. Later it became clear that there was a conspiracy by the Australians to contrive a trivial slight upon the old man who, since his crack about the Australian troops, had lived in lonely dignity in his bungalow on the hill. Strangers, particularly strangers fresh from the south – and one who had actually seen fighting in the Middle East – were pay dirt indeed for seven lonely men who had not been 'outside' in six months. To monopolize such strangers, wrongly and discourteously, would be a beautiful slap in the eye for the old man. I thought about it and decided: let the boys have their little triumph. It will mean a damned sight more to them than to him.

The 'garrison' was comfortably fixed in an airy bunglow built on tall piles. Its members lounged about in freshly starched and ironed uniforms. They greeted us with warm showers, whisky and English cigarettes (refugee cargo from Singapore).

The assistant district officer, second in command, was the most Irish-looking Irishman I have ever seen outside of the comic strips. He had a black, bullet head, beautiful navy-blue eyes, a pug nose, a comically long upper lip, a high, narrow delicate forehead which, like all true Irishmen, he was forever banging on lintels and cupboard doors.

He held the army rank of lieutenant. His pips were neatly embroidered lozenges, the work of the local nuns. His junior, also a lieutenant and the officer in charge of the signalers, was a quiet youngster – a university man with a passion for good music and books. *His* badges were bone buttons sewn onto his shoulder straps, so I took it he was an unregenerate Protestant and without influence at the nunnery.

After drinks we all sat down to table together, officers and men alike, for there was no formality and Christian names were used from the beginning. It was hard to get the men to talk about themselves when there was so much fresh war news in our minds and so much to say of blacked-out Sydney and Melbourne and the recently arrived American troops. But in the end, our persistent conversational acrobatics forced the poor devils back on their own weary ground.

No, nothing much ever happened at Yule Island, except when the Japs came over. Oh, yes, the place got raided. Last raid the Zeros had swooped down within 50 feet of the mission buildings. The missioners were two priests, two European nuns, and Brother George. Brother George was a great character. He wore an immense black beard, smoked trade tobacco in a huge calabash pipe, cursed blisteringly when provoked, and was a man of profound erudition and culture. He had a narrow escape the first time the Zeros came. Machine-gun bullets splintered the chair at his writing desk. After this attack the nuns were moved from the mission building to a native village hidden in the bush.

More troublesome than Japs, however, were the questions of native administration that keep cropping up all the while. Restlessness had run through the tribes since the old order passed and there had been an outbreak of feud warfare between some of the outlying villages. 'Payback' made pacification very difficult. A wrong was done. The wronged family paid back – with a little over for good measure. There was reprisal. And so it went on for generations.

It had been far harder to wean the native from his addiction to payback than it had been to cure him of a taste for human flesh. Supply the Melanesian with adequate proteins in his diet and he would lose his enthusiasm for cannibalism, but he gave up payback less willingly than a drunkard gave up his bottle.

The Irishman told a grim but amusing story of two clans who tired of a feud that had lasted 20 years. The score was very nearly even. Only one life was outstanding. So the headman of the 'creditor' clan paid a ceremonial visit to the headman of the 'debtor' clan and proposed settlement. The debt was admitted, and the debtor clan chose one of its young men by lot. He philosophically came forward for one of the creditor clan to knock out his brains with a stone ax. Thus was the debt paid – and they lived happily ever after.

The assistant district officer tried to bribe us to stay on a few days with offers of good crocodile shooting. The country, he said, would interest us. In the high hills on the skirts of Mount Lawson and Mount Yule, it was so broken, rough and steep that it was often possible for a man to shout conversation from one ridge crest to another man standing a *full day's journey away* on the crest of the ridge opposite.

It was past midnight when we stumbled down to the beach. My conscience about the old man was long since numbed. We shook hands all round and swore eternal friendship in the fumes of the whisky ...

'Don't forget – come back by St Joseph River!' they said. 'It hasn't been done yet!'

Solemnly I declared we would.

Gibson and Cyril appeared like afreets out of the perfumed dark. We pulled the dinghy clear. Suddenly there was wild shrieking and shouting in the native village, fires flared up, dogs barked, tin cans banged. No explanation. Personally I was too happily tight to care that it might be a full-scale rising of the tribes.

We got away at dawn. The redheaded sergeant, still laughing, came aboard at the last minute to bid us Godspeed and explain the commotion in the village. It seemed that some mission girls, feeling the spell of the night upon them, fell from sanctity and decided to visit the jail where they were surprised, in the middle of an erotic orgy, by a native policeman too aged to be corrupted by an offer to join in the fun and games. He smacked their naked hides with a walking stick and whistled for reinforcements. I had a shrewd suspicion Gibson and Cyril left the party just about at the right time – they had a glazed, faraway look in their eyes.

Yule dropped behind the horizon, and the peak, its namesake, vanished behind the rising mists. The island looked green and beautiful in the early sunlight. By noon it was breathlessly, blindingly hot.

In midafternoon, we sighted the launch *H. and S.* and signaled her to stand in. She was manned by filthy Hanuabada boys and had a native skipper. You could smell her 10 cable lengths down-wind. Grease, soot from cooking fires, scraps of food and spittle made her foul beyond description. The Hanuabadas had been indulging in a betel-chewing orgy and were half crazy with it – eyes glazed and eyeballs rolling, lips curled back slackly from blackened stumps of teeth. The red saliva drooled down their chins.

Bill bullied them into coming back to help discharge our cargo. Together we ran down into the lee of a point, where a portion of cargo in the main hold was transferred. The Kiwai were in their element, working stark naked in a furnace of golden light, viens standing out like black, knotted whipcord on their arms and suffering foreheads, chanting and panting each bale from its stubborn cradle. The sweat spurted from them until they shone with it like statues of wet coal. *'Ai-dee, ai-dee, hah, ho-ho! Ai-dee ai-dee, hah, ho-ho!'* over and over and over . . .

An hour before sunset the H. and S. was fully laden, cast off, and staggering away into the mouth of the Tauri. Her skipper promised to come back the next day to pick up the rest of the cargo.

Bill stood in as close as he dared and I took the whaleboat ashore with half a dozen of the Kiwai – more for the hell of it than for any desperate anxiety to find Lieutenant A., the white man reputed to be in charge of the river district. I thought a run through the surf and a mild exploration of the village would be a welcome break from the painful monotony of the pitching schooner.

Just before I stepped overside, Bill said casually: 'Oh, if A. isn't in the village, you'll probably find an old chap named Oscar. He acts as a sort of watchdog on the cargoes while they're waiting to go up-river. He speaks English, and he'll know where A. is, or when he's expected back.'

Fortunately, the surf was regular. Even at that it was a run through four lines of breakers. The whole village, men, women and children, rushed to meet the boat and steady her in the wash. Screams, wails, shouts, howls, and the roar of big combers thundering down on the hard sand . . .

A grinning face, emitting blasts of fishy breath, thrust itself at me over the gunwhale. Its owner signaled me urgently to climb on his shoulders. The boat swung side-on to the surf amid doleful shrieks. A wave slopped over the quarter and rushed forward. I leaped astride stinking brown shoulders and was borne away through a waist-high whirlpool, clinging with all my might. Hordes of children cruised through the foam like destroyers about a battleship. My human steed capered and shouted and set me dry footed on the sand, after a 100-yard sprint that barely made his fishy breath come faster. Not until I stood with feet on firm ground did I discover what made his shoulders so rough: from head to foot he was smothered in ringworm and to allay the irritation, he had covered himself with rancid fish oil.

The village headman, naked but for a black Trilby hat and a walking stick, discovered me scrubbing down with a handful of wet sand. The diseased steed looked on grinning.

The headman's Motuan dialect was much too fast to follow. I regretted not having brought Gibson, particularly when it became difficult to move for a press of naked children, who screamed at the top of their voices every time a timorous soul ventured to put out a hand and touch the white man's magic garments.

Finally, shouting them down, I roared at the headman: 'Picanniny *las*, you old bastard! Picanniny *las*!'

He got it, and laid about with his stick.

'Where's Taubada A.?'

Taubada A. was a long way away – a long, long long way away. He gave a performance calculated to indicate cosmic distance.

'Isn't Taubada H. here?' (naming Oscar).

'Yes, taubada.'

For a minute I was cheered – until I remembered the Papuan native's peculiar but logical habit of answering 'yes' to a negatively framed question when he wants to give a negative answer. So I tried again.

Where is Taubada H.?

At his house.

Where is his house?

A mile.

I knew all about Papuan miles. How long?

An hour.

I knew all about Papuan hours too. Very well, lead me to his house.

A procession formed. First I; than the headman at a respectful distance of four paces; then the adults; then the children. Mush!

The trail up the beach seemed reasonably clear, but the light was failing. After a quarter of a mile, an awful howling was set up. I turned back. The procession had halted and was bemoaning a great disaster. The white man had taken a wrong turning!

When this happened three times, I seized the headman by the walking stick and thrust him to the fore. He was greatly embarrassed and finally deputed the duty to an eight-year-old boy with the longest penis I have ever seen slung on human abdomen.

Progress was now more satisfactory. After half an hour's brisk walking, during which no single pair of eyes in the whole procession deviated by an inch from the middle of my fascinating back, we came suddenly upon a large, double-eaved thatch house set up on piles in the middle of a coconut grove. The place was in darkness, and there was no sound but the frantic barking of native dogs. Picturesque curses subdued the dogs. The silence of expectation followed.

Where is Taubada Oscar?

No one knew – not one.

Good. Then go and find him! Hurry! *Karaharaga!* (voice very loud and aggressive).

There was a wild scatter through the gloomy grove, screams, catcalls, shouts, and moans of 'Ossikar, Ossikar, Ossikar!' gradually fading away in the distance.

For 10 interminable minutes I stood in dignity on one leg and then on the other, watched unblinkingly out of the darkness by all who had not departed in quest of Oscar. The last light had gone out of the western sky and the mosquitoes came. They buzzed and pinged frantically around my exposed hands and face. Imperturbability was the best bet. I was imperturbable. I smoked cigarettes. At last there was a recognizably European puffing and panting and groaning among the bushes.

'Hullo, there!' I called down. 'Is that Mr H.?'

'What's left of me!' replied a querulous voice. 'What's left of me.'

Oscar sounded very ancient, 80 at least. It was so dark I could only see his vague outline. When I struck a match to light another cigarette, I caught a glimpse of a lined, grim face, yellow as a guinea. I told him my name and said I'd come off the schooner and had brought a bundle of mail for A.

God in heaven! The *Royal Endeavor!* Did she bring more cargo?

Yes, about 20 tons of it. Gasoline, oil, tents, mail and ammunition.

There were tears in his voice. Bill wasn't going to land it here, was he? There was so much cargo banked up, he didn't know what to do with it. He was working himself to death – no figure of speech that, literally working himself to death – trying to clear cargo banked up on the beach. You see, it had to be recovered from the surf when the whaleboat dumped it – rolled up the beach, stored, taken down to the riverbank, stacked on paddle canoes, taken to Moviave village, five hours' paddling away, transferred across the neck of land to the Lakekamu, and there shifted by launch or canoe to Terapo, another three or four hours' journey.

'What happens then?' I asked

'Then it begins its journey by small launch or canoe to Bulldog.'

'Well, there is no need to worry this time,' I said. 'Bill made the *H. and S.* turn back and has transshipped 10 tons to her for delivery at Terapo. He will transfer the rest tomorrow when she returns.'

'God be praised.'

'Where is A.?'

'Only God knows. Probably at Terapo.'

'The mail is very urgent. It contains orders.'

In that case . . . 'Hi you. Tagi. You Misi-Misi! Come here. You take this mail to Taubada A. Understand? You take a paddle canoe and go right now. Each boy will receive one shilling for the journey. I will pay him myself. Understand? But it is *karaharaga*. If you do not *karaharaga*, I'll cut your liver out with a jagged jam tin. Understand?'

Understanding was so perfect that the mail for A. had vanished through the coconut grove before Oscar had turned stiffly back to me and ejaculated: 'God save me!'

'You're not feeling so good, Mr H.,' I suggested.

'Not so good,' he sighed.

'Malaria?'

'No, an old complaint. I got a bad bout when I jumped off the roof.'

'Jumped off the roof?'

'Yes. I was mending the roof when the planes came over. I jumped off and nearly broke every bone in my body. This war is bloody awful. The planes keep coming over here and I've got to drop anything I'm doing to take shelter. This war is *bloody awful*, I tell you . . . '

'I didn't know the Zeros came as far up the coast as this,' I said. 'Or were they bombers? Did they machine-gun anything, drop any bombs?'

Oscar was indignant. How in the name of Lord Jesus did he know what they were! They were planes. That was enough for him. He heard them, and saw them, and he just naturally took cover. As far as he was concerned, all planes were the same. Bad. If they didn't drop bombs or machine-gun things, who was to tell that they might take it into their heads to do those very things the next minute?

I cocked an eye at the roof, a good 25 feet above the hard-packed earth of the little compound, and decided that Oscar was a man who had the courage of his convictions.

Business disposed, he apologized for not asking me indoors for a cup of tea, but he offered the service of the village policeman to guide me back to the beach. It seemed he was anxious to be rid of me, but promised assistance in getting native guides and paddlers if Parer and I should decide to make a canoe journey to Terapo. All that would be settled tomorrow.

And so back to the beach through clouds of mosquitoes constantly increasing in density. Mosquitoes! My God, I thought I knew all about mosquitoes at Moresby, but these made the air seem solid! Now I could believe the story that men in the swamps are kept awake by the sheer volume of noise made by the mosquito clouds. Happily they did not come out to sea. Once the whaleboat was afloat the sound died rapidly away.

The sea was luminous with phosphorescence. The surf lines shone like fire. The oar blades dipped as into a pot of greenly molten metal. Bill had hung a lantern in the shrouds to guide us, for the night was very dark.

Food. Canned beef, stale bread, biscuit as hard as iron. The schooner was rolling even more foully, for the river was coming out against the tide. Parer was cheese green with repressed seasickness. I wedged the three-legged table between the rail and the deckhouse, clung to the typewriter with one hand, and wrote home.

CHAPTER 8

THE DARK RIVER

FOR two days the *Royal Endeavor* lay rolling in the ground swell off the mouth of the Tauri. We would have gone ashore but for memory of the mosquito horde. It was so hot that pitch ran from the seams between the deck planks.

The second morning the *H. and S.* came back and lifted another load of stores for Terapo. Her villainous skipper promised to be back early in the afternoon, pick up a final load and Parer and me: but there was still no sign of the launch at sunset. When she was still missing next morning, I went ashore to consult Oscar by light of day.

Oscar, it turned out, was a Dane. He had run away to sea on a windjammer at the age of 12. He became interested in pearling and took employment as a deep-sea diver on the Thursday Island grounds, where he remained for many years earning – and spending – big money. He was regarded as one of the finest divers in North Australia. At the age of 40, however, he was burned out. Long jobs on the deep beds had given him diver's paralysis. With a little capital he went north to the New Guinea coast, probably hoping to make his fortune if the goldfields on the Lakekamu turned out a bonanza. He established a small trading store here at Kukepe and raised money in Moresby to buy a launch which he named the *Nance*.

For a time he did well, freighting stores up-river to the isolated mine at Bulldog, but then the mine petered out and he was forced to depend for a living on the Kukepe store, trading beads and lap-lap cloth, tobacco and canned beef and mirrors for the hard-earned shillings of natives who had returned to their villages after a period of service on plantations.

Many years ago Oscar had married a native woman, all legally and shipshape. That might have turned out well enough under the circumstances – but it didn't. Oscar's wife had a roving eye and a hasty temper – in fact so hasty that after one epic fight she burned the house down about his ears just to teach him a lesson. Oscar banished the termagant to her village and moved into the government rest hut until he could rebuild.

By drawing-room standards Oscar's career may seem patchy, but if he ever really incurred a debt to European society, he had paid it off long since. He was working like half a dozen coolies to keep the supplies for the troops going up-river. His understanding of the natives had smoothed over many a difficulty. He had paid and bribed them with his own trade goods and with his own money to keep the cargoes trickling in toward the mountains. I saw him straining his ropy old sinews rolling barrels up the beach, and the sweat pouring off him. He sent a note out by canoe:

BILL – DEAR SIR:
   I am doing what I can with that last cargo, but who the hell is responsible?

Respectfully yrs,
OSCAR

Oscar was 67 years old – *years*. In muscle and arteries he was 80. Work at 20 fathoms saw to that.

The third day was still and hot. At eleven o'clock a canoe came off with another note from Oscar:

The *H. and S.* stuck fast on the bar at high tide. No chance of getting her off until spring tides next week. Hope weather holds.

'That betel-chewing Hanuabada bastard!' was Bill's comment. 'He piled her up on purpose to get out of the work!'

Parer and I waited for further news until four o'clock and then went ashore with the gear. Neither of us felt capable of putting up with another night of rolling. The surf was steady but the whaleboat turned beam on to it when she grounded.

109

For a moment I thought Parer had lost his cameras and film. But in response to frantic bellowing and gesticulation, the cruising flotilla of children seized them and held them high and dry. Then they had fun rolling drums of fuel oil through the surf and up the beach.

Bill came ashore with us to stretch his legs. Oscar was speechless with indignation at the arrival of fresh cargo on the beach – cargo which he expected the *H. and S.* to move up-river. He said he would have to pay the villagers out of his own pocket again. Pale, small, rheumy eyed, knotted up, he squared his shoulders and cursed the army, navy and air force with a fluency I have never heard equaled. He said we had no chance of reaching Terapo before dark, but he didn't advise us to stay. Terapo would be more comfortable. We could believe that.

While we were discussing how many canoes to take, seven Flying Fortresses passed over on the way to Moresby. Oscar disappeared. One second he was sitting on a gasoline drum, talking. The next he had vanished. He did not return until the sky was silent again.

'It's breaking my health! Breaking my health!' he muttered. Then he rounded up six paddlers and two canoes to take us the first stage of our journey to Terapo.

We agreed to pay the paddlers one stick of tobacco each for the trip to Moviave. At Moviave, the local natives would meet us and provide another canoe for the final stage at Terapo.

We got away just before sunset The river estuary was about two miles wide, a stretch of placid, yellowish water. The canoes were 14 feet long, double dugouts shaped from single logs and fastened together by sapling crosspieces. Over the saplings a decking of withes and matting was laid. The paddlers sat slantwise, their feet in the dugouts. They propelled the craft with leaf-shaped paddles carved in one piece from light, strong palm wood. Every now and then one paused to bail with a gourd or half coconut.

As darkness came down, the river narrowed and the canoes slid in toward one bank to avoid a strong current. The light was too poor to see much of the country. It was mostly sago and nipa swamp. All one could discern was a tracery of fronds against the sky.

Suddenly we swerved and ran into a tunnel of foliage – dark and twisting as a serpent's gullet. The steerer said it was a short cut. How the natives could find a way in such narrow blackness was beyond me. Occasionally I flashed the electric lantern. It lighted a macabre labyrinth of hanging, rotten fronds, twisted roots and festooned creepers. Somewhere in the depths of the swamp a hunting crocodile barked. The frog chorus swelled to thunder. A few fireflies began to drift in the foliage. Here and there, where deadfalls abutted on the water's edge, were grottoes of glowworms. The paddles made a sucking sound. The boys began singing a canoe song in soft voices. An hour passed ... two ... three.. The darkness flowed like a stream. It had a tangible quality. It was hypnotic.

Without warning, the village came – the spit off Moviave. Fires glowed. There was a crazy landing stage of saplings. It seemed designed more to break white men's legs than to give any real help, but I revised that opinion when I stepped off the greasy grating of poles and sank below my knees in mud.

Shouted questions and shouted answers. A horde charged the riverbank, led by a man waving a burning branch. They seized the cargo on the canoe platform and began tossing it ashore, working – and looking – like imps of hell on a reception committee.

'Cargo 'e stop!' I screamed, gesturing frantically for them to dump the stuff together on solid ground. One package lost, and the whole expedition might fizzle.

'Policeman!' I demanded.

A near-naked giant stepped forward and saluted.

'I want six boys to take us to Terapo. Six paddlers and a canoe. I will pay one stick of tobacco for each man and two for the boss man.' The limb of the law nodded vigorously, turned and addressed an impassioned plea to the multitude.

Silence.

'Where are the Kukepe paddlers?' I waved a handful of tobacco sticks from the caddy.

At least 12 men jostled eagerly forward.

111

'Policeman!'

'*Io*, taubada!' Again a salute.

'There were six Kukepe paddlers.'

'*Io*.'

'Let them stand forward.'

Five men stood forward.

'Where is the other?'

Four jostled madly to be the sixth.

'Policeman!'

Three hung back.

I took a couple of wild kicks at their black behinds and thrust a stick of tobacco into the outstretched hand of each man who stood firm.

'Policeman!'

Salute.

'*Io*, taubada.'

'Choose six men to take us to Terapo!'

'Tonight?'

'Yes, tonight.'

Another speech.

Then it happened. The entire mob descended on a pile of 'cargo'. Within 10 seconds it had vanished. A singing, shouting, squealing crew trampled and scuttled and danced off with it in the general direction of the village. By grace of Providence I grabbed and managed to hold onto the haversack classified 'absolutely essential'.

'Come on!' I yelled to Parer. 'Quick.'

A man with an umbrella appointed himself guide. He led off across the break-leg causeway of logs at a jog trot. There were two stiles over sapling fences, then the village itself, a smell of burning coconut fiber and mosquitoes in swarms. Fires glowed on the hearths of nipa-thatch houses set on 15 foot stilts. Grunting, squealing pigs were running.

I tripped and flashed the lantern – a baby blinked up at me mutely from the mud. Then, in the beam, three tiny yellow puppies appeared. They turned tail and scampered off on their fat little bellies into the shadows. More houses. A glimpse of peering women, grass skirted, bare breasted, limbs tinted by

112

fire. One, pregnant, with the skirt band loosened under her great opulent belly, held up a child to see the shadows of passing white men. Musk. Aromatic smoke. Smell of sewerage, food, swamp mud, frangipani.

A small boy sidled up to me and asked, 'Me carry cargo, taubada?' He snatched at the haversack. I think he just wanted the honor of carrying cargo for a taubada, or was appalled by the indignity of a taubada carrying cargo, however trivial, by himself. But I said: *'Las, las!* This fella *pusa* (bag) *pourri-pourri* (magic).' He shied away and made off, eyeballs flashing.

Later, when crossing a log bridge over a deep ditch, I handed the bag to another child for a moment. He held it with all the care he might have shown 10 pounds of dynamite fitted with detonators!

The gear was assembled on the riverbank. I checked it and it seemed all there. Gibson and Cyril reappeared unobtrusively.

'Is all the stuff there?'

'We think so, taubada,' they replied gravely.

Just as the canoe was casting off there was a wild screaming on the bank. A child not more than six years old staggered forward, bent double under the weight of the brown gunny sack containing the bulk medical gear!

We arrived at Terapo in the early hours of morning, filthy and weary after a two-mile tramp through long grass from the canoe landing. The station turned out to a man, gave us hot shower baths, a mountainous meal of canned meat, sweet potatoes and fruit, and a gallon of black tea.

Terapo was a beautifully kept little post, manned by four whites. The houses were well built of ilimo saplings and palm thatch, not a single nail used in their construction. Joints were pegged or lashed with lawyer vine. The floors and furniture were made of peeled, closely fitting saplings, unsquared. A little settlement had been built with only two types of metal tools – bush knives and light axes. Yet there was comfort in it – even luxury – when one became used to the unevenness of all surfaces.

113

Most of the cargo from here was going up-river to Bulldog in two 90-foot dugout canoes powered by outboard motors. Each of these craft was hewn from a single immense log. Their sides were three inches thick and the bottoms an inch thicker. They drew only about nine inches of water when fully laden with from 60 to 80 men or with two and a half tons of cargo. They were ideal craft for haulage on a treacherous and changeable river, but wear and tear on outboard motors was heavy and breakdowns were frequent. Supplementing the two canoes were a couple of small launches that could make the run right into Bulldog only when the river was high enough.

We had been at Terapo three days, trying to make up our minds to resume the journey by paddle canoe because the dugouts were otherwise employed, when one of the launches, the *Toma,* came down-river unexpectedly and was briefed immediately to transport five tons of urgent cargo – tents and mail – to Bulldog. Her skipper John was 20 years old, a three-quarter caste with a magnificent thatch of brown, sun-bleached hair.

The launch was heavily laden. We traveled on the roof of the cabin with a load of stores. Soon after sunrise, John rigged up a large canvas umbrella for us, but the river wound so much that it provided shade only now and then. The sunlight reflected from the water was searing. All day long the glare increased until our eyes were red and swollen and our heads splitting.

The river was broad and tawny, with a six-knot current until it widened at the mouth. The whole delta was laced with a maze of little channels which short-circuited bends and ran from river system to river system. There were a few mangroves lower down. Regiments of lungfish were out on the aerial roots. They lay panting, living tableaux of life emerging from primeval slime. After two or three hours, the river narrowed and was half choked by great logs and snags among which the lion-colored water roared and snarled.

For the most part John kept the launch in channels under the banks and we had glimpses into the jungle lands behind the swamps. Many of the trees were covered in ropes of

114

crimson vine flowers and brick-red crotalaria. There were immense staghorn ferns, areca palms, plantain groves, banks of taro, towering ilimo and toon trees lording it above the lesser jungle, and festoons of thorny lantana.

There were ibex, storks, flights of clumsy hornbills, shrikes, tiny brown swifts, kingfishers, cranes, and crested doves crying sadly under the arches of the forest. Sometimes crocodiles slid hastily down from sandpits.

We saw the canoes of the solemn river people floating down-stream. They gave the launch a wide berth. Their outriggers were loaded with the produce of jungle gardens and the night's fishing. They were a light-colored people, slim and wild and graceful like animals. John said they were shy and avoided travel in broad daylight. No one knew very much about them.

At midday the second of the 90-foot canoes came round a bend ahead. Lieutenant A. was coming down-river unexpectedly. The naval man was still wearing a uniform cap with gold braid on it. He was sunburned the color of raw, bloody beef. At the prow, the canoe flew a large American flag. A. laughingly explained that it was more than a complimentary gesture to our ally. His police boys were very upset because they hadn't a flag to salute. No union jack was available, so why not Old Glory?

A. was doubtful about our reaching Bulldog that night because the river was falling. He thought we would get no farther than a sago-makers' camp near the village of Otomai. After all, he said, it would have been rare good luck to get through from Terapo in one day. By paddle canoe it would have taken us five or six days. Parer was jubilant about the shot of the American flag.

When the evening mists came down, the river changed from green and gold to pastel blues and browns, and was split by the wild rills of little rapids. A range of low hills slipped past . . . a glimpse of Mount Lawson, ponderous in the sky.

Just before sunset, the flying foxes began their evening migration. First one or two of the batlike creatures passed overhead – *flap, flap, flap* – cumbersome as archaeopteryx in the heavens of the dawn of time. Then scores. Then hundreds. Then countless thousands. *Flap. Flap. Flap.* A relentless, perfect rhythm in every wing. They passed so low over the river that one could see the hooks on their wing tips, the fur on their squirrel-like bodies. They were flying out to despoil the vine orchards of the jungletop by night.

The snags had got worse through the last hour of daylight. John came up to tell us he couldn't possibly make Bulldog that night. He would try to reach Otomai.

Then the launch hit the first snag. John backed off without much trouble, but he was worried. He went forward and, lying down with his head projecting over the prow, signaled the steersman with his hands. His skill at picking passages through savage runnels of water was amazing. He had a nose for safety in the river.

When it got dark, we went forward with torches and the electric lantern. The stream was now much more rapid and shallow. There was one terrific bump. The launch gave a lurch and the engine stalled. We could hear the angry sucking of the river, the muffled roar of rapids higher up. I looked overside in the beam of the lantern and calculated the possibility of swimming ashore if worse came to worse. It didn't look too promising. Weissmuller himself would have come to grief in the millraces that ran between the razor-sharp black snags. If we had been making more than a bare two knots against the stream, the launch might have ripped her bottom clean out. As it was, she was wedged firmly against a sunken tree trunk more than 100 feet long.

John came topside again. In a cold voice he asked: 'Do you wish to continue the journey, taubada?'

'Can you get her off, John?'

'Yes, taubada. In an hour or so.'

'What do you think?'

He shrugged, said with utter resignation: 'If you wish to continue the journey, we will continue, taubada.'

'Does it get better farther up, or worse?'

'Worse,' he said simply.

I should have called a halt to the journey at sunset. I was the taubada. Such decisions as starting journeys and stopping journeys remained inviolately with me.

'Is the launch in a safe position, John?'

'I do not know, taubada.'

'Then get a couple of men overside and find out if she is, damn you!'

He turned happily away and yelped at the crew boys. Two stripped off their ramies, took a rope end and dropped into the whirlpools where they splashed, grunted, poked and pried for 10 minutes or so, and answered John's questions.

'She is safe enough,' he said at last, 'if she does not move in the night.'

'Then make her fast with lines and see that she does not move in the night.'

'Yes, taubada.'

The mailbags were a lumpy bed and the mosquitoes were very bad. I managed to rig two nets, but neither was mosquito-proof. Parer had had very little sleep and in the morning looked ill.

John was slow getting the launch off the snag because she had bedded herself firmly in a tangle of wood. Eventually the boys managed to warp away and get through the beginning of a sizeable log jam. After an hour's run we passed the junction of the Kunimapai River and came into the bank at Otomai, just as the sun rose about the trees.

The sago makers were working on the outskirts of the forest. The village sprawled along the muddy banks of the river. It was in the stark, passionless light of morning, and I had seldom seen a filthier or more depressing human habitation. The houses were crude shelters with sides open to the weather. Smoldering fires were being coaxed under every thatch and the inhabitants squatted about them miserably, too torpid with betel nut, sleep and cold to take much interest in our arrival.

The physique, of the men in particular, was poor. The

117

cause was probably nutritional, since they lived almost entirely on sago. Few were free from fungus skin diseases – grille and sepoma. Parer went ashore for pictures and I went with him. The flies were just waking up. The place smelled abominably of wet human dung.

I inspected the sago cutters' work on the largest of the palms. The long spiky fronds were lopped off with stout axes, the log was split and its starchy pith hacked out. The chips of the pith were then pulverized in the hollowed log to a mass of fibre. Water was poured in at the top end and trickled out into bark containers at the lower end, depositing layers of sticky, brownish starch. This was dried off, formed into bundles about the size and shape of a cannon ball, wrapped in green leaves, and cooked. The finished product was traded up and down-river for other food, or for iron implements, cooking pots and tobacco. Sometimes the sago was mixed with small whitebaitlike fish dredged out of the river in fine coconut fiber nets. Sometimes it was beaten into flat cakes for cooking. It looked more like dirty kaolin clay than anything else.

Coming back to the launch I tried to make a short cut and nearly, very nearly, fell into the village latrine – a rough pit dug not 20 yards from the site of the sago making. It was a nerve-shattering experience.

Meanwhile Parer was getting shots of the children. Under three years of age they appeared healthy – delightful, black, grinning picaninnies of fiction, with beautiful teeth and clean skins. After that, they had all developed the pot bellies of chronic malaria and showed signs of skin diseases.

The naïve trust of a little group blowing up the fire in one of the shelters was touching. They could never have seen a camera before, but they accepted Parer without shyness. He wanted shots, so we got John to interpret. Once they understood, the mothers co-operated as heartily as Hollywood mothers at a screen test. They gathered the children together with the noises that mothers the world over make when gathering children together. Then they stage-directed the fire blowing with pride glowing in their eyes, chattering and

118

laughing. It might have been any baby show. Betel chewing had stained the women's lips in the caricatured likeness of lipstick.

Parer's final shot was of a newly born infant being lulled in a fish-net cradle. The little creature was the shade of a badly discolored sirloin of beef. It lay in the bag, as in the womb, doubled up and head down. The mother had been confined in the night. There was still blood on her grass bed. She was feeling poorly, muttering to herself and slapping the infant from side to side with her hands. The whack was audible 20 yards away and the fish net described a six-foot arc.

Before we left I gave some of the children a present of barley sugar. For the first time the mothers showed alarm. They grabbed at the candy anxiously, watched me eat one, raised their eyebrows, took off the paper wrapping, tasted them, then handed them back reluctantly to the clamoring offspring. A palisade of small, outstretched fingers, a battery of greedy, wide eyes, was my last impression of Otomai.

A few miles above the sago makers' village, the launch stuck finally. There was not enough water to carry her any farther. From another riverside village we obtained a canoe of the same kind that had brought us to Terapo.

John estimated it would take five or six hours' paddling to reach Bulldog. We transferred the gear and took leave of him. I gave him 40 American cigarettes in a burst of generosity and sentiment. He was complimented, but I doubt whether he smoked them, preferring trade tobacco in a *bau-bau* (bamboo pipe).

The next was the most trying stage. The canoe was crowded, and swarms of flies were attracted by a dead wallaby which the natives took with them for food – and by a very large, very dead, very charred fish.

The river narrowed again until it was a bare 100 yards across, and began winding insanely. It also became shallower and even more rapid. Paddling was slow and exhausting. After a time the crew gave up and started poling, zigzagging from

119

side to side to look for shoal water. By 10 o'clock the sun was fiercer than it had been the day before. I was feeling ill – from the heat, the stink of the paddlers, the wallaby, and the dead fish.

Parer tried to console me by declaring that low Arabs were infinitely dirtier than these people. I found it hard to believe, and not consoling. By midday I was beginning to cramp and shiver. It looked like a dose of fever.

'How far to go?'

'Close up!' declared the boss boy soothingly.

'How many points?' (bends in the river).

'Two, taubada.'

I sighed gustily and began to count. When we had passed six bends, I asked again: 'How many points?'

'Three, taubada,' replied the boss boy cheerily. 'Close up!'

CHAPTER 9

O WILD ELOA

TWELVE hours after John began to warp the *Toma* off the log jam, we poled into Bulldog. There were two white men in camp, Vic H. and Dick P. Vic was a hardened bushman long used to the rigors of New Guinea. He used to manage a line of 1,200 native laborers for a gold-mining company in the mandate. All his experience, tact, and toughness were needed here. The two men were managing to keep lines employing 600 natives filtering through the mountains. They were both rake thin, yellow, jungle weary to the bone. But they still had minds like rat traps. Dick was the first man since Moresby to ask us, politely but firmly, to produce credentials. He examined them thoroughly.

As an antidote to the appalling monotony, heat and discomfort in which they lived, they observed the formalities of race – dressed carefully and kept their clothes and quarters impeccably clean and tidy. They were punctilious about meal hours, insisted on a fresh calico tablecloth for every meal, and had trained their table boys to cook and serve their miserable rations in plantation-bungalow style. They lived in a small grass house that contained one room enclosed bodily in a huge mosquito bar. Within this enclosure was a dining table (packing cases) and a small bookshelf with very solid literature. The two men occasionally played cards together in the evening.

All about the house was a trim trench, four feet deep and about two feet six inches wide. It was crossed by two bridges, each doubly 'stopped' with a piece of corrugated iron set vertically into the ground. This trench prevented the entrance

121

of rats, scorpions and death adders which abounded in the surrounding kunai grass and jungle.

Here, at long last, we obtained a detailed, circumstantial account of the route to Wau. The distance was between 100 and 120 miles. It would take from five to nine days walking, according to the condition of the trail in the mountains, which condition would be determined by weather. There were six established camps en route – Dead Chinaman, Dead Kukukuku, Water Bung, Water Dry, Kudjiru, and Winnema. White men, we were told, were normally stationed at Dead Kukukuku and at Kudjiru, and would, of course, give us directions and assistance.

Water Dry Camp was approximately 9,000 feet above sea level. For the most part the going was extremely rough, streams being crossed either by logs felled from rim to rim of their gorges, by fording, or by bridges made from jungle creepers. The mountains were very wet and cold. Some of the climbing was difficult.

Vic and Dick were chronically energetic. Four or five hours' brisk walking was nothing to them. They took us out to inspect the overgrown airfield and a pandanus thatch camp they were building in the depths of the jungle for troop staging. It was wet and uninviting, but it was shelter. They looked upon the big, gloomy huts as temples of luxury.

They showed us the water vine that grows in these parts. It looked like ordinary lantana until you noted details of bark and foilage. Cut cleanly, a four-foot length of well-grown vine would quickly exude a pint or a pint and a half of clear, cool, pure water.

Vic and Dick were very proud that it was a tough country – and that they were tough citizens of it. Like most old hands they delighted in grim reminiscence. They told us about a German gentleman named Schultz who used to live in the hills. He had pleasant ways with the natives. When natives displeased him, he used to tie their hands, insert sticks of dynamite in their behinds, plug in a detonator and a length of fuse, light it, and order them to run at the point of a shotgun.

Schultz was hanged at Moresby.

Another pleasant fellow, reputedly the scion of a near-noble family of Australian 'squatocracy' used to hang up his recalcitrant servants by the thumbs. I thought: No wonder the Kukukukus are *shy!*

We had to sleep in the native hospital because heavy rain was threatening and no other thatch was proof against a real downpour. We rigged up platforms of piled biscuit tins, spread blankets and got nets slung.

There were four pneumonia cases in the hospital – one very bad. He wouldn't lie down. He sat on his bed cross legged – a thin, black man with a pink blanket round his shoulders. He moaned in time to his respiration – a sort of 'Ooo – *huh!* Ooo – *huh!*' His brother, tending him, squatted alongside, quietly massaging his back and chest. The eyes of both were frightened and wild.

Vic had been giving his pneumonia cases terrific shots of sulfapyridine and had saved most of them. But his supply of the drug was running very low. I resolved to spare him 50 tablets.

About six pneumonia cases came back every time a carrier line went into the mountains. The carriers were mostly coast boys acclimatized to heat and humidity. After a couple of crossings, the sharp cold of the mountains, the poor food, and the labor of lugging loads over the passes broke them. Vic was afraid that if the death rate increased he wouldn't be able to keep the lines going. He complained that the types of boys being recruited for the work were not selected carefully enough before they were sent in. He would like to see stout Koiari from the mountains at the back of Moresby instead of these thin, sickly coast dwellers.

At sunset I attended the evening sick parade and got my hand in dressing minor injuries. Every variety of tropical skin disease was paraded – also infected minor wounds of all kinds, pneumonia, pleurisy, malaria, cancer, dysentery, typhus, beriberi, yaws, cuscus, and so on. Vic's drugs were sulfanilamide, sulfapyridine, quinine, iodine, potassium permanganate, epsom

123

salts and castor oil. He had one scalpel, no probe, no artery forceps, and one pair of scissors. Before we left I gave him one scalpel, a pair of scissors and a couple of sets of forceps.

But by God, I will never forgive him for that night in the hospital! Try sleeping on biscuit tins with two blankets folded over them, in a temperature of 92 degrees, humidity at saturation point, rain pounding on a leaky thatch, countless millions of mosquitoes roaring – yes, roaring! – and a man dying of pneumonia going 'Ooo – *huh!* Ooo – *huh!*' over and over.

But at two o'clock in the morning the man with pneumonia stopped his moaning. He died. After he died I thought: I'd like to go down Flinders Street, Melbourne, with a gusty June southerly blowing and my wet overcoat flapping about my legs. I'd like to go home in a crowded suburban train and look at pretty girls' legs. I'd like to sit down in an armchair before a roaring fire. I'd like to go to bed in sheets so cold I would shudder – and get warm gradually. I'd like a hot bath, and lettuce salad, a plateful of porridge with cream on it! Then I went to sleep.

We made a start from Bulldog at nine o'clock. It was late, but there was a long sick parade and the carriers were difficult to load equitably. There were 93 in the line. We undertook the responsibility of getting them through to Kudjiru, tending those who were sick, maintaining discipline, preventing looting of cargo and judging disputes.

The line was carrying something over a ton of ammunition, tents, and mail for the 5th Independent Company. Most was packed in one-man loads of 40 to 50 pounds. Some of it was in two-man loads of 90 pounds lashed to a pole.

Vic said to go easy and save the carriers as much as possible. Fear of large-scale desertions was beginning to alarm him. But, save or kill, this load had to get through. There had been a long delay. Ninety tons of cargo for Wau were banked up. Much that had already set out from Bulldog had been damaged, pillaged or lost. Only half of it actually got to the front, so it was providential that at least one line would be traveling, with a couple of white men to keep an eye on things and report the condition of the trail and the probable points of leakage.

(Diary notes best tell the story of the journey from Bulldog to Kudjiru.)

June 15 – For about two hours this morning the going was reasonably good. The forest was fairly open and clean. The trail wound along the side of a wavering, flat-topped ridge. The grade was gentle. Everything was soaked by overnight rain, and roots were troublesome, tripping me every time I lifted an eye off the ground. The only way to see anything of the country, to check direction and grade, is to go like hell, head down, in quarter-hour spasms, then stop and have a good look round.

In these lower reaches the trees are tall, sound, and with huge, flared buttresses evolved by the species to give support in deep, soft soil and mold. I can recognize only the commoner types – ilimo, toon, okiri, and a few myrtles. Here and there are stands of timber that look like rosewoods and peppermints. The larger underbrush is unknown to me except that there are a few wild clove bushes and nutmegs. Palms are rare so far from the coast, but there are arecas, soft pandanus and the omnipresent wild plantain.

The stories of the forest are hard to see. Nearly all the big timber is smothered in saprophytic vines and ferns, which spread out over the treetops and are looped and interwoven into a coverlet so dense that the sun never gets through to the floor of the forest.

It is wrong to call this country jungle. The real jungles are simply porridgy masses of growing things, whereas it would be possible to travel off the trails in this mountain forest without much cutting. But I would not care to try it. All the usual checks on directions are useless. One cannot see the sun. There is no wind. It is not even possible to see the main forks of the trees. One travels in a dim, religious light, soundlessly – and by compass!

June 16 – We did not reach the new Kunda bridge over the Eloa River until after midday. It was far less wild than Vic had led us to suppose – a new bridge. The remains of the old one could be seen a few hundred yards downstream, an insane structure that sagged in the middle until its 'decking' brushed

125

the water. The new bridge had been reinforced with a wire rope and was decked with slats about 30 feet above water level at the lowest. It swayed and jumped, and pieces of the vine handrail stripped off.

The Eloa here is a most beautiful stream. Perhaps the word stream is inaccurate – rather it is a series of rapids and water-falls over slaty boulders. In a few places where the water is not churned up, it is deep green, ice cool and pure. Any man or animal who fell into it would be dashed to pieces in the rapids.

During this afternoon there were one or two rather tricky log crossings of the tributary creeks. It is extraordinary how sure footed these natives are. Their sense of balance is superb. Without a fraction of a second's hesitation they can swing onto a nine-inch log – greased with mud as slippery as mutton fat – and stride along its 60-foot length as firmly as if they were walking the broad highway. No doubt, in time even I will become more confident and stop worrying about the consequences of making a misstep halfway across.

We took the last couple of hours very steadily and I had a chance to potter off the trail. The vine flowers that drift down from the top story are beautiful – exotic things that are electric blue, yellow and white, and scarlet.

The jungle fruits thudding from the top story are queer, too. Some are like too perfect pears, apples or peaches. They have a deceptive, waxen color. The New Guinea police boy – a doleful, rather brutal-looking boy, but physically magnificent – assured me that they are very poisonous. How typical of this country! Never could imagination conceive a clime where beauty and death, plenty and poverty, action and decay are such close bedfellows.

On the subject of fruit: I experimented with one species. Came unexpectedly on three blue-crested cassowaries having a feast. They crashed off into the bush and I examined the debris – a peculiar fruit more like a woody-skinned rock melon than anything else. The flesh was peach yellow, and the seeds large and black. The flavor was astringent yet sweet, perfumed of eau de cologne. I ate about four ounces of pulp in half an hour. Nothing happened. There is quite a lot of this fruit, so

126

I've added one more item to the possible diet if we have to come back this way (or some other way) without provisions and with Jap patrols on our heels.

I am more confident than ever of being able to live off such country as this. There are snakes, pigeons – indeed, birds of all kinds – fish like mullet in the streams, wild taro and yams, wild bananas, areca, chillies, cassowaries and wild pigs. Probably getting a living would be a full time job because of the dense nature of the bush, but it *could* be done far more easily than in the Australian mountains.

If worst came to worst, fern roots and fern tips would provide a meal.

The tragedy of those poor devils who came down the coast from Rabaul and nearly starved to death on the way!

We checked in the cargo at six o'clock and held sick parade. Result: dressings for four galled shoulders and two cut feet, fifteen grains of quinine for a malaria, and six kicks in the backside for malingerers.

The carriers are delighted that there is a *lik-lik* doctor[1] with them. My stock is high.

June 18 – A wet miserable morning and two nasty jobs on morning sick parade. Top joint of a big toe to come off (he didn't report last night). It was gangrenous and the leg was swelling. Made a neat flap of skin and jointed it rabbit fashion. Stitched the skin back with gut, doused it with sulfa and bound the whole foot. The boy said he would carry on.

Second job was to lance an abscess in a blind eye that looked cancerous to begin with. I ended up by removing most of the eye, which was putrid, cauterizing the socket, plugging with sulfa and booting him back down the trail for Bulldog.

So far the novelty of the forest has kept me from getting depressed, but depression is creeping on. It's three days since we've seen sunlight. The mold underfoot stinks of epoch-old decay. In a thousand years the sun has never shone on it.

Queer things I saw today:

[1] Medical assistant.

127

1. A peculiar flower with fleshy, liver-colored sepals that looked like fungus.

2. A white, spindly fungus like a ground orchid.

3. Spiders three inches across the *body*, waiting for butter-flies and insects in great golden webs strung between the trunks of trees (Who said spiders have more than two eyes? I know better than any zoologist. These bastards had two eyes and they *looked* at me! Hell, how I hate spiders!)

4. A pitcher plant.

5. A sensitive mimosa that fell 'dead' when I brushed it.

6. The skeleton of a Chinese crouched in a hollow tree, the bones green, the empty sockets of his eyes staring out – oh, so dispassionately – on the walls of his green-walled living tomb. He gave the name – Dead Chinaman – to the staging camp. He fled with the miners from Bulolo when the Japanese came. He died of pneumonia in the tree where he took shelter from a bitter mountain storm. A miner gave 2s. to a native to bury him. The native contented his conscience by piling green palm fronds over the entrance of the tree's hollow, but they fell away in decay more rapidly than the Chinese. He now keeps lonely watch.

June 20 – Three pneumonias. One chap was running 105. I don't know about the others because Gibson, blast him, steri-lized the thermometer in boiling water! You can't mistake the pneumonias – plugged up and gasping.

One doubtful pleurisy. He'll have to go on because I can't spare him. It's hard enough distributing the loads of the men I've had to send back already. At this rate the sulfapyridine isn't going to last very long.

The sick men are making up a party to go back together to Bulldog. It is better that way because sick carriers have a way of vanishing into the bush when they travel alone. Either they go *long-long* (mad) and wander off to die or the Savage Kukus snap them up for their heads.

Half a dozen of these little head-hunters plucked up courage and came into camp tonight. They gave the call from which they derive their name – a sound like the beginning of the cry of the Australian laughing jackass. The party that came into camp were all young – little chaps under five feet high, with very black skins, compact, brutal faces, shortish lank hair, incipient beards, eyes that darted this way and that – and saw everything.

The men develop tremendous calf muscles from hunting in the hills. They carry short powerful-looking bows and bundles of poisoned arrows.

I took no notice of them for a long while. Then a sheepish carrier who spoke a little English came up and said the Kuku boys wanted to trade sweet potatoes for rice. I walked over and got the carrier to explain there was no rice for trade – taking care to stick the .38 in my belt. I wanted the Kukus to see it. One was wearing a tattered khaki shirt. Lord knows what a trade history it had before it got up into these hills. Perhaps the little devil had stripped it off some sick carrier.

They are charming children, these Kukus. The last white man they killed for his head was somewhat cavalierly treated. After clubbing him they discovered he had no knife. Neither had they. So they thrust his head into a narrow tree fork and kept twisting the body until the head came off. They then went off contented.

In appearance they are much like the aboriginal Sakai people of the Malay Peninsula, but they are even more primitive and much more savage. The Kukus are sturdy, well-nourished nomads, moving periodically from garden to garden. They terrace out a little land on some slope of the lower ranges where the jungle is not so thick and grow crops of bananas, pawpaws, yams and taro. The method of agriculture is primitive: the digging is done with a pointed stick; there is no attempt at cultivation after planting; they eat out a garden, replant it and then move on. They are also great hunters and fishermen. They never build permanent villages and range over hundreds of miles of the central mountains, mostly at temperate altitudes of between 3,600 and 5,000 feet. The natives of the plain are terrified of them, and they have been a thorn in the side of the administration because it is almost impossible to locate them for punishment after they have staged a raid for trophies or human flesh.

In Moresby, government officers tell a story to illustrate how difficult it is to deal with the Kuku problem. A certain well-known patrol officer, after years of work, succeeded in persuading a Kuku to return to *dim-dim* (white man) civilization with him. He was given light work to do (no Kuku had ever been known to work before!) and was shown all the *dim-dim* wonders, like motorcars, steamers and phonographs.

The Kuku was very docile and very impressed. After six months the patrol officer suggested that he return to his own people to spread the good word. The Kuku was still docile. He agreed. The patrol officer and one white companion, a prospector, went off with six police boys, the Kuku boy jubilantly in the van as a guide, interpreter and friend. Nobody ever saw or heard of any of the party again.

Knowing this story, and to soften the blow of refusing rice, I got a packet of salt and doled out a handful to each of the party. They licked it up then and there to the very last grains and pleaded for more.

Despite their bad reputation, I don't think Kukus would be dangerous to white men if left strictly alone or, if that were impossible, dealt with firmly and fairly. Old hands always warn about the danger of sharp practice in trade and of taking food from a native garden without payment. Few natives resent your getting food from their gardens if you need it, provided only you make some small payment.

June 21 – Mary be praised, a white man – and an Irishman at that!

We're in Dead Kukukuku Camp, the guests of Harry O'K., who knows all the Parers of New Guinea down to the last set of twins. Dead Kukukuku is also known as Central Camp. Harry is stationed here permanently to keep the carrier lines moving. He has with him Errol S., a redheaded youngster who is away at the moment looking after step making on the trail through the hills.

The plan of military development for this route is becoming

clear. It calls for the construction of good staging camps, trail improvement to the extent of putting in rough steps on the steeper slopes to assist infantry and carriers, and the building of proper bridges and cuttings where the route runs out on the side of gorges.

So far the country has not been really difficult and the grades are reasonable. Still, although I know little or nothing about military engineering, I am willing to swear it will be years before wheeled traffic can get over. A mule trail for pack artillery, possibly – but a military road? Never![2]

Another problem! Can white troops be moved through these hills in large bodies? Unless they are thoroughly hardened to tropical traveling and tropical living, wastage through exhaustion and disease will be high. Effective hygiene for large numbers of men is practically impossible in this climate and terrain.

Note for engineers: River scarps show the *soil* in places to be 30 feet deep! It rains every afternoon and the storms are of great violence. Maintenance of even a foot trail will need big labor gangs if there is any volume of traffic.

Harry is one of the most delightful characters I've ever run into. He is black haired, blustering, animated and company-loving, childishly grateful for the chance to talk. He is a miner who has made and spent fortunes, who always comes back to the jungle and the hills because they, and the wild life, are in his blood. He's well on in middle life, but his physical condition is excellent except for a few bad leg ulcers caused by tick bites. He has spent nearly 30 years on the territory and seems to have had fun out of every day.

After dinner I couldn't resist Harry's wistfulness. I produced a bottle of whisky – the worst whisky that ever came out of a bad Australian distillery. The light in his eye, the way he passed his tongue over his lips, was reward enough.

'Holy Mary, Mother av God!' he exclaimed, after the first long luxurious sip. ''Tis a trifle on the raw side to be sure, but 'tis niktar no less! Niktar off av Olympus!' In the next four hours I had four moderate drinks and he settled the bottle. He

[2]I was wrong. Australian Army Engineers completed a jeep track over these hills by the end of 1943 but it was never used.

was not tight. He was glowing, happy, in love with the world and everybody in it.

The stories he tells, with his Celtic instinct for point and picturesque gesture, are inimitable. Yarns flowed from his rich tongue in a never ending stream. His eyes twinkled and his laugh reverberated through a muffling of stained and molded canvas, echoing back from the trees where the fireflies shone.

Never was a bottle of whisky better spent!

June 22 – Bath in the icy Eloa at dawn. I've not been feeling too well. Possibly it's fever, but more likely it's weakness through sweating so heavily. Am trying salt tablets.

The trail has been getting steadily steeper. We're now at 3,000 feet, having left the river valley and wound up slopes of increasing severity. On this stretch there were some bad patches along the sides of creeks, where it was possible to keep going only by clinging to greasy roots and swinging like a monkey from clay ledge to clay ledge.

A trivial injury could be disastrous out here. One can consider with reasonable equanimity the prospect of dropping 300 feet down a greasy cliff and breaking one's neck – but not the humiliation, pain and anticlimax of a badly sprained ankle.

More and more the carriers amaze me. How they can edge two-man loads round those corners is incomprehensible.

Log crossings are getting stiffer.

Just after midday I poked off the trail and found a spur about two miles down. It ran out on to a bluff overlooking the Eloa valley and I looked up to the crest of a great unnamed mountain. There can be nothing like it anywhere in the world. The mountain must be more than 11,000 feet high, because the timber line ends 1,500 feet below the summit. Over this summit, rank upon rank of great rainclouds tramped like the armies of God marching out of all space and time.

From 6,000 feet to eye level, moss, alpine scrub and forest swept down in an unbroken avalanche of green. Then it was held by limestone precipices. They gleamed white, like snow. Below them the forest dropped again, tier on tier of trees, looped in flowering vines of crimson and yellow and blue.

Deep through this tilted, eternal savagery of growth was cut the cleft of the river. Three thousand feet below, it wound like a white snake in leafy canyons – a mighty, roaring stream glutted with the clouds' burden. Rapid upon rapid, fall upon fall, whirlpool upon whirlpool. Ten thousand bombers could drop their cargo in that valley and there would be no visible scar. Nor would a billion trees reck so trivial a shattering, for here since life began the forest has been growing and decaying, growing and decaying. Until all forests end, it will still grow and decay, and the white river groan under the spilled loads of heaven.

June 23 – Tonight we camped in a rickety shelter with a leaf thatch and a pole floor. An hour ago I was writing by the light of the lantern. We heard aircraft. The sound became clear and unmistakable – the buzzing of Japanese bombers. Mechanically I turned out the lantern and went into the open. The forest all about was bright with a cold, pale, spectral light.

Beneath the falling, rotting logs about the camp and under the floor of the shelter itself were grottoes of glowworms. The trees, the rocks and the deadfalls were picked out with faint luminosity – every twist of branch, every convoluted knot, every twig angle. All green-blue, shimmering, phosphorescent. Between the branches and the fronds of the ferns were pulsing myriads of fireflies – cold little ghosts of long-dead fire in the hills.

Disney at his most inspired never designed a frame of such eerie and macabre beauty as this.

June 24 – Up and up and up and up. Nine carriers gone in the last two days – pneumonia, broken legs, collapse.

Countless thousands of 'steps.'

Saw 'Blue', who is in charge of a section of the route. Twenty years old, carroty-haired. He used to be a shipping clerk, but he has taken to the hills and the hills have taken to him. He walked seven miles up the trail with us on the pretext of inspecting a construction gang. Then he admitted he had come just for the pleasure of having a talk with someone from the outside, and started to walk back. He was very cheerful because a fortnight ago he received mail from home – the first in five months. He's a fit companion for merry Harry, vital, imperturbable, simple of spirit. There are no bad men out here. Bad men don't last.

The character of the forest has been changing. It is subalpine – cold and dripping.

I forgot to record that I saw the Dead Kukukuku at the camp – a small bark-wrapped corpse on a spindle-shanked platform in the bush. The Kukus bury their dead that way. Beside his burial platform half a dozen magnificent aspidistras were growing. Aspidistras growing by the mummy of a pygmy cannibal is something else that could only happen in this country.

The aspidistras were recalled to me by the other familiar plants in these hills – kidney ferns, maidenhair, umbrella fern, tuberous begonia, calceolaria, stinkwort, wild mint, rasberry and tansy. The cedar trees are smothered by giant white and mauve clematis.

Blue said that from Water Bung Camp the trail gets really bad.

June 25 – We've passed the boundary between Papua and the Mandated Territory. A crazy-looking brush fence across a creek marked the old division of administration in the British end of the island. How and when it was put there or by whom – I don't know. It does not extend more than 20 yards from the creek banks.

The inevitable rainstorm broke at four o'clock and caught us on the wrong foot. I haven't been properly dry since that grilling on the Lakekamu and my feet are spongy and inclined to blister. Mockas[3] are hell, but I've managed to keep infection down with iodine. Am keeping to the rule of never going to bed without washing, powdering and disinfecting feet, armpits and crotch. Adhesive plaster and iodine on the slightest scratch. Touch wood, but so far it's worked! I don't want ulcers like

[3] Minute bush ticks.

Harry or Blue. This personal care takes about an hour a day. Can troops be disciplined to observe like precautions?

The carriers are getting more difficult to handle and keep from straggling. There are more malingerers on sick parade. Perhaps it is unfair to call it malingering because there is hardly a man on this line who is, by European standards, fit for heavy work. Nearly every one of them has an enlarged spleen. Without exception they have diseased skins. They are louse ridden, ill nourished, and most have some infected injury or other – wild, dusky, graceful creatures with melting brown eyes, corded limbs and an odor like a circus cage!

Their labor is incredible. I cannot fathom how they perform the work they do on a daily handful of rice, a can of meat a week, a little sugar and a little tea. They would rather work on this carrier line than eke out a miserable existence in their own villages. Yet I don't think the carrier line provides them with better food or greater comfort than the village. It provides only more work. They prefer it because they are *paid* – in tobacco, certainly, but paid. They have an opportunity to acquire 'wealth'. Work on a carrier line represents progress and enterprise. For crossing the mountains, carriers are issued with one thin, pink, trade blanket. They take all their worldly belongings with them in a little bundle wrapped in calico and slung on a stick. They sleep on the sodden ground, sometimes under shelter, but more often in the rain.

They are not interested in this war. They don't know what it is all about. They have not even seen a Japanese, but they have seen and are interested in white men. Why is it that a white man's eye, the magic of his presence, can so hypnotize these savages that in all essentials they are more faithful to what is entrusted to them and are willing to endure more suffering than white men themselves?

If there is a war in New Guinea – and there are times when I believe any war to be negligible against the face of this land – *these* are the people who are fighting it now. The polers and paddlers, the Johns and the Wasurus. The people of the rivers and swamps and hills who come and hire their bodies for tobacco, and die of pneumonia, exposure, exhaustion, in the

135

evil mountains; who carry the white man's burden – a load of death – into a far, strange land.

I do not understand. No ordinary loyalty moves them. They have perhaps heard of the king. They have been told that the Japanese are bad men who would enslave them. They have never known liberty to want to save it. Before they were the slaves of white men, they were slaves of the inexorable wilderness. They have not evolved beyond slavery. In Kukepe I was received like a king. Here I am obeyed like a god.

June 26 – Today the going became terrible, truly terrible. Beyond Water Bung the trail reared itself up a greasy precipice for four or five thousand feet. Grade of one in two, with occasional vertical patches. Then sharp equally precipitous drops.

Up this appalling hill the carrier line staggered and heaved, groaned and panted. Their black legs corded. The veins on their heads stood out. Sweat rushed out of them. They cried out with the agony of effort, always struggling up and up. Ridge after ridge. Greasy mud, looped roots, thorns. Still up.

Just before 11 o'clock, the Papuan police boy – who is a decent sort of black boy and quite kind under his bullying manners – came panting up to me in a great state of agitation. The two-boy loads, he declared, had 'buggered up'. They said they wanted to go back. This was serious! There were about 20 two-boy loads, representing half the line.

I went back quickly. The stragglers were lying face down on the trail. Something had got into them. The New Guinea police boy was raging up and down, kicking and screaming. They ignored him. I signaled him to stop and he stood back reluctantly, disgusting little flecks of foam at the corners of his mouth.

'Stan' up, you boy!' I roared.

Half a dozen stood up, panting.

I kicked three recumbent men in the ribs. They clambered to their feet, groaning and rolling their eyes. Most of the rest followed them.

'What for you bugger up?' I demanded.

The New Guinea boy snapped the question in dialect. A babel of voices.

I took the Papuan policeman to one side. 'What is the trouble?'

One boy had 'buggered up', he told me, and the rest caught it.

I stood for a moment, working up steam. 'Which boy?'

He led to a poor, shriveled devil doubled up, muttering and groaning. I felt his head. No fever. Felt his pulse – rapid, shallow. Felt his legs. They were relaxed. Rolled up his tightly shut eyelids. He goggled at me and groaned again.

Exhaustion. No doubt of that, but there was apparently nothing else wrong with him. The carrier *had* to go on. He *had* to go because 20 cases of small-arms ammunition had to go with him.

Suddenly I kicked him hard in the ribs. He screamed and buried his head in his arms. 'Catchem cargo!' I howled. 'Catchem cargo, you black, double-died, scrimshanking, bloody bastard! Up! Up! before I kick your gizzard from here to Kingdom Come! *Catchem cargo!*'

He pulled himself slowly to his feet, eyes rolling pitifully. Another boy lifted his end of the pole and put it on his thin, galled shoulder. Leaning on his climbing pole then, he took half a dozen staggering steps forward. Up and down the line – raving, cursing, foaming.

'Too much heart b'long me soft all-e-time!' I ranted. 'Too much you bloody kanakas *koi-koi* (humbug). Sposem boy sick, I give medicine. Sposem boy *koi-koi*, I'll ram his guts down his own throat and pull what's left out the other end.'

Standing on a log, the brutal-faced New Guinea policeman gave a translation for those who needed it.

When the line was going again I marched past it, gritting my teeth, shaking my fist under every clotted nostril. The line shrank back from me. They were more terrified than if I had killed one of them. Far more terrified, because it was now clear that a boy who 'buggered up' made the white man insane.

Fifty yards ahead of the leader I passed a finger over my

137

lips. Yes, foam. Nice, nice work, White! No wonder you swallowed your vomit.

June 27 – Nine thousand feet of altitude. Not a breath in a lungful of air. The cold is piercing.

Water Dry Camp – six miserable, open-sided shelters with slat floors that have an inch of air between the slats. Bath in the creek, but it did no good. I'm damned near done up. Even Parer is gloomy.

Bright-green ferns and mosses clothe the trees to their topmost branches. The creek bed, composed of frost-shattered rocks from the peaks, is like a geological museum after an earthquake. Mica, olivine, schist, serpentine, granite, gneiss, porphyry, quartz, felspar, crystals, limestone, slate, chert, volcanic agglomerates, quartzite. These ranges would drive a real geologist mad with curiosity.

Cold, *piercing* cold. Hell, what a night *that* was!

We got Cyril and Gibson to build and tend a fire under the hut directly below our bedrolls, which were sodden. We ate canned beef and biscuits impregnated with trade tobacco, and turned in.

All the wood was pulpy wet and emitted far more smoke than heat, but it was better to lie there in a little warmth and smoke ourselves black than to shift over and shiver. The slats were so ridgy that in the morning I was almost too sore to move. Our eyes were puffed and rheumy. All night the carriers coughed and groaned and cried out in their sleep. Drenching rain fell – not far off, hail.

The morning's camp was the most miserable I have ever seen. The carriers crept about with their pitiful pink blankets draped round them and tried to get warm at the stubborn fires. The poor, improvident devils had eaten the last of their rice issue and had to go breakfastless. More was to be drawn at Kudjiru, a day's journey away, but I couldn't bear the thought of them starting the descent on a completely empty belly. I gave the police boys a pound of our reserve stock of tea and a couple of pounds of sugar, and told them to see that every boy got his pannikinful. They grinned and bowed and scraped and held up the pans for me to see. They danced about the fires.

'You are a good man, taubada,' said the Papuan police boy gravely. 'Very nearly all boy he *all* bugger up. But now it is down the hill and there will be rice tonight.'

Just before we were due to leave, the police boy came back again and complained that a carrier would not go. I went down, cursing on principle. No, he wouldn't go. He crawled out of a miserable lean-to, supported by two others, with his pitiful arms clasped over his guts. He was doubled up in agony. His eyes were protruding and suffused with blood. He moaned incessantly and his nostrils were plugged with mucus.

For one ghastly moment I thought it was the black boy I had kicked in the ribs the day before, but it wasn't. The police boy told me a load had fallen on him but he had not complained, just carried on.

There was no doubt about it – ruptured spleen or bowels. I gave him a hypodermic of two-thirds of a grain of heroin – above the maximum dose, but it will make him feel good. He had been in great agony all night. And very soon he will die. I gave permission for a friend to stay with him. All the carriers have a friend to stay with them when they are dying. To the friend I gave a handful of barley sugar to be given to the dying man if he should get hungry, and a five-grain tablet of caffeine – to be given to him if, by some miracle, he should get strength enough to set out on the descent. I don't know any more.

So – down. Down and down and down. We have crossed the great range and are going down into the valley of the Bulolo River. Somewhere ahead is sunlight and open country. The voice of wild Eloa is behind the hills, unheard.

CHAPTER 10

THE HAPPY VALLEY

WE MADE good time from Water Dry. A few hundred yards out from Kudjiru Camp, the jungle was cut off as if with a giant knife. Ahead, as far as eye could see, was a rolling, grassy valley between mountains. How good it was to feel the sun – a crisp, not too savage sun, like home. We spent a day drying the gear, doctoring mocka bites, greasing boots.

There were six white men at Kudjiru, sorting, clearing and dispatching such cargoes as came through. The carriers were there rested, treated for illness or injuries and sent back without loads to Bulldog. New Guinea carriers took the loads to Wau. They were blacker, sturdier and more healthy than the Papuans. Many were free altogether from skin diseases. They were more stupid, therefore more courageous.

While we were resting at Kudjiru, a circumstantial account of the first two commando raids on Lae and Salamaua came in. The Salamaua show had been notably successful. Eighty raiders went in at three o'clock in the morning and caught the Jap sentries napping. Scouts slit the throats of three, and the main force got almost into the town before being discovered. They sprayed everything in sight with tommy guns, threw bombs into the houses, dynamited stores, and withdrew before the enemy could organize resistance. They killed more than 100 Japs and the sole casualty on our side was one man shot through the hand.

The Lae raid was not so successful. The officer in charge and two other men were killed before the force reached its objective. After that, co-ordination went to pieces and everyone had to get out. Native dogs kept enemy outposts awake and the element of surprise was lost. Forty Japs were killed but the material damage done to their dumps and buildings was small. Fearing large-scale attacks, the Japanese then began bombing and shelling the jungle in every direction, blindly. Wau and Bulolo took another heavy pasting from the air.

Rats are my only unpleasant memory of Kudjiru. There were hordes of the brutes. They came down from the bush and paid particular attention to the rice storehouse where we were quartered. They ran over the blankets all night, sat on one's face, dropped with soft thuds from the thatch – sounds horribly reminiscent of the noise made by falling snakes – and generally played hell.

If there had been no rats I wouldn't have minded staying there indefinitely. The outlook was magnificent. The climate was cool and comparatively dry. There was fresh food. The men themselves grew crops of cabbage, lettuce and tomatoes in record time – ten days for radishes and about a month for the others. However, there was a New Guinea boy line going out in the morning and we went with it.

A few miles out on the trail we met a number of sick and slightly wounded New Guinea riflemen and commandos. They were the forerunners of a party on their way out to the south coast. They looked dreadful, poor devils – the commandos particularly, though they had been in the jungle only a few weeks. They were thin, fever stricken and nervous. They said there had not been a plane into Wau for nearly two months and food was running low. Even at the base there was an acute shortage of everything but canned beef and rice. Apart from that, there had been trouble with the carriers, who had been made nervous by the bombing and by the tales of Japanese atrocities in the coastal villages.

The sick men had news, too, of the commando party that preceded us overland. There were 55 of them. They had followed much the same route as we did. They had been sent in overland purely as an experiment, for it was realized that the rate of travel and physical condition of miners and other bushmen gave no measure by which to gauge the effect of overland travel on troops trained in Australia. Now the result of the experiment was known. Forty-seven out of 55 men required hospital treatment when they got to Wau – for bush ulcers, infected wounds, malaria, dysentery and exhaustion.

The Independent Company men I had seen training in Moresby were fine types, in good heart, and trained to a hair – trained to shoot, strangle, knife and bludgeon; to run with full equipment over obstacle courses; to swim rivers and dynamite bridges. But they were *not* trained to look after themselves in tropical jungle; not trained to save energy instead of expending it recklessly, nor to powder their feet and wear gloves and face nets on sentry duty at night.

Jungle toughness is only in part muscle toughness. Jungle toughness is primarily a condition of mind and of a blood-stream with antibodies in it.

Just after we left Kudjiru, a carrier came through with the news that the boy with the ruptured spleen had died. Six natives from the following line dropped their cargoes and were carrying his body back to Bulldog for burial in friendly ground. That sort of thing could be avoided only if white men accompanied every cargo.

The going at this stage was easy – through shallow, open marsh or rolling kunai country with the mountains standing on the skyline. There were a few patches of clean forest, and, finally, a low range of hills which, if the map was right, was really the main watershed of the Owen-Stanleys. Over the hills was the valley of the Bulolo proper.

Gibson brought me a spike of dendrobium nearly three feet long – every waxen, creamy flower on it perfect. The perfume was overpowering. The butterflies were even more gorgeous than in the high hills. Most common were the big electric-blue variety, some of which were nine inches across. There were violent orange species with black-speckled markings; sooty blacks with fringed wings; and brilliant midgets of scarlet, pink, and sulphur yellow.

It was a pleasant and peaceful-seeming land. I wondered what the early explorers and prospectors must have thought when they first came upon this valley after weeks of struggling in the swamps and forests. The mountains, many towering above 10,000 feet, stood around it like ramparts topped by cloud. The subtle play of gray and green and gold in the folds of the grasslands overwhelmed the eye with beauty. The air was cool and sharp. In the beds of the creek, lush little coppices and splays of emerald grass were springing. The Bulolo was brawling mountain water among shingle and boulders. Here and there on its banks were tall strands of hoop pine. But for the graceful pawpaws and groves of wild bananas, one might have imagined this valley in the South Island of New Zealand.

In Winnema Camp we met Corporal G., one of the three cattle drovers who, after war with Japan started, brought 700 head of cattle from Madang, a 300-mile trail up the coast through the Ramu valley into the valley of the Bulolo. This must surely have been one of the most remarkable cattle-driving feats in history. The beasts had to be driven through dense sago swamps, swum over crocodile-infested rivers, have paths hacked for them through tangled jungles, and be coaxed up and down razorback ranges. Yet they were delivered with trifling loss. The guerrilla force of the valley had been eating fresh meat for months.

The corporal was a gloomy soul. He said there was less than three weeks' supply of food in Wau. Cultivation had stopped and many natives had gone back to their villages. Boy rice was getting short. The commandos were cracking up fast down at the front, and the men of the New Guinea Volunteer Rifles were burning out one by one.

The last stage into Wau was over dry, hard ground. First sign of journey's end was Kainde Mountain, where the fabulously rich Edie Creek goldfield was discovered. It rose – a huge, blue-black, precipitous bulk – out of the folded valley. A couple of hours out of Winnema was the junction with the Salamaua 'road', the hilly kunai country where six months later the 17th Brigade of the Australian Imperial Force were to drive the Japanese back into the jungle, broken and defeated.

There was a little wayside telephone box there. The corporal, who had obligingly walked back with us, rang headquarters for a truck to come out to Crystal Creek, at the head of the motor road. We rounded up the last of the carriers and hurried on.

It was queer to ride again. All along the road were burned out wrecks of motor vehicles destroyed on that memorable night when Wau was told that the Japanese would arrive within hours and that a scorched-earth policy must be applied ruthlessly. My old friend Major T. was then commanding officer of the area and he made a job of it. Men still referred to the 'Night of T.'s Terror.'

Wau is, or was, a sprawling rural settlement under the shadow of Kainde, in an undulating hollow between two mountain ridges. Most of its dwellings were weatherboard and corrugated iron, built on high stilts and austerely furnished in cane, rattan and local soft woods. They differed little from working-class homes in any North Australian town. Certainly there was nothing about them to suggest the wealth of many of the miners who lived in them – or that they cost thousands rather than hundreds of pounds to erect.

Indeed, Wau was remarkable only when one came to know the conditions and circumstances under which it had been built – and destroyed. It and its smaller sister town, Bulolo, were humdrum islands of white habitation in an ocean of picturesque wilderness. They had no connection by land with the outside world. Their streets led into no highway, but into the jungle.

They were towns built solely by virtue of man's conquest of the air. Every nail, sheet of iron, weatherboard, spot of paint, pane of glass, crock, wire or sheet of paper was carried in by air – at freight rates varying between 4*d*. and 1/5*d*. per pound. The wrecked trucks that now dotted the highways, rusted out and twisted by fire, were brought in by air. The billiard tables at the hotels were brought in by air. Easy chairs, refrigerators, bathtubs, stoves, dynamos, linoleum, carpets, garden statuary, even great mining dredges, bulldozers and power shovels – all were brought by air, and this in a decade when most people in Australia were still thinking it adventurous to take a five-minute joy ride over an airfield.

Wau and Bulolo were now the pitiful ghosts of towns. Their rough streets were scattered with blackened debris, the charred uprights of razed houses poked into the sky, the footpaths and paddocks and yards were pitted with bomb craters. Kunai grass was closing in on the cultivation. The creepers in the gardens had run riot and invaded the houses. Doors were wrenched from their hinges. Everywhere was a strange odor compounded of burned wood, dynamite, charred fabrics, rain and sweet-smelling flowers ...

Kanga Force headquarters invited us to dinner after we had reported. Colonel F. was looking into things at Bulolo, but Captain John W., a young Staff College officer serving with the commandos as intelligence officer and whom I had known in Moresby, gave a summary of the situation.

White men available for service in the area totaled about 800 – including New Guinea Volunteer Rifles and commandos. Many of the N.G.V.R. were beyond military age, but could not be spared because local knowledge was so precious. Of these 800 men, only about 300 were fit to fight. The commandos were going down in droves with malaria, dysentery, pneumonia, and infested sores. Ammunition and foodstuffs were getting very short. The European ration at the front was rice and canned beef. There was no sugar, biscuits, tea, jam, powdered milk, flour, or any other staples. In the valley here conditions were a little better, because a few 'luxury' goods were left over from peacetime and it was possible to get fresh fruit and vegetables.

Only enough carriers to supply the frontline men with ammunition and bare necessities could be mustered. Native food-stuffs were getting desperately short, too, because the Europeans were making more and more inroads on them. The Lakekamu route was delivering about three tons of cargo a week. No one expected to improve this rate for months. There had been no plane in for eight weeks. Message after message had been sent to Moresby asking for supplies, but aircraft were too few to be risked.

Captain W. thought that unless help came soon disease and starvation would probably soon put an end to this remarkable venture in warfare. If the Japs moved in strength, the defenders would be able to do little more than sell their lives dearly.

So far the men had done an astonishing and heroic job. They had bluffed more than 12,000 enemy troops into believing that the hinterland was held by strong forces. The guerrilla patrols had been so active that the Japanese dared not venture more than a few miles inland for fear of being wiped out by ambushes or picked off, one by one, by concealed snipers.

Even more important than that, the guerrillas had maintained watching stations of such efficiency that not a single enemy aircraft could land on or take off from the Markham valley or Salamaua airfield without the fact being reported almost immediately to Moresby.

Lastly, because the Moresby command had not retracted its orders to stage an offensive war, the raids on Lae and Salamaua had been carried out.

Debilitated by fever, half starved, living under the worst conditions of war, the men of New Guinea and the tough, green youngsters who belatedly reinforced them had already done service which should make their country deeply proud and grateful. Those who were not actually at the front were working like slaves to supplement or conserve foodstuffs, plan and construct defenses, recruit new native labor or work what they had. Those who had enough bush experience were maintaining constant patrols of the native villages, preserving the forms of European government as far away as the mouth of the Sepik River, the Hagen Mountains and the Ramu.

My notebook entry under the date July 8 is interesting. It reads: 'It is now apparent that there are not enough men here to make a really serious attempt to retake either Lae or Salamaua – and there are not likely to be enough men until we have established unchallenged air superiority and developed more fields to which troops can be flown, through which they can be adequately supplied.

'In peace time these jungles could be conquered only by the airplane. It is doubly evident that they can be conquered only by airplane in time of war.

146

'It is my belief that the Allied command will have to get a new slant on air war, or rather the part it can play in New Guinea.

'All the same, the offensive uses of air power are limited. I have seen a good deal of bombing and machine-gunning in Moresby, and I believe that bombs alone cannot blast the Japs from their footholds in this country, or inflict very heavy casualties on troops in jungle. If troops can be confined within a restricted area, well and good. Bombing and machine-gunning may then be effective. But their restriction to an area postulates the use of ground forces, which must be taken to an operational base *by air* and supplied from that base *by air*.

'The ground troops should not necessarily be required to root the enemy out – but to confine him. Then air superiority can attack him and interrupt his supplies. The country itself will do the rest. Blitz methods will cost us more lives than we can afford.

'Another thing seems plain. Large formations cannot be profitably used in the jungle. Small formations taught the art of reducing the supply problem by "living off the country" and of independent offensive action when cut off from the main body – these are the ground troops that will win a war in New Guinea.'

Parer and I both enjoyed the lazy days in Wau. After sending out a few dispatches by native runner over the Lakekamu I began poking back into the hills and wandering around the pathetic town. In the ruined and looted houses, there were a thousand relics of days forever gone. Parer searched his brother's house, which was damaged but still standing. He found some felt animals he had sent from Cairo to his little nephews and nieces and a precious family photograph or two. For the first time his long, sallow face became grim, with a shade of wistfulness. He bundled the toys together. 'They'll be surprised to get them back,' he said simply.

Early mornings were best. There were a number of out-sized spiders in the house. One spun his web across my bed-room window. I hadn't the heart to break it. The amber lace

147

was very beautiful with the light of the morning sun on it. In the overgrown garden, other smaller spiders made great communal webs that covered a quarter acre with finely spun entanglements.

In the early morning, too, I could watch birds of paradise in the bush on Kainde Mountain, and enjoy walks in the cool rain-refreshed forest.

Nights were an anticlimax. Natives had taken up unofficial quarters under the house, overflowing from the compound a mile down the road. They talked vociferously and sang and squabbled any old hour of the day or night. Even Gibson objected to the racket and asked permission to sleep in the kitchen. 'Too many persons come and too many persons go,' he explained with dignity.

One night I went out and blasted them in rough and rocky pidgin. They were unimpressed. The moment I was inside, they started jabbering away again. I then poked my head out of the window and fired my .38 into the air. This silenced them. It also put out every light in the district. I had forgotten that one shot was the signal for an air raid.

The days of leisure brought increased knowledge of Gibson Duluvina's talents. While Cyril was away with Parer at Watut, he suffered the tortures of the friendless man in a foreign country. A state of armed neutrality existed between him and Jacowe, the cook boy, whom he resented as an interloper. On his part, I rather suspect Jacowe looked upon Gibson as a soft mug from a sissy tribe.

One evening Gibson concocted a pawpaw pudding to put me in a mellow frame of mind. After dinner he came in and wanted to talk. I signed him to sit on the floor and gave him a cigarette. We got on famously. I asked him about his village and people, subjects on which he had hitherto been reticent to talk. I wanted to find out if there were any historical traditions, folk tales or mythology among the tribes in the southeastern end of the island.

It was uphill plugging. The most I learned was that the details of tabu customs and tribal laws were handed on by word of mouth from one generation to the other, but tales of war

148

or storms or earthquakes died after a couple of generations. In his village, for instance, the only known history came from the tongue of a very old woman who was a girl when the first white man's ship came to Port Moresby. Gibson didn't think her tales were particularly interesting. He had no idea what his tribe had done before her time, what wars it had fought, or where was its original home.

'Taubada,' he said suddenly. 'White people say that they know just what happened a thousand years ago. Is it true?'

I assured him it was.

'How do they know?'

I told him it was all written down – that it had been written down for hundreds and thousands of years. He was silent in reflection.

'Taubada, I can write,' he said.

I knew that. He wrote a beautiful copperplate. It was closer to drawing copperplate. He once wrote me a note subscribed: *'Yrs in the blutherhod of Xt, Gibson Duluvina.'*

'Yes, Gibson, I know. You write very well.'

'Taubada, when I write, it is too hard very much to write the truth. To write the words is hard, but I could never write *all* the words to tell *all* the truth. To write at all I must make all the things seem easy. Then, when it is written, it is not all the truth. Some of the words are not the right words, because I am tired with writing. Do you think men who write history are like that? Are *you* like that when you write, taubada?'

Against that searing examination of white man's culture was the story of Ba-pe, a Bessema village boy who received permission to go through the Japanese lines to visit his family. When the intelligence officer questioned him on return, he expressed great delight over his earlier decision not to work for the Japanese.

'Japan! 'E no good. No good all 'e time!' he declared.

'Why, Ba-pe?' the intelligence officer asked him.

He spat betel juice on the ground. 'Japan! 'E dirty bugger all-e same kanaka,' he said contemptuously. Then, to make it amply clear: ' 'E dirty bugger all-e same ME!'

CHAPTER 11

ROAD TO SALAMAUA

WAR in the New Guinea mountains – the fighting that was to come for the Owen-Stanley passes, the landward approach to Salamaua and the Finisterre Mountains – was to demand more from the body and spirit of white infantrymen than any campaign in modern times.

On these jungle fronts, what could not be compassed by human effort and fortitude could not be compassed at all. There were no machines to take the weight from human shoulders or the strain from human nerves. The man, the soldier, was the only machine which the tilted bypaths of the forest would tolerate.

For long periods the fight against the Japanese was almost incidental – a few minutes of blind action when patrols met by chance or design to contest some trivial path, or when some long and arduously prepared move against an enemy stronghold flashed into climax. The real fight was an incessant battle against exhausting terrain, climate, disease and accident.

Parer and I had gained some appreciation of what the mountain war was to be like on our trip over the high ranges. We had set out to do that after months in the despairing stagnation of the garrison at Moresby. Now, having completed the journey, we were to complete the preview on the battlefields to be – the kunai downs about Wau, the echoing gorge of Mubo, the precipices of Mount Tambu, the black thickets of the Bitoi flats and Komiatum.

After a week in Wau we decided to spend at least a fortnight with the scouts before Salamaua, then return, rest for a few days and carry on with the trip through the Waria valley and eventually across the Owen-Stanleys to the south coast again.

The first day's journey from Wau to the 'front' was to Bellam's Camp, 13 miles through open country. Eight miles out we sighted a party approaching us, traveling fast – a white man and two natives. The white man was Captain S. He said he had made 30 miles since dawn. A thousand Japs had left Salamaua. The forward scouts' radio had been silent for 36 hours. Troops must be called in from rest billets and deployed to defend the airfield. Every man who could stand would have to be used. The Captain was very excited. He spent five minutes on his back on the ground and then charged off down the track as if the Japanese were already in sight.

But the men at Bellam's Camp were not very impressed. They seemed more interested in mail or the prospect of getting sugar. They had had no sugar for six weeks and it was becoming an obsession with them.

It was a good, dry camp on high ground with a fine outlook on the valley for defense. We spent a dreamless night. At sunset a native runner arrived with a message of correction. 'For 1,000 (one thousand) Japs read 100 (one hundred).' The mistake occurred because the forward scouts' radio broke down and a note was sent with a native. It reported that a Japanese patrol of about 100 men had left Salamaua and was pushing up the trail past Komiatum Hill. There was a rainstorm, the note got wet, and was almost illegible when it reached company headquarters at Mubo.

Before sunrise next day we plunged into hill forest again. The Kuper Mountains gave promise of being even wetter than the central ranges. It poured rain all day and the trail was in appalling condition. Some sections of it were more than knee deep in greasy slush covering a matting of treacherous roots.

At 6,000 feet, we passed the watershed and temporarily deserted staging camp, the Summit, partly built and then abandoned because of labor shortage. Here we met 'Paddles' W. He was a commando – 220 pounds, six feet, three inches. His feet made Parer's look dainty. He was covered from head

151

to heels in scrub itch and infected sores. He was cook at Mubo until fever got him – now he was through.

With him was a small, pot-black native about four feet nine inches tall, nicknamed Lik-Lik – a cheerful-looking creature with a grin that spread right round his head. Paddles said that Lik-Lik was being sent back in disgrace and told us about his offense.

In a raid on Salamaua on July 1, Lik-Lik begged to be allowed to carry ammunition for his boss. Eventually permission was given. During the raid he behaved with great steadiness and courage as 'No. 2 to a tommy gun'. He killed two Japanese with a bush knife. Then he disappeared. Our troops had withdrawn by nine o'clock in the morning. Lik-Lik was missing at the rendezvous. Just before the last men moved off, he arrived exhausted, dragging a bulging copra sack. It contained 13 Japanese heads. He then had the effrontery to ask for leave so that he could take them back to his village in the hills and hang them on the pole of the *darimus* (men's clubhouse). When, in the course of his dressing down, it was pointed out to him that very little credit would devolve on him for cutting off the heads of men killed by other warriors, he replied simply: 'But they were not dead, boss. They were only wounded.'

The next camp, Skin Dewai (pidgin for 'tree bark'), was reputed to be the most comfortable in the area. It was a miserable habitation. Its appointments were more primitive than Dead Kukukuku. Its situation was infinitely worse. The rain pelted down all night and most of the day. Everything was cold, sticky and sodden. There were six inches of stinking mud on the ground. When it was not raining, it was misty.

Something else woke me. I don't know what. Maybe it was Parer turning over. A minute later someone flashed a torch and said: 'Five o'clock.'

It was hard to wake up. Outside it was raining still, and dark. The rain had started again at eight o'clock the night before. The bark roof of House Sleep didn't keep out rain as heavy as that. But Parer and I were lucky. We found a bit of rotten tarpaulin and stretched it over the ridge pole and slept without drips worrying us.

House Sleep was supposed to have beds for 50. It was an opensided shed with no space under the roof but that taken up by a double tier of bunks made of peeled saplings, with the mattress part a four-inch mesh of split-green cane. After sleeping on a platform of bare, slimy slats at other camps, it was luxury – until someone turned over and the whole business bounced wildly. Someone was always turning over.

An officer lit the lantern and roused the men out. God, but it was cold up there at 8,000 feet! I didn't know it was so cold till I moved – so cold and so utterly damned miserable.

The mocka bites started to itch again and I dabbed with iodine. One looked as if it were going to infect. It was the size of a 50-cent piece, red and angry.

I was dopey after the march of the day before and had forgotten to check my shoes when the rain started. They were under a seam in the bark and were half full of water. A greenish slime had grown on the mud on them overnight. Served me right. I had been in the country long enough to have learned to check on my shoes.

Sleeping in wet clothes and blankets makes men stiff. The troops were straggling off to House Cook for food. You could almost hear their knees clicking. House Cook was 200 yards away, down a flight of steps that were timber rungs pegged into the steep, slippery slope. All through the camp the mud was ankle deep. The huts were tucked into little caverns in the deep undergrowth, so they could not be spotted from the air. Dawn was coming. It came slowly through the leaves and festooned monkeyrope. In House Cook there was a fire, smoky and red. There was a sharp smell of wet wood burning, cutting through the moldy stink of the forest. Parer and I shouldered in and crouched down to the flame. Someone yelled: 'What's for breakfast?'

That was good for a laugh. The food was in two blackened kerosene cans. One had rice, brown and burned. The other had a curry made of canned beef broken down with water and curry

153

powder added. By rights, this stuff the cook boy ladled out into my mess-tin ought to have turned my stomach. But it didn't. My mouth was watering for it. But when the spit started to run I could suddenly smell mud on House Cook floor. It smelled sweet and hot and filthy like a boardinghouse gully-trap. Down forward the men had had rice and bully straight for six weeks, washed down by unsweetened tea. No sugar, salt, pepper, jam – not even an army biscuit to vary it. Breathe through your mouth and cram it down. Every extra ounce you could cram down was going to be useful fuel by nightfall. It was not the tasting, it was the swallowing you enjoyed.

The rain was easing. The clouds were lifting from the valley. There was a thick, drenching mist. A ragged slit trench of morning showed through the treetops. The timber ran up to it like dim palisading, all covered with fern and fungus and creepers.

The carriers moved off. We laced our shoes, slung on knapsacks and followed them. The first half hour of traveling in the morning was always the worst. Tick and mosquito bites started to itch and burn all over again. Even the best pair of shoes rubbed somewhere. The mud squeezed in and out between your toes with a gentle, hot, maddening tickle. It took a while to get into the trick of balancing on mud slopes. Every time you slipped you wrenched something.

The trail looked rough. It led down to a log crossing – an 18-inch log caked with clay from the carriers' feet over a gully 60 feet deep. In these hills there might be five or six such crossings in a mile. Some of the logs were not more than nine inches thick. Crossing them, the main thing was not to falter or lose rhythm.

Quarter of an hour out – and the first climb. A wet, slanting tunnel through the green, leading up the razorback edge of a ridge. Every step waist high, and over the steps a dripping cascade of mud and spring water. Maybe two or three thousand steps. I counted up to 4,000 once without even 10 yards of letup. It was just lifting one leg after the other, feeling for the tricky roots with your foot, then hoisting up the rest of you. After 1,000 steps or so it started to burn the muscles in the top of the

154

thigh like hot needles. All you could hear was the pounding of your heart and the rasp of your breath.

We passed the carriers. They stank to high heaven. The man ahead killed a black snake with an orange mark on its head. It was about a foot long. He threw it into the bush. Five minutes later the leader killed another snake – then another. I picked off the first leech, a striped brown fellow two inches long and full of fight. He vomited blood. I had forgotten to roll down my sleeves.

The fellows on the trail behind seemed to be feeling good. I could hear them singing and yelling curses and laughing when they stepped into a hole and the mud ran down the top of their gaiters. But the man at my back was not feeling so well. Fever, he said.

There was a noise from somewhere up above the mist. We all stood still and listened.

'*Balus* (airplane) 'e come!'

It sounded like a big force of planes traveling in the direction of Moresby. Ours coming back, or theirs going. We were over the crest of the ridge then, and glad to go down, even if descent jarred your legs where they had burned before.

Four hours out. The lieutenant in charge called the first spell. Down there the air was warmish – just about the temperature and dampness of a greenhouse in the early morning, with the same smell. It looked like a greenhouse in the early morning – that same, over-green, steamy look. The creek where we drank was choked with white begonia. And all the greenhouse plants were there – those slick dark-green things that all greenhouses have, the velvety, particolored ones, coleuses, cyclamens, a hand's breadth across, green and brown-striped slipper orchids.

On again. Still down. At one o'clock the lieutenant signaled to pull in for a half-hour spell. The first of the carriers caught up and got a fire going. We made tea. Four men from the forward area came in, on their way back to Wau with bad feet. With them were two wounded natives on sapling litters. The kanakas were casualties of the Japanese wholesale bombing of native villages after the guerrilla raid on Salamaua. They looked nearly dead, and the Europeans not so far off, either.

155

They were thin as rakes, with transparent yellow skins and eyes shiny with fever.

Some of the troops had saved rice from breakfast, wrapped it in leaves, and now were eating it in big, sticky, brown mouthfuls, swilling it down with tea. Two of them shaved up a stick of trade tobacco with a rusty razor blade, mixed it with shreds from a bundle of native leaf and cooked it in a pan over the fire. In 10 minutes it was dry enough to smoke – rolled in a newspaper.

In these foothills were occasional open grass patches. It was fine to feel the sun and look back up the great valleys where the rivers come through – hard to believe we had actually come over that purple mountain with the cloud still hanging over it like an untidy tablecloth.

From midday the trail lay along flat ledges on the side of a slate cliff that dropped away to treetops four or five hundred feet down. The man with the fever was making heavy going of it. His knees started shaking on the narrow pinches and he complained of feeling lightheaded. He was sweating so heavily I could have wrung out his shirt. He said it was the damned slipping, slipping, *slipping,* all the time that got him.

In the end he fell over a log and did not get up. The lieutenant came back and looked down at him lying like a dummy in a wet bush. There wasn't much expression in the lieutenant's face. 'Come on,' he said in a flat sort of voice. 'You're supposed to be a bloody commando, aren't you? Well, you've got two hours to go until camp.' The sick man got up.

Just before nightfall we came to the sequel of the '1,000 Japs' scare – a patch of open kunai, trampled, scattered with the obscene yellow-white of discarded field dressings. There were little yellow candy wrappings, too; packs, rifles, letters, a notebook. Pools of rusty-colored blood were soaking into the churned earth. Also there were natives, four dying and two dead.

What had happened was this: A patrol of 139 Japanese left Salamaua in the morning. They wore jungle-green uniforms, carried rifles, light machine guns and pony-skin packs with a week's rations.

Scouts saw the enemy across the Francisco River. They sent back runners to warn our posts, and shadowed the patrol through the jungle. The Japanese were led by a renegade police boy (one of the two natives killed) and five other natives who had probably been conscripted from the village of Bessema. All day long the scouts kept with the patrol until it reached the clearing, where the Australians had set up a Vickers and three Lewis guns. They rightly judged that the Japanese would be tired and depressed from nine hours' slogging through the jungle, and would welcome the clearing as a place to rest.

The enemy was caught in a murderous cross fire. Twenty or thirty of them were mowed down by the first bursts. But they were crack marine troops and took cover quickly. They returned the fire within a few seconds and then retreated into trailless jungle in small parties, carrying their dead and wounded with them. They abandoned only the unfortunate natives, upon whom our men had particular orders to concentrate. We could not – dared not – tolerate local natives guiding Japanese.

CHAPTER 12

MEN AND THE JUNGLE

As PARER and I were noncombatants it was considered proper to offer us the most comfortable quarters available in Mubo – beds in the hospital. The hospital was a dank hut set back in the protecting bush. There were eight occupants. The beds were copra sacks stretched on poles. The blankets were wet and could not be dried. The floor was inches deep in mud. Even at midday the light was so poor that dressings had to be done by kerosene lanterns. Quinine was the only drug in plentiful supply.

One of the patients was a serious pneumonia case. He was a New Guinea Volunteer Rifles man with valuable local knowledge and refused evacuation. He said he was used to conditions like this and would be on his feet again in 10 days. But the sulfapyridine treatment made him vomit. He vomited violently at about 20-minute intervals into a kerosene can beside his bunk. Nobody took much notice of him except to give him water and empty the tin. There was nothing else to do.

Another patient had a broken ankle. He smashed it when he fell off a log crossing and had to be carried back on a stretcher. When the bearers were passing through a patch of open kunai, the Japanese seaplane, which every day ranged up and down the gorge trying to spot our troop dispositions, passed directly overhead. The natives carrying the stretcher dropped it in the middle of the trail and bolted. The man with the broken ankle curled up, waiting for the guns to blast him. But the Jap observer merely leaned out of his seat, peered down, waved, and flew on.

By now I was working up to a bout of fever and was con-

158

vinced in good earnest that the hospital was the best place for me. Parer was still going strong, though I never saw a man who *looked* more ill. The black beard, now assuming formidable proportions, bristled wirily and gave him the appearance of an escapee from some medieval bedlam.

'White, my boy,' he said with that crazy laugh of his, 'one might fairly say conditions is awful!'

We sought assiduously, each in his own way, to record something of the eerie, sneaking war going on in this maze of valleys, rivers, swamps and mountains. On July 15 I reconstructed in detail a typical encounter between patrols. It was a story that epitomized the quality of Australian resistance to Japanese efforts to penetrate the hinterland at that time.

The day was no different from any other day. About midmorning there was a break in the clouds and the sun came out. The heat became more oppressive. It beat down into the narrow slit in the jungle with breath-taking pulsations – a weight on the shoulders, a constriction about the skull.

The trail slanted down the steep side of a sawtooth ridge into a river valley. Thence, from comparative straightness it began to twist in and out among stretches of swamp, hillocks where the trees were violently cut off as by a feller's ax, and sundrenched expanses of elephant grass. Along this path two parties of men were approaching each other, each unaware of the presence of the other.

The first, a party of Japanese marines traveling southwest, was between 50 and 60 strong. It was moving at a rapid, steady pace, with 12- to 15-yard intervals between each man. Each Japanese carried a rucksack made of hide with the hair on the outside to shed the rain, ammunition bandoleers, side arms, a rolled raincoat ground sheet, and either a stubby submachine gun or a bolt-action Mauser-type rifle.

The uniforms of this force blended excellently with jungle coloring – overalls of dark-green cloth, close-fitting steel helmets daubed with green paint, black canvas boots with rubber soles, and canvas gaiters.

Everything about the patrol – its equipment, pace, order of

movement – indicated that it was a force specially selected, trained and fitted out for just such an operation as that on which it was now engaged. Four natives preceded it as a scout screen by about 50 yards. Several more natives, bent under heavy loads of food and medical supplies, traveled in the center of the column, prodded firmly in the buttocks with a rifle muzzle every time they showed signs of slackening.

A separate file of Japanese carrying two small mortars slung on poles brought up the rear. Four files behind the leader, a man carried a small, silk Rising Sun flag on a bamboo staff. Its folds drooped limply in the windless, humid air.

The rubber-soled shoes made no sound in the mud and leaf mold underfoot, and there was not even the faintest rattle of equipment. The party would have traveled with astonishing quietness but for the constant, shrill jabber of conversation passing up and down the line.

The Australian patrol comprised six Europeans and three native police boys. One police boy walked about 70 yards ahead of the main party, keenly scanning the mud for fresh trails and sometimes pausing to listen intently.

The leader was a tall, thin man in a shirt stained with sweat and mud and in shorts that had once been khaki. This tattered 'uniform' had been doused in green dye, now faded by sun and rain into irregular mottlings. When he stood still in sunlight and shadow his body was almost invisible against its background. Like the other Europeans, he also wore a battered slouch hat with a pigeon feather stuck in it, and his face had a three weeks' stubble which he claimed protected him against insects. But his legs were bare from thigh to ankle and blotched by tick bites that had been dabbed with scarlet mercurochrome antiseptic.

He carried, slung on one shoulder, a Thompson submachine gun and on the other a small, dingy yellow haversack containing field dressings, a can of beef, a packet of moldy biscuits, clips of spare ammunition, a bottle of quinine tablets, and 'money' – a dozen or so sticks of trade tobacco.

His shoes were mud-bleached leather, the soles heavily spiked to give purchase on greasy clay slopes and slippery logs. He walked with a free-jointed, long, loose stride that contrasted oddly with the shuffling pad of the two natives who followed close behind him.

The two patrols steadily approached each other. At noon the police boy scouting for the Australians stopped at a sharp bend and moved into the cover of a thicket before continuing. He saw the Japanese scouts before they saw him, at a distance of about 200 yards. Like a flash he turned and sped back, gesticulating with panic-stricken urgency to the leading white man.

'Japan 'e come! Japan 'e come, kerose-up too much!'

The tall man unslung his tommy gun and waved back the rest of the party.

'Nips!' he told them succinctly. 'Scram!'

There was no need to ask how many. The Japanese seldom if ever patrolled in parties of fewer than 50. Without a second's hesitation the Australians fled at full speed up the path, floundering and slipping and cursing in the wet patches.

Quarter of an hour back – measured by normal pace – there was a small forest clearing where once natives had planted a grove of bananas and cultivated a patch of sweet potatoes. Vines now choked the trees, and runner grass and kunai had smothered the potatoes.

The Australian patrol made the distance in seven minutes at a wild gallop. Then the leader gave a low whistle between his teeth and his men pulled up panting.

'Okay. You two with the tommy guns, get up there behind the cedars. I'll take the bamboo clump. Jim and Harry down the trail under cover of the big deadfall. Jerry, lie where you like, close in. You, Yacone (to the leading police boy), you stick somewhere close to me. Tell other fella policeman walkabout along number-one master talk 'im Japan 'e come kerose-to. Savvy?'

'Savvy too much, master.'

'Okay, then. Get going, boys.'

In 30 seconds the clearing was deserted, utterly still under the sun. The leaves of the kanaka bananas hung shiny and limp, casting blue-black pools of shadow. A flight of white cockatoos

161

settled among them, screaming. The kunai stood stiffly, unruffled by even the faintest wind. Had one listened very carefully, one might have detected sounds foreign to the voice of the forest – a scuffling and snapping of twigs different from the noise made by a traveling cassowary, the only forest dweller who *is* noisy. But in a minute even these sounds died away. Only the quarreling cockatoos could be heard.

Suddenly they rose up from the bananas, screaming angrily. The native scouts and the first Japanese came into the clearing. They halted and called questions back. Another dozen arrived. Another. The ruined garden was swarming with small, green-clad figures.

Down in the bamboo clump, the tall man waited very patiently. Then he slid his tommy gun forward, propped it, slipped the catch, squinted, grinned – squeezed ever so lightly. A stutter of fire ripped out and thundered back from the sounding board of jungle treetops.

The first spray of lead split a party of four or five Japanese standing together. Two went down, squealing. Before the rest could even drop into the grass for cover, the other two tommy guns from the cedar grove opened up, and rifles began to crack.

It was perhaps 20 seconds before the Japanese recovered from the surprise and began to fire. But that 20 seconds of confusion had cost them 10 dead and 6 wounded. Then when it was apparent that only a small force opposed them, they got over their initial panic, took cover in the undergrowth and began systematically to locate the points from which the Australian fire was coming. The remainder of the Japanese force then began to break up the ambush, point by point.

The Japanese method hardly ever varied in dealing with inferior forces in concealed positions. Having taken cover, they wriggled out fanwise through the undergrowth, searching the target area methodically and monotonously with a moving arc of submachine gun fire. Such tactics made it impossible for small groups, however well concealed, to maintain their positions. Sooner or later a bullet was bound to find a man who tried to stand his ground – or else he would be pinned in a steadily contracting circle of the enemy.

The Australian patrol made no effort to stand, once the Japanese had rallied. Every man moved rapidly and quietly away, invisible behind a muffling green screen of foliage and inaudible in the echoing thunder of fire. Those who were actually behind the enemy simply found themselves convenient hiding places – in tree forks, under logs, in particularly dense thickets – where they settled down patiently to await the enemy's withdrawal.

For more than an hour, the Japanese continued their systematic scouring and surrounded one position after another only to find the quarry escaped. Then they improvised litters for the dead and wounded and made off down the path in the direction from which they had come. Six pairs of eyes watched them sardonically through leafy peepholes, and six pairs of jaws munched steadily on canned beef and moldy biscuit.

Until sunset, the Australians forbore to move. There was no need to move, for the day's job was done. Besides, the Japanese might have tried a double ambush and left snipers. So they waited, one watching a little black snake sunning itself on a stone, another a trail of red fruit ants climbing into a wild lime tree. The others . . . who knows?

When darkness came the tall man rose, straightened out his cramped limbs and scratched himself thoughtfully, listened, whistled to the police boy.

'What place other fella master 'e stop?'

'Behind him walkabout, master.'

'Longa Mubo?'

The police boy nodded.

'All fella master?'

'Yes.'

The tall man grinned to himself, stepped out onto the trail and began walking, feeling for roots in the dark with a sensitive boot toe.

Such warfare selects, rather than develops, men of exceptional talents. Only freak constitutions could stand for long the strain of intense physical effort in such a climate, particularly when fed, housed, clothed and doctored as crudely as these men then were.

Most of the work was still being done by the New Guinea riflemen. The commandos had just come into the 'line' and were learning the hard way. The officer commanding the Salamaua force, Norman W., held the rank of captain. He was a man with a streak of tempered steel through him, and a brain that thought precisely, neatly, quickly – and not too deeply. He knew what he was up against. For 17 years he had been a planter in Java.

Like the stalwarts of Bulldog, W. gave an ineradicable impression of preserving the properties and accepting the white man's burden. He was tall, sandy haired, thin and yellow complexioned, with a faintly supercilious English face – and he lived up to all the more complimentary things that have been said about the 'English face'. He had the reputation of being a terrific walker, second only to some of the top-notch scouts, the few picked reconnaissancers of this guerrilla force who could reel off 40 miles a day, day after day, even along the fearsome gutters they called trails. His men had affection for him, and he had their utter confidence.

The scout force, particularly, comprised men of remarkable physical qualities. They were tireless on the trail, skilled in living on and in the country. Their chief, McA., sometimes traveled barefoot and practically naked, and was immune to malaria and other infections. Many of them were former forestry officers with bushcraft in their blood. They could read trail signs with the skill of a red Indian or an Australian black tracker. They had made themselves familiar with every ridge, creek and gulley for 50 miles along the watershed. They could conceal themselves like leaf insects and move with the silence of a cat.

The scouts' proudest boast was that they had been fighting the Japs for more than six months and had never once fired a shot. They amused themselves thinking up new ways of silent killing. One was the use of a loop of fire-hardened, razor-sharp bamboo. If flung skilfully enough over the head of an unsuspecting sentry and pulled with the right twist, the loop would slit his throat from ear to ear without a sound. The idea was borrowed from a certain western tribe, notorious for the same subtle way with enemies.

The scouts' resources were well-nigh limitless. McA., for instance, understood natives thoroughly. He coveted the exclusive use of a tract of country for small supply dumps, defensive foxholes and observation posts. He did not want natives of doubtful discretion wandering in it. So, with a great deal of impressive mumbo-jumbo, in the presence of selected witnesses, he put a tabu on it. He made it devil-devil ground. The result was that not a kanaka on the whole of the north coast would dare to enter McA.'s sanctuary.

McA. was a six-footer, 32 years of age, with a patriarchal auburn beard. He was a health crank and neither smoked nor drank. In his estimation, a 40 mile walk was just good exercise.

There was one redoubtable scout on the enemy side, too, a German named Hoffstader. His knowledge of the territory dated back to 1914. All through the between-war years he had remained a rabid Anglophobe but refused to get out.

It had not been certain precisely to what extent Hoffstader was co-operating with the Japanese, but he was known to have considerable influence with the coastal natives. Recently he had disappeared and everybody believed the disappearance boded ill for someone. Just as our scouts could spy on Japanese without ever betraying their presence, so could Hoffstader spy on our forces. He was a miner and prospector and he knew these hills as suburban gardeners knew their own back yards.

Hoffstader persuaded many of the villages to trade fresh fruit for Japanese canned meat and fish. He was, in all probability, chiefly responsible for natives' guiding Japanese patrols. Listed as Public Enemy Number 1, Moresby had a price of £200 on Hoffstader's head.[1] The scouts were willing to break their tradition about shooting if they ever spotted him, and the commandos were slavering to get his bulk in their sights. Apart from being probably the only European on the enemy side of the line at Salamaua he was easily recognized – a stout,

[1] They never caught him. He is believed to have escaped in the Japanese retreat to the west in 1944.

square man about 50 years old, wearing a black spade beard. He had never been seen to go abroad without suspenders to hold up his pants and gumshoes on his feet.

The scouts and combat patrols forward of Mubo lived in kurukuru shelters set in the deepest jungle they could find. They took elaborate precautions to avoid leaving tracks that might betray the camps to the enemy. Many could be approached only by wading for miles in streams and diving abruptly through carefully preserved screens of vines and undergrowth.

If living in Mubo was hard, living forward of it was hell. Here at last, it seemed, were the penultimate rigors of war. In Townsville they spoke scornfully of 'loafers' in Brisbane and Melbourne; in Moresby of the 'bludgers' of Townsville; in Wau, of the 'base boys' in Moresby. In Mubo, they curled their lips at the luxury of Wau. At the forward scouts' camps they thought company headquarters lived the lives of sybarites.

Men on patrol existed like wild animals, and amphibious animals at that. They spent their days and nights in clinging mud, yellow water and drenched undergrowth. There was a dreadful nervous tension in their every movement. Their voices were hushed. The jungle, the heat, the ever present menace of surprise and death brooded over them. They slept with hand grenades in their trouser pockets, lightly and as still as cats.

There was a 'scout tree' a few hundred yards from the Salamaua airfield. Observers climbed into its spreading branches before dawn and remained there motionless until nightfall. But the observation post most used was farther off. Thirty or more camouflaged rungs led up to a swaying platform which commanded a comprehensive view of the airfield and the isthmus. Results of all bombing raids could be observed at leisure and in detail.

Our bombing had been disappointing. Nearly all of it was, up to then, from high level. During the much publicized Fourth of July blitz on Salamaua – the first mass aerial attack by the Allies in New Guinea – only two bombs fell in the target area. The Japs had taken a leaf out of Moresby's book – and improved on it. Waterfront posts at Moresby could always be certain of a meal of fresh fish after the Japs raided the harbor. After the Americans raided Salamaua, a Jap launch put out, collected the stunned fish and took them back for treatment at a small portable cannery.

A few months later, however, the raw air crews had learned their work, and the life of the Japanese garrison on the isthmus must have been sheer hell.

Nevertheless, even in those early days all the explosive was not wasted. A freighter was aground and sullenly burning near the isthmus. She looked to be about 4,000 tons.

Moresby had good reason to thank the Huon Gulf scouts for this constant surveillance of the enemy. Air and sea traffic to and from Lae and Salamaua, and along extensive stretches of coast, was observed and immediately reported. Not only did the Allied base receive long warning of raids, but it also had a reasonably accurate day-to-day approximation of enemy strength.

The R.A.A.F. maintained a special observer in the area. He was Leigh V., a former patrol officer – a small, dark man with doggy brown eyes and an ugly, sensitive face. His temperament, courage and patience were a combination that made him great. At that time he had been sitting for five months in his jungle hide-out, where he could observe both Lae and Salamaua. Naturally enough, V. did not encourage traffic to and from his post – but when visitors did arrive, in the face of his discouragement, he almost wept with gratitude.

By local standards he was provisioned most liberally – almost luxuriously – with canned foods and books specially dropped by air. He just sat, watching, from daylight to dark. He had amused himself by breaking down his stocks of provisions into a multitude of small packages marked with the month, week, day, and meal in which they were to be consumed. All luxury goods, such as chocolate, jam and the more palatable canned fruits, he had apportioned separately and marked 'Visitors'. He did his watching through a little 'window' in concealing foliage, seated on a prim, homemade stool. Dependent upon a long hanging vine was a pair of massive naval binoculars and, by their side, an ingenious little contrivance for holding a book. He would read a chapter gravely, reach for the binoculars, study the view, flick the binoculars away with a contemptuous turn of the wrist, and continue to improve his acquaintance with English literature ...

Only one man in a million could have endured such strain and monotony. The Japs knew he was operating because they could hear his radio set, but they could never locate it – although they tried again and again.

A month or two after we saw V. he was relieved, given home leave and decorated by General MacArthur for outstanding gallantry and devotion to duty. He returned to New Guinea and was killed on a reconnaissance flight over Lae.

One night, camped in the high hills behind Mount Tambu, we heard the sound of distant bombing and gunfire. The explosions echoed in the gorges and it was impossible to determine the direction from which they came.

It was common enough to hear the American mediums and heavies dumping a modest ton or two on Lae or Samalaua, but this time the noise was of such volume, so prolonged, and so distant, that it was apparent a large-scale engagement was taking place of which the local command had no knowledge.

There was a good deal of speculation next day in the jungle camps, and wild rumors made the rounds. The first story was that the Japanese had heavily attacked Wau and were landing paratroops; the second that an enemy force had landed at Morobe Harbor down the coast.

Twenty-four hours later the mystery was solved. Broadcasts were picked up announcing the landing of Japanese forces at Buna Bay far to the east and the unsuccessful attack by Allied bombers on the invasion convoy. It was hard to believe that the detonations of bombs and gunfire should have been audible at so great a distance, but there was no other explanation.

The Buna landing canceled our plans to go on by way

of the Waria River valley to Kokoda. It was now necessary to return to Moresby as quickly as possible and cover the fighting that was bound to develop if the Japanese advanced along the old post trail through Kokoda.

It was awkward, being marooned in the jungle 200 miles from the war one was supposed to be reporting, and with only your legs as a means of transport. I realized I would be lucky to manage the trip back in 10 days – and that only by dint of traveling double stages.

To make matters worse, the bout of malaria I had been fighting off for a fortnight with near-lethal doses of quinine was beginning to catch up with me. Luck and Kanga Force headquarters solved the problem. A runner brought a note stating that if Parer and I wanted to get back to Moresby for the 'fun', New Guinea Force expected to get a transport plane into Wau within a couple of days. There would be seats on the return trip if we wanted them.

Parer decided there was no use leaving his job half done, even with the prospect of more important action elsewhere, so we parted regretfully at Mubo. He made for one of the scout trees with a hand camera, and I set off for Wau with the pious resolution to cover the 60-odd-mile trail to Wau in a day and a half. As a personal experiment, the next 60 hours will remain in my memory as an 'all-time low'.

I started from Mubo just after dawn feeling well enough; met two Independent Company men walking back with fever, stayed with them five miles, and pushed on because their pace was too slow. Just at the foot of the first steep climb, the fever hit me.

Gibson hadn't kept up. He was carrying my pack. I remembered being shown a short cut into Skin Dewai Number 2 and for some crazy reason decided to take it. It was just a series of muddy waterfalls. After a couple of miles I fell down – the first time in my life I had fallen down simply because my legs were too weak to hold me up.

I rested half an hour, made another 200 yards and fell down again. After that the memory of the journey is very hazy. I can recall taking 10 grains of quinine and, about half an hour later, five grains of caffeine. I was worried about having left the trail, and it seemed to be getting bitterly cold. Just after eight o'clock at night I saw fires in the valley, and reached camp in short spurts. A party had arrived from Wau on the way to the front. There was some mail. I wrapped up in four damp blankets, took another 10 grains of quinine, read the letters without noting or remembering one word of their contents, and went to sleep.

In the morning I was feeling better, having sweated very profusely in the night. So I got away at six o'clock and walked in a daze all day. Twice I used caffeine to keep me going.

Gibson was hopelessly lost. I passed Bellam's Camp in mid-afternoon and reached Wau at nine o'clock. Some Australian Imperial Force men took me into their quarters – a house near the airfield – and provided a meal of beef, rice and unsweetened tea.

At headquarters a couple of hours later they gave me a hot bath and a luxurious, quilted dressing gown of pink satin salvaged from some bomb-wrecked-boudoir in the town. Howls of delighted laughter greeted my appearance at the mess poker game. But my sense of humor was as dead as my legs. I politely howled with laughter in reply, but did not think anything about me in the least funny.

About 1.00 a.m. I went down to quarters, collected a few odds and ends, stowed them, and went to sleep after arranging for a truck to call on its way to the airfield at dawn when the plane was due.

At four o'clock Gibson reached town and came to the house. Without resting he scraped up an American chocolate emergency ration and made me a hot drink. He understood that I wanted to catch the *balus* and must be awakened in good time. His feet were cut to ribbons and his ankles were double their normal size. 'I am very tired, taubada,' he said. 'But I do not wish to miss the *balus*.'

It was tough telling him he wouldn't be going in the *balus* at all. Yet he took it without batting an eyelash. He refused to go to bed and insisted on coming to the airfield to carry the haversack and see me off.

We waited for three hours watching the clouds. It rained steadily. Twelve bad malaria cases were scheduled for evacuation. They huddled together, shivering in the ruins of the M.A.L. hangar. Just after nine o'clock there was a break in the clouds, but simultaneously a message arrived to say that Moresby had canceled the plane. It was pitiful to see the faces of the men who were due to go out.

I had just returned to the truck when the mutter of a motor sounded over the hills. A plane roared down from Kainde Mountain and circled. The field sprang magically to life. Hundreds of natives appeared from nowhere and started clearing the runway of oil drum and log obstructions.

The transport made two circuits and landed in the lane. The pilot didn't even switch off. The gang unloaded in three minutes. A ragged cheer went up when it was found that the bulk of the cargo comprised sacks of sugar, caddies of tobacco, and mail.

The malaria squad, endowed with sudden energy, charged the transport's open door in a solid phalanx. Gibson laid violent hands on me.

'Quick, taubada, quick!' he yelled.

I scrambled up. He smiled wistfully, waved, and shouted something that was lost in the roar of the slip stream as the pilot thrust the throttles forward. Wet grass-blades blew back.

A harried man yelled 'Zeros!' – and slammed the door behind me. The plane gave a convulsive bound and was off.

I saw no Zeros, thank God.

At 15,000 feet, just before the transport punched for cover into the big cumulus cloud where air currents were so violent that 30 rivets sprung in the port wing, I caught a glimpse of shining, silver sea, and the rolling jungle ridges that led down to the valley of the Markham and the isthmus of Salamaua.

Part Three
FORESTS OF DREADFUL NIGHT

AFTER more than four months spent regrouping their forces from the conquest of Malaya, the Netherlands Indies, and the Philippines, the Japanese at last launched an attempt to complete the conquest of New Guinea as a preliminary to the invasion of Australia. The first move was the Buna landing and the dispatch of strong patrols inland toward the passes of the Owen-Stanley range. Australian militia engaged the patrols but were forced back. Troops of the 2nd Australian Imperial Force, recently recalled from the Middle East, were then rushed into the mountains to defend the passes and try to recapture the strategically important Kokoda airfield. American bombers and some American equipment were by now supporting the Australian infantry. The Japanese brought up their main force and the Australians, untrained for their task, were practically annihilated. The lesson was too costly and bitter for even a classically conservative command to ignore. Allied strategists at long last changed their minds about jungle fighting and started to train men intelligently and realistically for it. The death and agony of many brave men was the price paid for this progress . . .

CHAPTER 13

WAR BASE

MORESBY had changed almost beyond recognition when I returned from Wau early in August, 1942. The dry season lay over the savannah like a blight. The grass was tindery and there were great, black blotches on the hillsides where fires had burned down to the raw earth. The leaves of the gum trees were limp and thickly powdered with dust.

Dust and fire and Australians in slouch hats have an affinity. Men of the 21st Brigade of the Australian Imperial Force had moved in to reinforce the garrison. All day they rolled up the road from the harbor in open trucks, bound for foothill camps. I spent a good deal of time sitting on the porch of Correspondents' House, watching them. Their appearance was inspiring. They were men who had played a leading part in that grim side show in Syria the year before – where Australians wore their slouch hats into battle because the French were 'on our side' and steel helmets might provoke 'incidents'.

These troops were tested and selected by war. They were scrawny muscled and burned to the color of leather by desert winds. There were no weeds among them. They betrayed no enthusiasm. They did not cheer and catcall. They knew what fighting meant and they were going to fight.

The trucks bristled with Bren guns on antiaircraft mountings. Batteries of snub-nosed 25-pounders roared by, and a procession of carriers, jeeps, battle buggies, and olive-green trucks loaded with ammunition and grenades.

After eight months, the 'Tobruk of the Pacific' had at last become a war base. Tent cities were springing up in sheltered acres. The Seven Mile airfield, once a raw landing strip, had been expanded into a military airfield, and satellite fields were coming into commission, one by one. At times they were literally jammed with aircraft. All day and half the night, American bombers in formation roared over the House. We became blase. We did not look up. How many aircraft were available for the test? I used to ask myself that, sitting on the porch, watching the shadows of planes speed over the scorched fields. Enough?

One morning I rose before dawn and went down to the Seven Mile to see the unheard-of total of 27 heavy bombers set off for a raid. It was very dark. The sky was clear and strange stars were burning. All the hills about the field were inky blue. A sad wind was blowing. There was a smell of dust and dew, and gasoline and wood smoke. The aircraft were crouched like big, stunned bats on the ground, black and potentially terrible.

The crews had been sleeping by their planes inside little brown mosquito bars. They were unshaven and bleary eyed – American boys, gallant and eager but not yet hardened to the rigors of operating from 'an advanced base'. You could see the poor devils wondering where the hell breakfast was – and what it would be like two hours hence, when the flak started to throw up puffballs into the sky. It was their first combat mission.

Dawn came. There was a morning feeling. This was the brief time when Moresby is almost cool. A lemon glow, cold and passionless, spread in the eastern sky. Then it changed to apricot and suffused the zenith. The dust-smothered guns leaped into view, fold upon fold of them over the savannah.

The air crew drank coffee out of their thermos bottles and gnawed at iron-hard biscuits.

It was morning – morning with no enemy in it. Somehow that got under my skin. It got under my skin even more than the whispering war in the terrible gorge of Mubo; even more than the sight of toiling, dying carriers under the shadow of Lawson.

These men were the products of a civilization utterly removed from the country in which they now found themselves.

They were healthy, cared for – the products of well-endowed civilization. They were inspired to resolution by a vague but complicated ideology. They believed in something called democracy. Their machines were skillfully and complexly contrived by the triumph of human intelligence over nature – hollow metal tubes into which they, civilized men, inserted their pale bodies and, like genii, flew out into the morning to deal with death – because they believed. War made no sense in the morning, only a sadness.

The field was very shabby when the planes had gone, shabby and lonely. Then the sun came up over the hills. The apricot glow faded. The drone in the sky melted into the wind.

As yet, the presence of the approaching Japanese 'over the hill' did not seem to worry anybody very much. Men thought it a pity that the enemy had beaten us to the gun – two battalions of militia troops had been on their way to garrison Buna when the Jap landing was made – but things like that happened in the best regulated wars.

Still, the first battalion to contact the enemy, the 39th, was doing well considering its strength and supply difficulties. One platoon had actually arrived in the Buna district when the Japanese landed. Hopelessly outnumbered, it fell back, joined the rest of the company and fought a delaying action all the way to the village of Oive, about 40 miles from the coast, where the first real stand was made.

The Japanese moved considerable forces inland very rapidly. The defenders of Oive Ridge were overwhelmed and forced to retreat. The colonel of the battalion was killed and was replaced by the young Australian Imperial Force officer who had escaped from Rabaul and led the Salamaua rear guards.

We all agreed the Japs meant business and were determined to capture the Kokoda airstrip site, the only available landing place in the area, but what would develop was hard to foresee at that time. No one believed they would strike at Moresby through the mountains, particularly as we now had enough troops to defend the passes. The Buna move must be part of a much wider plan. Personally I thought it probably had the

177

force of a diversion in the rear, and that the real attack would come, as it had always threatened to come, from the sea.

The whole Southwest Pacific war theater was stirring. News came that the Australian forces at Milne Bay had grown very substantially. Were they there defensively or offensively?

Then in August landing of American marines on Guadalcanal was announced. Again, was this a stroke on the offense or defense?

It was useless to speculate on the general situation. There were too many factors unknown in Moresby. I turned to the problems of the jungle war that was now bound to develop in the Huon Gulf around Salamaua and Buna and reached two conclusions which events promptly proved wrong. The first was that the Australian army had learned the lessons of Malaya. The second was that the Japanese would not seriously try to penetrate the Owen-Stanley range until they were ready to launch an amphibious attack on Moresby.

Even when Kokoda airfield fell to the Japanese and the 39th Battalion was forced back into the mountains, with instructions to defend the foothill passes to the last man, I was surprised to hear that the 21st Brigade had been ordered to go in over the hill. I sought enlightenment from the new commander, Major General R., who shrugged and said frankly: 'As far as I'm concerned, I'm willing to pull back and let the enemy have the rough stuff if he wants it. I'm willing to present the Jap with the supply headache I've got. But there are those who think otherwise. We need a victory in the Pacific, and a lot of poor bastards have got to get killed to provide it!'

There were now 17 or 18 war correspondents at Moresby – English, Australian and American. Most of them were energetically hitchhiking bomber rides to and from Townsville, anxious to detect which way the cat would jump.

Chester Wilmot of the Australian Broadcasting Commission, beefy veteran of the Western Desert and Syria, agreed with me that a fight on hand was worth half a dozen in prospect. He was something of a tactical expert and persona grata with brigade headquarters. We applied for permission to accompany the main body of the Australian Imperial Force and were refused.

We tried subterfuge. There was going to be a massacre of the Japs, we suggested, when the 21st Brigade really got among them at Kokoda. Was a nice massacre of Japs to go quite unrecorded in the world's press and radio? It seemed a pity. Having sown the seeds, we went back to waiting and trying to be wise.

The fight for the Gap was going promisingly. The 39th Battalion counterattacked from its first hill position. One company reoccupied the Kokoda airstrip for three days, until it was forced to withdraw through lack of food and ammunition.

In flying weather, P-39's and P-40's strafed enemy-held villages and river crossings. There was no Zero opposition. But the dark shadow of supply hung over the jubilation about making a fight for it in New Guinea at last. The question was how to maintain an army 100 miles from its base, or even 50 or 20 miles, when the intervening country was so rugged that no military engineering could pierce it with a road capable of carrying wheeled traffic. There were only two answers – air transport and sheer manpower.

Transport planes were not yet assembled and dropping places not yet mapped. The main weight must be borne by manpower. Between 5,000 and 6,000 natives were conscripted as carriers. With their labor and the half dozen transports at first available, it was just possible – theoretically – to maintain a force at brigade strength on the far side of the range. If we could build up a sufficient reserve, it was hoped to launch a counterattack to regain the Kokoda airstrip, where troops could be landed.

Sketchy knowledge of the exact nature of the country between Rouna and Kokoda – indeed an almost complete ignorance of the terrain on both flanks of the old post trail – was hindering the preparation of the offensive. Belated attempts to assemble and collate the information possessed by peacetime administration men were being made, but the quality and precision fell far short of military requirements. I remember the spirited description of the route given me by my old friend, Major E. S. of the Australian New Guinea Administration Unit. It seemed extraordinary, indeed almost criminal, that no adequate reconnaissances had been made after eight months of large-scale military occupation, under constant fear that the Japanese *would* land at Buna. But a spurt to make up for lost time was certainly going on now.

Wilmot and I were at last able to get maps and details of the trail at headquarters and we studied them carefully. The road through Rouna Pass had been pushed out a little more than 30 miles from the port. Clearly it could not be pushed very much farther, except possibly as a corduroy road, unless new grades could be surveyed and suitable metal found.

As a walking proposition, the route looked formidable. From roadhead to the present brigade position at Deniki village, the surveyed distance was about 80 miles – in practice, 100 miles of walking – but infantrymen passing over this route would not merely walk 100 miles. They must climb and descend an aggregate of 20,000 feet on the rain-drenched razorbacks before going into action.

Staging camps were being built at native villages not more than 10 miles apart on the post trail – Uberi, Eoribaiwa, Menari, Nauro, Efogi, Kagi, Templeton's Crossing, Eroa Creek, Isurava, and Deniki. At Myola in the high mountains, reconnaissance parties had discovered a large, dry lake bed that was too rough for an airstrip but on which supplies could be dropped from transport planes. A reserve of stores and ammunition was being accumulated there.

The strategic importance of Kokoda airfield was now becoming painfully apparent. In Japanese hands it made any plan to bring large forces against them in the Buna area wholly contingent upon our ability to supply our troops in mountain jungle, *without unchallenged air superiority and without an adequate fleet of transport planes to drop supplies.*

After the final retirement of the 39th Battalion into the Gap passes, two battalions of the Australian Imperial Force, the 2/14 and the 2/16th, immediately moved out to reinforce them. As we learned later, they were to make an attempt to recapture Kokoda before the rest of the 7th Division and

United States army units were deployed to deal with the Japanese centered on Buna.

A party of correspondents went up to the rubber belt to watch the 14th Battalion march out into the jungle. An acre of men were resting in a green meadow flanked by rubber trees. Their shirts were off and their backs were sun tanned, rippling with muscle. They had set up Bren guns against surprise strafing – an automatic precaution that marked them as veterans. Some were singing, some writing letters home. One group had borrowed a small grindstone from the plantation house and were sharpening their bayonets, slouch hats pulled rakishly down and their eyes bright and reflective.

But I could not help noticing that their packs weighed 65 pounds, although they believed their personal equipment was cut to the minimum; that they were half naked when they should have been covered; that their uniforms were the color of desert dust and not the color of green jungle; that their webbing shone white from long bleaching in the desert suns.

For the first time, the shadow of a doubt crossed my mind. I dismissed it. Lesser fighters might fail, but not these – not the best assault infantry in the world!

The only hurt was the thought of how many of them would never again see this quiet grove, the trees tinged red with brief winter, or feel the caress of the coarse grass, or lie on their backs watching the trade-wind clouds race over a sunny sky.

Parer returned by plane from Wau the second week in August with a fearsome growth of black hair and eyes that looked as if they had been burned into his skull with a red-hot poker, but he was still free of malaria and bubbling with energy. He wanted a place in the party for Kokoda. He said that the arrival in New Guinea of a fleet of regular transport planes had temporarily relieved the supply crisis in the Bulolo valley, but freights were erratic again. With Lake Myola's maw gaping for 25 or 30 tons of dropped supplies daily – and only half a dozen aircraft to feed it – the unfortunate commandos should soon be drinking sugarless tea again.

One bright spot remained in a gloomy prospect. The Japanese had been unable to develop a fighter strip at Buna, and our transport ought to be free of fighter interception. The loss of three or four transports, particularly at this stage, would be a major disaster.

I decided to have a look at Myola from the air and begged a plane ride that gave me more unpleasant moments than most bombing missions. The transport crews were then working without fighter escort. They kept down to treetop height to escape being spotted by the enemy. This meant hugging the vertical contours of the range in rough air and often in poor visibility. It meant flying through drifting mist at so low an altitude that if the undercarriage had been down, it would have ripped creepers from the jungletop. It meant flying up twisted canyons, hoping to God and the gremlins that the next patch of cloud did not conceal an unmarked mountaintop.

There were two main lakes at 6,000 feet in the Myola basin. Both were deep, drying saucers of marsh and kunai. The westerly clearing was being used.

Approach was difficult even in clear, still weather. In wind or cloud it was murderous. Only aircraft with power to climb out on the prop could get low enough to drop accurately. When the pilot came out of the run with throttle at full gun, the clearance between the belly of the plane and the ridgetop trees was seldom more than 10 feet. A plane took four to six runs to unload a full cargo.

I worked as unloader, tied with six feet of stout rope to a ring bolt opposite the unloading hatch. We hurled over the switchback of jungle at zero feet, rushed into a green vortex as the plane slipped off height over the lake, and flinched from rock faces and timbered scarps. Once the run began, I hadn't time to worry but my ears strained for the sound of a falter in the overworked motors.

The copilot signaled me to start dropping. A strip of kunai flashed into view, spinning slowly to the left. The pilot took the runs with one wing down, so that the blanket-wrapped bundles might be hurled more quickly and easily through the hatch. While the nose of the aircraft was still down, it was hard work heaving the cargo up the incline, and kicking and shoving it clear. But when the nose came up, half a ton of stuff began slowly to slide down the duralumin floor and all one had to do was kick, punch or deflect the bundles into space.

In the excitement of the first pass I went half through the hatch myself and jammed my fingers clawing back. Then the plane climbed almost to stalling point, flipped dizzily over and circled for the second of five runs.

New Guinea air is as treacherous as New Guinea ground. Throughout the trip, the transport never felt as if it were fully under the pilot's control. It skated, skidded, staggered, slithered, rocketed its way through air that was as rough and solid seeming as an angry sea. One such adventure was quite enough. I stepped down on Seven Mile field with a chastened admiration for the crews who made half a dozen of these missions a day.

On August 19, the thing we had all feared happened. Our run of luck broke. A notebook entry of that date tells the story best. It reads:

'Well – it's come! Three hours ago, 35 heavy bombers, with a big Zero umbrella, pasted hell out of Seven Mile.

'It was the first raid for more than a fortnight, and our fighters and ground defenses were caught with their pants down. Even the 3.7 antiaircraft boys, who had turned off many a dangerous looking run at the last minute, had an off-morning.

'The Japs did the best bombing they have done since the sinking of the *Macdhui* in Moresby Harbor. Using 500 and 1,000 pound demolition and antipersonnel bombs, they straddled a long line of undispersed transports and bombers. A stick ran the entire length of the runway, finishing up in a dispersal area. It wrecked operations room and holed the road at several points.

'Casualties were not heavy, considering the number of men caught on the airfield. But 28 aircraft were either destroyed or seriously damaged. – *including the entire available fleet of transports.*

'What reserves can be brought from the mainland I do not

183

know – but the delay alone will put the troops over the hill in a serious position. An S O S has gone out for replacements.

'The raid was pretty grim. The bombers came in, out of mountain cloud, at about 23,000 feet. They kept two tight V formations.

'Over the field the sky was clear. They looked like opalescent dragonflies. The three-inch antiaircraft pointed them, but as far as I could see no fighters were up.

'They made only one run and released all together. The detonation was terrific. An immense cloud of reddish-yellow dust swirled from the field – then spurts of fire, and columns of black, oily smoke. Delayed-action bombs started to explode, and a fuel dump went up.

'The strip was a tragic sight. The wrecked aircraft burned fiercely. Grass fires had broken out in a dozen places. Drums of gasoline kept popping. An ambulance had overturned on Hellfire Corner. The only sign of its occupants was a pool of blood gathered under the dashboard.

'The entire runway was ankle deep in debris – fragments of blackened and twisted duralumin, shattered motors, parachute packs ripped open and the silk blasted into pieces the size of a pocket handkerchief.

'Half a dozen Flying Fortresses from the mainland had just made landfall. They made a single run over the ruined field at low altitude, climbed out and started to circle disconsolately.

'For awhile we wandered about, spotting duds for the bomb dispersal squad, surveying the destruction. Dazed men clambered out of slit trenches, sooty and filthy.

'Then gangs were organized to clear the worst of the stuff from the runway. Bulldozers and scoops came puffing and snorting out of the scrub and began filling in craters.

'We went back to the House, depressed beyond words.'

The day after the big raid, Parer, Wilmot and I received permission to go to brigade headquarters at Myola or Isurava. The only stipulation was that we must not use fit native carriers and must carry five days' rations ourselves.

We held a last conference with Major General R. He made no secret of the fact that he had misgivings that the task of recapturing Kokoda might prove too much for even the 14th and the 16th.

I recalled from somewhere in my schoolboy reading the Roman emperor who planned roads by calling for a map, a straightedge and a stylus, laying the straightedge between town and town, drawing a line and saying: 'Bid the engineers build it *thus!*'

CHAPTER 14

MARCH ON KOKODA

WILMOT took the radio sound truck as far as the roadhead, which had then been pushed out through the fringes of the rubber country almost to the village of Uberi.

There were already signs of the great adventures in military engineering that were, within a few months of this date, to alter fundamentally the haphazard nature of New Guinea campaigning. Roadmaking in such country was a Homeric undertaking. Bulldozers, scoops, power shovels, graders and rollers were ripping a canyon through the jungle and a wide, deep gutter in the glutinous soil. Thousands of tons of metal, crushed coral, pumice, logs and gravel were poured into the seemingly limitless belly of the road's foundations. Even so, it was still a river of mud in which every wheeled vehicle but the unconquerable jeep sooner or later stuck fast or skidded into the ditch.

But afternoon rains had been exceptionally light for three or four days, and the sound truck made it. We were spared a 15-mile slog through morass. We had stopped at the native labor compound on the way to pick up three native reject carriers to carry half loads of Parer's camera gear. It looked then – and proved later – to have been hardly worth the trouble. They were Pari boys, ruined by tourist and poor missionary influence. The second day out, we kicked their behinds down the trail and carried the gear ourselves. It was a bad thing in principle, but it saved hours of precious time.

It did not take me long to realize that carrying a 50-pound load up and down razorbacks demanded quadruple the en-

186

ergy expended in straight, unburdened climbing. We made Uberi after three hours' scramble over a stiff ridge. The forest was comparatively open and the trail in fair condition. No rain had fallen for nearly a week. The main body of troops had gone through four or five days before. Since then there had been just enough traffic on the drying ground to settle the clay.

The engineers had done considerable work on the old native path already. Before that, traveling had been almost impossible. On one clay slope elements of the 39th Battalion were reported to have taken 17 hours to travel 600 yards. They had to cut their way up the chute as mountaineers would cut a traverse on a snowfield.

In spite of the improved route the second stage was a long, extremely hard day. After leaving Uberi the route lay along the river flats for awhile. Then it slanted up a razorback into which more than 1,000 steps had been cut. In three or four miles it rose 2,000 feet. From the crest was a magnificent prospect of ranges sweeping down into the valley of the Brown River.

The formation of the trail had psychological drawbacks. The more or less regular steps seemed to make the going more difficult than an unimproved native trail, where stepping from root to root broke the monotony even if it slowed progress. At the foot of Uberi ridge a severe rainstorm caught us in the early afternoon. Parer started worrying about his film again, but I found the rain refreshing, the violent claps of thunder stimulating.

Eoribaiwa village stood on top of a 2,500-foot ridge. The engineers had let in 4,000 steps on the approach. That night I saw what the country could do to raw troops. A detachment of engineers came in behind us in full marching order. Most of them were big men and fit by normal standards. They made the last few 100 feet climb out of the valley in 5- or 10-yard bursts. Half of them dropped where they stood when they reached the plateau. Their faces were bluish gray with strain, their eyes starting out. They were long beyond mere breathlessness. The air pumped in and out of them in great, sticky sobs; and they had 100 miles of such traveling ahead.

Parer again distinguished himself for guts. Clipped by a sharp dose of fever – his first acute attack – pale, streaming profusely with sweat, and at the same time shivering violently, he refused stubbornly to stop. In the morning, almost forcibly, I made him split his pack between us. He would stop every hour or so, reeling on his feet, and protest that he was capable of carrying his own gear.

The 'beef' was vanishing from chubby Wilmot before our eyes. His technique of travel was amusing. Downhill he took terrific, two-yard strides that would have broken my ankles. He went like a whirlwind, outstripping the rest of us by miles. But when we struck the next hill, we drew even. Halfway up we would pass him hoisting one leg after the other with agonized slowness. Three hundred yards away his grunts, groans, whistlings and profane cries were audible. He clawed his way to the crest and fell flat on his face. If he had not been strong as an ox he would have scrambled his guts. He was the wrong build for this sort of work – but the right temperament. He was still grunting, cursing and whistling at the end of the day – and still traveling.

There was rain every afternoon. The nights were getting chillier as we climbed, and the staging camps were yet inadequate. I could hardly believe that 2,000 troops, raw to such conditions, had passed that way and left so few stragglers. They were men of great heart.

The Koiari villages, used as a basis for the reconstruction of the staging camps, had originally been only half a dozen poky, palm-plaited huts, with bamboo flooring. Now most of the men had been recruited for carriers or had 'gone bush' in the hills.

The Koiari were a fine people, very dark skinned with a peculiar hair-do – a bun worn squarely on top of the head. Physically they were robust and more free from skin diseases than any other Papuan natives I had seen. Despite close proximity to Moresby, they had resisted the 'civilizing' influence and until a few years ago the coast villagers lived in terror of their raids. The tribe showed surprisingly little resentment of the sudden and bewildering invasion of their domain by a white army. The men, accepting the patrol officers' explanation that the Japanese were bad people who would loot their gardens and steal their women, were serving willingly on the carrier lines. The women were employed weaving palm thatch for troop shelters.

When the main forces moved through, however, only about a quarter of the troops could be got under shelter at night. They had been forced by the severity of the going to discard more of their already cut-to-the-bone equipment. Hundreds of men slept in the mud. They had been issued one blanket and one ground sheet to six or seven men. They had already been drenched to the skin by the afternoon rain. Sometimes the downpour did not ease off but continued half the night and was followed by a piercingly cold, early-morning wind. Open fires were forbidden, and, in any case, could scarcely have been tended. The march to Myola had taken from seven to ten days. It was not hard to imagine the condition the men were now in – long before beginning the serious business of fighting the Japs.

The third day out, fever started to creep up on me again. I declined to emulate Parer and stopped at Menari village to give the quinine a chance to work. We were all glad of the break. All day I lay on the veranda slats feeling half dead. I had a bad cold and a painful cough.

The natives here were restive because some of the troops had been raiding their banana and pawpaw patches. The patrol officers were worried because the headmen demanded not compensation but punishment of the culprits. They refused to accept beef and rice in payment for the damage done. They wanted justice.

This was the type of minor slipup in discipline that could have had very serious consequences. Few people realize how completely we were dependent on native goodwill.

After leaving Menari we met two wounded men coming out from Kokoda and Deniki – men of the 39th Battalion. One had been shot through the foot, the other through the left eye. The bullet had passed obliquely and shallowly through his skull from just above the cheekbone, and emerged behind the ear. He complained of severe headache, but said the wound itself was not painful. The man with the bullet through his foot was leading him. The pair had walked 113 miles in 16 days. They expected to reach the roadhead in another five.

A little later we passed three more wounded men. The first was shot through the shoulder, the second through the thigh, and the third had a badly shattered hand. They were jubilant because they had wounds that would earn them home leave. They had been nine days on the trail.

None wanted to talk about the Kokoda fighting. They merely said that the Japs were hard to see in the bush, but that the 39th had got amongst them in the rubber plantation and inflicted high casualties. What impressed me most deeply about these wounded was their apparent desensitization. They were completely inured to suffering. They accepted it as an integral part of living. Pain was as much a part of their day as eating and sleeping. True, they wanted to live. If they had not wanted to live they would have fallen down and died. That would have been easy. But they did not want to live *too much*. They were not afraid.

Swinburne's prayer 'From too much love of living, from hope and fear set free . . . ' had a new meaning to me now. I knew why a medical officer in Moresby said forebodingly: 'God knows how we are going to get the wounded out. It doesn't bear thinking about.'

To make up for the day lost at Menari, we decided to travel a double stage at Lake Myola. It was a 15-hour walk. I sweated heavily. My very skin ached. It hurt me to breathe deeply – yet it was strangulation to try and moderate that painful breathing.

Blue valley after blue valley. Ridge and valley, and valley and ridge. Mile upon endless mile of hills seen from open patches of grassland. There was a detour about Kagi – a russet, round-thatched village clinging to its jungle crag. There were pole fences about overgrown yam and sweet potato fields. It was blue country, all covered with a mantle of majestic cloud and mist.

We went up a dizzy ridge that rose and kept rising, topless. The sky was growing black with night. The storm of the afternoon merged into one continuous downpour. The last four hours' going was along the gutterlike detour.

On Myola ridge the forest was very dense and the trail laced over by huge roots and frantically wide tree buttresses. The passage of troops and carriers had churned the footway into a knee-deep glutinous quagmire. A sentry challenged. He stood out and flashed a torch over us. His steel helmet was already red with rust. He had wrapped a ground sheet around him for warmth. He was saturated and plastered with mud from head to foot. He had not been dry since he left Moresby. Behind him, three others had managed to get a small, smoky fire going. They were crouched over it, too dispirited even to look up. The rain trickled in streams from their backs and helmets.

Headquarters was a mile farther on. Ten miles would have been all the same to me. It is difficult to describe the abysmal depression that had me in its grip. The rain did not vary in intensity for as much as a minute – an endless, drumming, chilling deluge. It roared and rustled and sighed on the broad leaves of the jungle top. It soaked through the green pandanus thatches of shelters and spilled clammy cascades upon the bowed backs of exhausted men. It swamped cooking fires. Creeks ran in every hollow. One's very bones seemed softened by the wetness.

We reported at the command post. We were given lukewarm stew and rice in a muddy messtin, and I drank three mugs of tea that tasted rankly of rotten leaf mold. We were assigned shelter. The camp had been erected too hastily to allow such luxuries as slat floors. Bed was a ground sheet and blanket in four inches of mud. The mud would have been liquid if it had not been bound together with rotten fern fronds and sticks. In the morning the rain stopped for the first time in a week. I spent a few hours soaking up sun and drying out gear, but my cold was steadily getting worse.

The 'lake' was 300 or 400 acres of kunai grass and reeds on a mud pan. But for the danger of Japanese aircraft, it would have been infinitely preferable as a camp site to the dank jungle skirting it. Nevertheless the 14th Battalion had crept cautiously out of the bush and made a collection of tiny grass shelters hard to spot from the air. They were full of scorpions and beetles, but better than the depressing green huts under cover of the forest.

When the rainclouds started to collect again I stirred myself and gathered a large bundle of reeds which, laid latticewise on the mud floor, kept the ground sheet and blanket clear of the muck.

The second morning at Myola I was lying in the sun sound asleep when transport planes started to drop supplies. A wild Australian flying an old DH 86 nearly brained me with a case of canned beef. The Lodestars and the DC2's could come in low enough to drop accurately. They had the power to climb out steeply. But the unhappy Australian had to unload his cargo at 500 feet, and most of it fell well out in the bush. It was fascinating to watch cases of canned beef explode as they hit ground. The gold-colored cans scattered like shrapnel.

Most unenvied job at the lake was that of 'marker'. The marker had to stand perilously close to the dropping area and take compass bearings on bundles that undershot or overshot clear ground. The bush was so dense that only a small percentage were ever recovered, even though scores of natives were employed searching. The total loss, including food or material damaged beyond use by the fall, was about 25 per cent of the cargoes. Even so, the transports put down as much as 25 tons in a day. Supply parachutes, then scarce, were used only to deliver mortar bombs and fuses and machine-gun ammunition.

The force now had five complete three-inch mortars and about 300 bombs. These had gone down front. Everybody was reassured by the presence of 'artillery!'

News came through that the 39th had been forced back from Deniki and that the 16th was relieving it on a line that ran through the village of Isurava. This meant that the Japs were at last getting into the Owen-Stanley's themselves and that something was wrong.

Supply difficulties were self-evident. Planes were reported to be making experimental droppings at the villages on the trail between Myola and Moresby. Several men had been killed or injured by packages crashing through the grass roofs of the huts.

The third day at Myola we heard that the situation at Isurava was deteriorating. The Japs had anticipated the push on Kokoda and had hit first. We decided to move forward immediately.

From Myola to Templeton's Crossing was the worst stage on the Owen-Stanley trail. For long stretches it was precipitous – no more than a muddy cleft in a clay cliff, down which one swung on lawyer vines and supple branches made ragged and greasy by thousands of pairs of clutching hands.

More and more wounded or sick were coming back along this fearful route. Most of them were walking skeletons. Their eyes were bright with fever. They traveled a few yards in a burst, then paused. You could see the loose skin on the sides of their necks palpitating like a lizard's throat. Their greeting was unvaried. They said 'Good day, dig. Pretty tough, eh?' and grinned. The grin didn't mean anything – or did it?

Templeton's Crossing was a dry camp with kunda bunks by the riverbank. We stayed the night and pushed on.

I will never forget the scene as Eora came into sight halfway down the last ridge. Hundreds of men were standing about in mud that came up to their shins. The whole village, built of pandanus and grass, looked as if it were about to founder in the sea of mud. The huts leaned drunkenly. There were piles of broken-out ration boxes and firewood half submerged. The men were slimed from head to foot, for weeks unshaven, their skins bloodless under their filth.

Lines of exhausted carriers were squatting on the fringes of this congregation eating muddy rice off muddy banana leaves. Their woolly hair was plastered with rain and muck. Their eyes were rolling and bloodshot with the strain of long carrying. Some of them were still panting.

It was Mubo Gorge over again – only this time there was a whole army in the jungle instead of a few bands of elusive scouts. Machine-gun fire was almost continuous. A Jap .50

caliber was going *dub-dub-dub*, away in the east. They said the Japs were gradually cracking us. The 2nd/16th was moving into position. The 53rd militia had broken on the right flank and was on the run.

CHAPTER 15

RETREAT IN THE MOUNTAINS

IT TOOK great effort to write coherent notes on the happenings of the next few days. It was impossible to say: 'This happened, and then this happened.' Everything was confusion.

Parer, excited by so much cinematic material at Eora, decided to stay there and get it on celluloid while he could. Wilmot and I joined a small party of stragglers from the 16th going down to battalion positions. All distinguishing insignia had to be taken off because the Japs were reputed to have an uncanny ability to spot officers. Losses among commissioned men had been disproportionately high. We went down, stumbling and teetering over bad log crossings. Machine-gun fire sounded, without intermission, from the hills on either side.

The Japanese were 'infiltrating'. Their patrols had penetrated far into the hills on the flanks of the trail positions. Indeed, they ignored the positions we were anxious to defend, and were striking out boldly into the trailless forest of the hills. Our men were not prepared for such tactics. The bulk of them were troops trained for desert warfare. They were more than half afraid of the country. You could see that in their movements, in their whole attitude. They were far more afraid of the country than the Japanese.

They were continually worried by the idea of being 'cut off'. To their minds, being cut off meant that one must wander in the jungle, wander in the hills, wander in the valleys . . . up and down and up and down those heartbreaking razor-backs, until one died of hunger or exhaustion.

You could *see* them thinking that way. The commandos on Huon Gulf thought that way until they learned better –

until they learned that it was almost as easy to move off the trails as on them. A bushman thought of these hills as friends to conceal and protect him; a formally trained soldier thought of them as deadly enemies eternally ready to baffle and trap him.

I traveled for a while with a young officer belatedly going down to join his unit. He had gone off into the bush at Myola to look for an overshot load of air-dropped mortar bombs. He had not gone a half a mile before he lost himself. He wandered for four days before he managed to get direction again from listening to the sound of the planes dropping loads on the lake. No one could blame the man for lack of bush-craft. But the troops were being led by such men as he – men never trained to be bushmen; men who never could be bush-men, because they lacked the instinct.

Machine-gun fire became more intense as we went on. Most of it was on the flanks, but some was dead ahead and we heard one or two bursts directly behind us. The Japs had moved on without opposition to Kagi Ridge, and it seemed as if Myola itself might already have fallen to a flank attack. Occasionally there would be the dull, echoing crash of an exploding mortar bomb. Absolutely nothing could be seen.

It was uncanny. The bullets made a strange noise among the leaves – a low, deadly whispering. The whispering could be heard before the rattle of the discharge. The enemy was holding positions on the other side of the river and kept up an intermittent fire on every clearing. There were numerous clearings, and to pass them we divided up into twos and threes and dashed across them bent double.

After a time my nerve broke under the constant gauntlet running and I refused to play. Every time we approached an open space I would detour into the bush and scramble along the clay scarps under cover – or worm a way through the dense undergrowth. This proved just as rapid a means of getting to the other side of the clearing as the more direct method. More and more wounded and stragglers were coming back. The entanglement was becoming really heavy.

Three hours out from Eora, we learned that the Japanese

had been mortaring the brigade headquarters position. Elsewhere they were using .50-caliber guns to clear fields of fire. Large sections of the forest were rotten with fungus and it was possible to cut down sizable trees with a few well-placed bursts.

The whole battle had become a blind groping in a tangle of growth. One party came in with a story of having traveled for miles just under the crest of a steep ridge, parallel with a party of Japanese. No one on either side was willing to show his head against the skyline for a shot, so they fought it out by tossing grenades at one another over the crest. The Mills grenade won. It had real, lethal quality. The Japanese were using a light grenade. One man on the patrol had his teeth knocked out by a Japanese grenade striking him in the mouth. It fell to his feet and exploded. All he suffered in addition to his loss of teeth was a peppering of shrapnel in one thigh.

It was seldom that anyone got a glimpse of the enemy. Most of the wounded were very indignant about it. I must have heard the remark 'You can't *see* the little bastards!' hundreds of times in the course of a day. Some of the men said it with tears in their eyes and clenched fists. They were humiliated beyond endurance by the fact that they had been put out of action before even seeing a Japanese.

Yet the 39th Battalion saw Japs – plenty of them. They had been in Moresby from the beginning and had a smattering of junglecraft. The others simply didn't know how or where to look.

So it went on. . .

One could visualize what was happening, but one could not *see* it. Somewhere out in the green, clots of Australians were defending localities which they believed to be important – the 'key passes' of the Owen-Stanley range. They believed, because they had been told, that if they held the trail they would hold the range. The Japanese knew better. The Japanese knew that the key to the Owen-Stanley range was high ground, not a valueless trail. Our men were constantly under the fatal misapprehension that if the Japanese *surrounded* a position, that position was inevitably lost. The humiliating part of it was

197

that any pack of damned fools could surround a position in this country. Our men were being beaten by affection and superstitious respect for the cookhouse! Why couldn't they realize it would cost them less to hang on without supplies – and take their chance of spending a few days, or even a few weeks, in the bush!

The sole consolation was that wherever the enemy dared to launch frontal, man-to-man attacks, we beat him. But most of the killing was done 'on the blind'. Someone saw movement. An entire force opened fire in the general direction of the movement, using all available automatic arms. Sometimes I wondered how anyone got killed in this blind shooting, but since our patrols had suffered heavy casualties from it, it was a safe assumption that the enemy had suffered even more heavily. Our small arms were more deadly. The Japanese apparently had no serious supply problem. They were burning up ammunition at a terrific rate. They didn't seem to care.

Wilmot and I reached the brigade position just as it was decided to evacuate. The enemy had broken through on both flanks and was making an enveloping movement. The 53rd Battalion, on the right, had folded up completely across the river, and machine-gun duels were going on six or seven miles in the rear. It looked just about as dirty a spot as it was possible to get into.

A long line of stretcher cases were being brought out under fire by native carriers. Machine gunners, bent double under guns and ammunition, staggered up the hill with the sweat and mud rolling off them.

My belly felt like lead. I had passed being afraid that a bullet would come out of the leaves and account for me; but I was deadly weary and deadly discouraged – appalled by the sense of being a partisan spectator to a disaster. Also I felt lonely. Everyone else had a job to do with his hands and his fortitude – except me. Everybody else had orders, to go or to stay – except me. My only job was to watch, and nobody cared the price of a matchbox in hell whether I watched or not.

The sequence of events is inextricably confused. I remember pulling myself up every now and then and saying: 'You'd better remember *how* things happened and when – after all it *is* your job. Even if nobody cares whether you do it or not, it *is* your job.' But even though I made painfully conscious mental notes, nothing stuck.

Wilmot was very anxious to find Brigadier P., whom he knew personally. But before we found P., the brigade major, Hugh C., found us. He ordered us to get out – and get out fast.

C. was the only man in that weary, straggling procession of retreat who looked to be still mentally alert. He was ghastly, mudsplashed and sweat drenched – but his eyes were still alert and roving. He had been detailed to select a new position for brigade headquarters. You could see him trying to project his mind – to cast his aliveness and alertness like a net over the whole bloody, disintegrating, invisible confusion. You could see him trying to draw in the net of his perception and make its contents cohere, so that they might be used to achieve order and positive purpose.

We traveled together for an hour or so, not saying very much. C. selected as a temporary site a kanaka garden that commanded one of the main bends of the river.

Halfway through the afternoon it had begun to rain again. Everything was sodden, but it was not so cold as it had been higher in the hills. No one had so much as a pup tent or a ground sheet as protection from the weather. One by one the brigade staff came in. They dropped where they stood in the dripping undergrowth.

Wilmot said he would wait for the brigadier. I decided to go back to Eora. I believed the brigade would drop back there within 48 hours and I wanted to know how the retreat on the flanks was going.

The whole defending force seemed to have fallen to pieces. Stragglers from a dozen different units were making their way back, like sheep, to the trail. The wounded were coming onto the trail from both sides of the river. A few natives were held as stretcher bearers for men who could neither walk nor crawl.

I calculated the enemy was moving troops under cover of darkness well up onto Kagi Ridge and on the spur that dominated the Myola lakes. I left the brigade just after darkness fell. There could be no doubt now. The force that had been sent to recapture Kokoda had been broken and enveloped. The tragic truth was this envelopment would have signified nothing if we anchored our defense on properly prepared positions and had known anything about the general lay of the country in which we were fighting.

All night I kept passing lines of wounded men. It was pitch dark. They shuffled at a snail's pace, holding onto each other in long, pitiful strings. They were in the last stages of exhaustion, but somehow they kept moving. They were constantly sorting and resorting themselves. The strongest, the least seriously hurt, overtook the weaker, the more seriously hurt. At the tail of every string, men would drop off and lie face down in the mud. Then the next string would come along. The leaders would help those who had collapsed into the bushes by the side of the trail.

Some died there. Some recovered a little strength and moved on at the tail end of another string. There were piles of forest refuse that were host to the same phosphorescent fungus I had seen above Dead Kukukuku. Sometimes a man would find a resting place on one of them. One could see the black shape of his body against the diffuse luminescence. He lay upon a pyre of heatless embers.

Sometimes a voice, weary and quiet, would come out of the thicket: 'Dig, I say, dig . . . are you going to Eora? Then tell them to send a light down the trail, will you? Tell them to send a light, digger! Tell them to send a light!'

This was their sole complaint – that, in chasmic darkness, there was no light to guide them.

A time came when I could pass them no longer. I had hoarded a worn-out flashlight against direct emergency. I flashed the light sparingly – only when the trail petered out into a clay scarp, or when there was a log crossing. A line of wounded men, 100 yards long, formed up behind me. The man who walked at my back, his hand on my shoulder, had been shot twice in the chest. Behind him was a man with shrapnel in his forearm and thigh. Every now and then I would stop and turn around and flash on the light to encourage them. They saw nothing by its light that would help them, but it gave them heart. They were led by a man with a light!

After two hours the flashlight battery gave out.

The man who had been shot in the chest said: 'I'm pretty tired. I think I'll wait till daylight.' I gave him a nip out of my brandy flask and he was asleep, lying in the arsenic weed, before I had straightened up from bending over him. I started to cry. The tears rolled down my face, burning. Now there was no light. The line fell away, disintegrated. I was alone.

Just before dawn I met up with a patrol going out to reconnoiter the Kagi Ridge, and traveled with them for a time. They were raw troops and moved very clumsily and noisily. We at last reached a ridge opposite a Japanese position. The Japanese had built a long line of decoy fires just beyond the crest.

The patrol had orders to take up a position at the junction of the spur and the main ridge and from there observe and report enemy dispositions. I stayed with them until just before sunrise. I was very tired and irritable. Their noisiness annoyed and frightened me. It was a relief to be away on my own.

Recollection of the next day is very confused. My cough was troublesome and breathing seemed to be getting even more painful. I didn't know it then, but I had a dose of pneumonia.

The battle remained without form. By now practically the entire available force of Australians had been thrown in, and one by one their main positions were overwhelmed by the enemy. I don't think that the Japanese were much superior numerically, but they contrived to be superior numerically wherever it counted. Position after position was abandoned because it was held to be in danger of being 'surrounded'. At every stage the enemy avoided frontal attack.

We had no fresh troops. At no stage did we ever have fresh troops. Every man who took part in the battle for the Owen-Stanleys was exhausted by a march over the range and by living conditions in such camps as Myola. Worse than that, what forces we had were being fed in piecemeal, and defeated in detail. The enemy was completely in command of the situation.

Early in the afternoon I got back on the trail, still congested by streams of wounded, retreating remnants of units, and by fleeing native carriers. I reached Eora village about nine o'clock at night. The natives were still bringing in stretcher cases. Walking wounded were lying or sitting in the mud about the dressing station waiting their turn for attention. I made a halfhearted attempt to help the orderlies for awhile but had to give up.

Word came through that a general withdrawal had been ordered. This meant that most of our forward supply dumps would have to be abandoned – and now there was no limit on rations. Everybody who wanted to eat, ate his fill.

Even though I had not had a meal for 48 hours, I was not particularly interested in food – until I started to eat. Ten minutes or so after cramming down a messtin full of hot rice and beef, I got ravenously hungry. In the next hour I stowed away two cans of army stew, two packages of army biscuits, liberally spread with cheese and apricot jam, and washed down this gluttonous meal with about three pints of strong tea. I began to feel well – wonderful! The army biscuits had just been broken out and were like iron. My mouth was sore and bled from chewing. I slept for an hour, woke up hungry, and ate more biscuits and jam. Then I wrapped up in three wet blankets and didn't stir for six hours.

Among reactions to exhaustion this was a new one. But, healthy or not, I felt almost fit next morning, and the cough was easier.

Wilmot came in about 10 o'clock in the morning with a story of complete collapse down front. We discussed the situation and decided the only thing to do was to get back to Moresby with the story as fast as possible. We also heard about the Japanese landing at Milne Bay and that the position of the United States marines on Guadalcanal was critical.

The affair out here – now that we had failed to retake Kokoda – was becoming of secondary importance. The remnants of the force would probably withdraw to the Moresby perimeter, and present the Japs with the problem of feeding through enough men to create a sizable diversion.

Next morning Parer put up another extraordinary performance lugging his camera and gear out of Eora. He threw away all his personal equipment – not even keeping as much as a spare pair of socks. Even so, he had too much weight. A few miles up the trail he threw away the leather case and accessories of his Newman camera. Then the tripod went. Then a Graflex still camera. But he clung grimly to the Newman and his exposed film – staggering with weakness, pale as a ghost, and smiling quietly to himself.

'An army in retreat, my boy,' he said, pausing and bobbing his head at the pitiful procession strung out along the trail. 'Not very pretty, is it? I wonder when we'll start to win this war? I've seen so many retreats. Greece was a picnic compared with this.'

No, it was not a pretty sight. At Eora the wounded had been like clots of flies round the dressing station. They were forever moving restlessly in the mud, and the yellowish rain pelted down on them. The dressing station was a hut with a partition across the middle. One side was reserved for the dying and the other for an operating theater and surgical ward.

The surgeons performed amputations during the night in the light of flashlights held by orderlies. A canvas stretcher covered by a sheet dipped in disinfectant served as an operating table. The surgeons worked kneeling. There was one mercy – a plentiful supply of anesthetics.

The only cases that could expect more than perfunctory dressing were those completely immobilized by the nature of their wounds – mostly men shot through the abdomen or head. Limb wounds, unless very severe, were not considered to immobilize the soldier. If with the aid of a stick he could prop

203

himself upright, he had to make his own way back.

It is surprising how much it takes to immobilize a completely determined man. Many did not wait at Eora for attention, but pushed resolutely through toward Templeton's Crossing and Myola. They knew they had no chance of getting stretcher bearers, and they preferred to take their chance of dying by the side of the trail to the certainty of falling into Japanese hands if they gave up the struggle to keep moving.

The night I came back from Isurava I passed a man who had had his leg blown off just below the knee by a mortar bomb. He had ligatured the stump, applied two shell dressings, and wrapped the remainder of the leg in an old copra sack. He crawled and hopped vigorously. He said he was quite strong enough to reach Eora.

An hour after leaving Eora for Templeton's Crossing, 48 hours later, I passed the same man. He had obtained a dressing at the aid post and gone on. I offered to try to round up stretcher bearers for him, but he said fiercely: 'If you can get bearers, then get them for some other poor bastard! There are plenty worse off than me.'

At Eora I saw a 20-year-old redheaded boy with shrapnel in his stomach. He kept muttering to himself about not being able to see the blasted Japs. When Eora was to be evacuated, he knew he had very little chance of being shifted back up the line. He called to me, confidentially: 'Hey, dig, bend down a minute. Listen . . . I think us blokes are going to be left when they pull out. Will you do us a favor? *Scrounge us a tommy gun from somewhere, will you?*'

It was not bravado. You could see that by looking in his eyes. He just wanted to see a Jap before he died. That was all.

Such things should have been appalling. They were not appalling. One accepted them calmly. They were jungle war – the most merciless war of all.

I was convinced for all time of the dignity and nobility of common men. I was convinced for all time that common men have a pure and shining courage when they fight for what they believe to be a just cause.

That which was fine in these men outweighed and made

trivial all that was horrible in their plight. I cannot explain it except to say that they were at all times cheerful and helped one another. They never gave up the fight. They never admitted defeat. They never asked for help.

I felt proud to be of their race and cause, bitterly ashamed to be so nagged by the trivial ills of my own flesh. I wondered if *all* men, when they had endured so much that exhausted nerves would no longer give response, were creatures of the spirit, eternal and indestructible as stars.

On the hills above Templeton's Crossing we parted with Parer. He decided, on hearing that 1,500 feet of fresh film had been dropped for him at Myola, to stay and photograph the retreat. Apologetically he asked if we could leave him a spare shirt, a pair of socks, and some quinine! He clutched the rain-soaked Newman in one hand and his cans of exposed film in the other.

I think Parer must be a genius. It is certain that he is a man of immense character. He is a devout Roman Catholic. I think I understand, now, the quality that makes him say his prayers without fail, night and morning, wherever he is.

One night – at Skin Dewai, I think – he said his prayers kneeling in a hut where 50 rough, tough, cursing commandos were going to bed. Someone, who didn't notice, called out: 'I say, Parer . . . '

Parer looked up. 'Just a minute,' he said mildly, in a clear, penetrating voice, 'I am saying my prayers.'

There was silence until he had finished – and no word of comment.[1]

[1] On September 24, 1944, when this book was in galleys, the following notice appeared in the New York *Times*:

'Damien Parer, 33 years old, Paramount News war correspondent, has been reported by the Navy Department as having been killed in action by enemy machine-gun fire on Sept. 17 while filming front-line operations at Peleliu Island, east of the Philippines . . . '

CHAPTER 16

LAW OF NATURE

WILMOT and I went back to Moresby in the second week of September. Parer stayed with the troops to film the retreat. It was a hard, fast trip out – 60 hours from Myola to the roadhead with the first 'eyewitnesses'. At the end of it, I wasn't much use to myself or anyone else. From a professional point of view I had timed my run poorly. The climax of the campaign was still to come. The battles that would be remembered were still to be fought.

Near Uberi, they were already manhandling the 25-pounders into position to cover Eoribaiwa Ridge. I doubted the necessity of falling back so far, for I was certain much of the range could be successfully defended by a small body of competent jungle troops. Yet news of local defeats kept coming through.

At Eoribaiwa, we met the 2/27th Battalion of the Australian Imperial Force going up the line. I remember them unkindly because someone stole my only shirt from the stake where it was drying by the cookhouse fire, and I arrived at the roadhead clad in a pair of pants and a tin hat.

Moresby was very jumpy. Big things had been happening elsewhere, and to anyone who had never been over the range, the approach of the Japanese was disturbing.

The first of the 'big things' elsewhere had been a Japanese landing at Milne Bay on August 26. Milne Bay, 250 miles to the southeast at the tip of the island, controlled the seaward approaches of Moresby, and the Japs needed it before they could attack the key base. A fierce touch-and-go battle between the Jap invaders and the Australian defenders had raged in coastal jungle and coconut groves for a week. In spite of the numerical superiority of the defending troops, the work of low-flying fighter aircraft was probably the deciding factor in breaking the stubborn Japanese onslaught. Australian P-40's and American P-39's ranged up and down at treetop level and did bloody execution at the enemy's bridgehead near Moebuli, on the north side of the bay.

It was evident that the enemy completely miscalculated the strength of the defenders. On the night of August 30, a Japanese cruiser and eight destroyers landed substantial reinforcements, but even this was not enough. Moresby's bombers about the same time beat off and dispersed another convoy, sinking a gunboat and a transport. By September 2, the battle had reached the mopping-up stage, and bulldozers were burying the piles of rotting Japanese dead.

Milne Bay was notable as the very first considerable land victory won by Allied troops against the Japanese. The failure of the enemy to consolidate positions, and their eventual annihilation, robbed the advance of Japanese patrols-in-force across the Owen-Stanleys of any significance – unless disclosure of Australian unpreparedness to fight in the jungle could be classed as significant. If Milne Bay had fallen, the patrols might have given valuable support to a frontal sea assault on Moresby, by harassing in the rear of the garrison. With Milne Bay still in our hands, they were merely a nuisance factor.

Moresby was never seriously threatened by the Japanese advance across the range per se. It could have been threatened gravely had the enemy been able to launch an attack by airborne troops, but the qualitative superiority of American bombers and the increasing numerical strength of the Airacobra and P-40 fighter squadrons ruled out the chances of such an attack.

The miserable patrols who doggedly followed the retreat of the exhausted and unsupported Australian troops after the fall of Isurava and Myola never constituted any peril to Moresby. Once they got within range of field artillery they were

207

finished. They had to die or to get out – or both. In the end they did both.

I have always been annoyed by the widespread impression that 'the Japs got within 30 miles of Moresby before they were stopped.' The Japanese did get within 30 miles of Moresby – but in such numbers, with such equipment and such forlorn hope of support and supply that they might just as well have been within 300 miles of it. Their halting near the village of Eoribaiwa was not a feat of defense. It was a law of nature.

The Owen-Stanley range, trumpeted as 'impenetrable', proved impenetrable – at least for sufficient troops, artillery and supplies to attack a strongly held garrison area.

Similarly, I have always been annoyed by the prevailing belief that the Australian troops rallied magnificently and, beating the Jap at his own game, fought their way inch by inch back to Kokoda and eventually to Buna, Gona and Sanananda, in face of desperate opposition. The Australian soldier needs no fictions nor propaganda to justify him as a fighting man.

The Japanese fell back through the range from Eoribaiwa because their efforts to establish supply were doomed to failure from the start. They fell back because they were exhausted, diseased and starving. They had no combat air support, no artillery except a few mountain guns hauled in pieces up and down muddy precipices, no transport planes to drop them food.

When the Milne Bay force held tight, when Japanese pilots failed to break the Allied air blockade, the Battle of Moresby was won, and at the same time the fate of the Buna-Gona bridgehead was sealed. From then on it was only a matter of time – time to have a second stab at recapturing Kokoda on the plan that had failed before, time to edge troops for flanking attacks along the northeast coast from Milne Bay, time to let the enemy rot soft for mopping up.

I did not see either the second advance of the Australians to Kokoda and beyond or the four months' campaign by Australian and American troops to liquidate the Japanese at Buna,

Gona and Sanananda. The first combat units of the United States army arrived in New Guinea just as I left. In October, 1942, I was invalided to Australia and in December assigned to the South Pacific area. For information of the sequence of events in New Guinea thereafter, I have had to depend upon official communiqués and the dispatches of fellow war correspondents.

The facts of the campaign were fully and accurately reported, according to scores of soldiers to whom I have talked since. It is, however, open to question whether the campaign was fairly and accurately interpreted by the world press. In the first place it was interpreted as a great tactical victory. In the second place it was interpreted as having weighty strategical importance. Both interpretations are disputable.

At the time the original landings were made at Buna, there were certainly not more than 20,000 Japanese troops in the whole of New Guinea, inclusive of the regiments that landed and pushed across the range. Not more than 3,000 men were used in the march against Moresby. When this force was drained by the country, the remnants fell back to the coastal strip on the farther side of the mountains and prepared for a 'suicide defense'.

The Japanese force that defended Buna-Gona-Sanananda was officially estimated in November to comprise between 5,000 and 8,000 men, including a few reinforcements brought in by barge.

Against them were deployed elements of the 7th and 6th divisions of the Australian Imperial Force with Australian militia in support, and the elements of the 32nd Division of the United States army. The total strength was more than 25,000 men.

Allied planes by now held almost complete control of the air, closely blockading the Japanese, ceaselessly bombing and strafing them, and protecting our air transport of troops and supplies.

Artillery and tanks, particularly in the later stages of the campaign, were freely used against the enemy. Yet despite all these advantages, it took from October until January to evict him from his main system of defenses. Further weeks elapsed before the remnants were cleared from the improvised positions to which they retired after the fall of Buna, Gona and Sanan004anda. It is difficult to see cause for jubilation in this performance, judged tactically.

It is equally difficult to see that the recapture of the airfield sites about Buna, which the command in New Guinea had ignored consistently for nine months, and which only the Japanese had been enterprising enough to develop after their landing, was a matter of great strategic importance at that stage of the war in New Guinea.

The enemy had failed at Milne Bay in a major move against Moresby. He had shown that no troops, however tough, could attack Moresby overland from north-coast bases. He had been forced to acknowledge Allied air superiority in New Guinea skies.

What, then, was the reason for energetically attacking Buna, Gona and Sanananda with 25,000 troops untrained in jungle warfare and dependent upon difficult land and air supply routes? The same result could undoubtedly have been achieved by continued air blockade and by maintaining holding forces until such time as a full-scale amphibious operation could have been mounted from Milne Bay, by now firmly in our hands.

If education and experiment – the trial-and-error method of solving the problem of how to fight the Japanese – were the motive behind the Papuan venture, the Australian and American troops paid dearly.

The 21st Brigade, A.I.F., went into action 2,000 strong and came out with 400 fit men. The 18th Brigade at Milne Bay emerged a mere skeleton after the August fight and its subsequent march against the eastern flank of the Japanese earthworks at Buna. Exhaustion, malaria and neuroses decimated the 32nd American Division.

The tragedy of the campaign was not a tragedy of men required to make bayonet charges against deep foxholes held by a fanatically brave enemy. It was a tragedy of men unprepared for the peculiar rigors of such a life, struggling with bulging eyes and knotted veins to heave their packs and weapons to the top of dizzy sawtooth ridges; of men shivering in bitter mountain cold, sweating and tortured by insects in steamy swamps; of men whose fiber was made rugged by the strain of peering and listening in inscrutable bush for the enemy.

Communiqués recorded the fall of one jungle village after another, each a bomb-blasted heap of sticks. They recorded territory regained, and prognosticated repeatedly that the enemy was on the point of annihilation. The headlines looked significant. Commentators suggested that the tide had turned, and the sweep might go on to Salamaua, Lae, even Rabaul.

Only the men whose breath rasped on the razorbacks, whose strength was sapped by the everlasting wet heat, filth, mud and discomfort until they were like skeletons covered by yellowing skin, knew that what was happening was not the winning of a great victory. It was only the elimination of a minor expeditionary force, which had been cut off in hostile country by the failure of a wider combined operation planned by the Japanese command.

Yet it would be prejudiced to contend that the Buna-Gona-Sanananda campaign was of no value. It proved on a scale sufficiently large to defy ignorance:

(1) That air power was a dominant factor in island campaigning – so dominant that it could offset a multitude of other sins.

(2) That the Japanese could not, or would not, commit properly balanced and powerful forces at the end of strained lines of communication in New Guinea.

(3) That enemy strategy did not now really envisage holding northeast New Guinea, but that the Japanese were willing and anxious to fight a delaying campaign which would impress the Allies with their desperation and inflict every possible damage.

(4) That Allied ground troops were not yet the man-for-man equal of the Japanese in jungle fighting, and that the training of American and Australian troops needed revolutionary revision.

(5) That for months – possibly even years – the Allied command's only prospect of success against the Japanese in jungle

defenses lay in its ability to concentrate against them an overwhelming weight of war machines – planes, tanks, guns, ships, and transport.

Proof that the lessons were realized was given by later developments.

Until the cost of Buna-Gona-Sanananda was counted, the New Guinea command spoke freely of developing a serious attack against Salamaua and Lae on overland lines of communication. Mopping-up operations at the mouth of the Kumusi and Mambare rivers were undertaken with that object in view. A patient movement of troops west along the north coast persisted until Allied forces were actually within striking distance of Salamaua in the coastal sector.

Yet no attack was launched until September, 1943, nearly a year later, when a properly organized aero-amphibious expedition went to Lae and the tottery structure of the long-strained enemy defense crumbled.

Allied concentration on land warfare pleased the Japanese. They reacted smartly to the Buna-Gona affair, seeing a chance that defense of the northeast coast of New Guinea would pay dividends beyond their wildest dreams. They began industriously to develop bases farther west along the coast, from Finschhaven to Hollandia. They endeavored to reinforce the Lae and Salamaua garrisons, both of which sprang into activity.

Harassing tactics by the ghostly guerrillas of the Markham River and the Kuper Mountains had made the enemy timid, but the indifferent performance of the Allies in Papua gave them fresh encouragement. The result was a thrust by 3,000 Japanese troops up the Salamaua road against Wau.

The guerrillas were no longer in any condition to put up much of a fight. They retreated, making waspish sallies, but the Japanese came steadily on. They were within sight of the Wau airfield when New Guinea Force did a little 'reacting' on its own account. With control of the air assured, it sent in the whole 17th Brigade, A.I.F., by plane to Wau.

Here was something that suited the Australian soldier down to the ground – open, rolling, grassy country, a reasonable climate and plenty of Japs. The first comers leaped from the planes and were in action in five minutes. Airborne 25-pounders were supporting them within an hour or two. There was no question of not seeing the enemy. It was a 'fair' fight. The Japanese were cut to ribbons in a few days, and the last of them bolted shrieking into the jungle from blood-soaked Wandumi Hill.

The Wau move was the soundest and most enterprising maneuver yet made in New Guinea. It was risky, unexpected, positive and well timed. But it fizzled out once the Japanese were in the jungle again – down in the steamy, dripping greenness of Mubo Gorge. The advance to Mubo and beyond, the battles on Mount Tambu and among the confused foothills, later of the Ramu valley and the Finisterre range, were an Owen-Stanleys campaign all over again – with one difference. The Australians were at last beginning to learn – not in camps but by hard experience in actual warfare. The Americans learned on the seacoast and on New Britain.

Men with enough guts can be taught to put up with almost anything, and no one could accuse the American or Australian soldiers of lacking guts. Besides, they were spurred by the humiliation of being outwitted by an enemy they regarded as despicable. And they had discovered a valuable truth: in spite of the excellence with which the Japanese army is designed as a machine to perform a specific type of task, the Japanese soldier is himself stupid and his leadership in adversity as unintelligent as it is courageous. A Japanese post will die to a man rather than surrender; but a Japanese post will seldom improvise and act quickly enough in crisis to enable it to live to a man and succeed.

Even so, and notwithstanding the Allies' improving capacity in jungle, it is unlikely that Salamaua would have been recaptured without many months of extreme attrition and the final blow of the Lae landings. All else being equal, it is incomparably easier to defend jungle positions than to attack them.

Although this fact must have been plain from the beginning, endeavors to establish a 'land front' in New Guinea died hard. For a long time engineers battled to make the Lakekamu route work as a supply line. A road was built. Then the necessity vanished. The jungle closed in again.

Air power continued to win the New Guinea war while the troops and their leaders slowly digested bitter doses of jungle lore. The Battle of the Bismarck Sea – in which 30,000 Japanese troops on their way to Lae died by the bombs and bullets of irresistible American and Australian bombers and fighters – doomed enemy hopes of holding the Huon Gulf and the peninsula.

A final coup by the Allied forces, however, awaited the evolution of methods far different from any yet employed. I was to watch the evolution of those methods elsewhere.

CHAPTER 17

THE PROBLEM OF THE PRIMITIVE

THE close view is seldom or never the broad view. I left New Guinea depressed, ill with malaria and the aftereffects of pneumonia. Too easily remembered were the personal tragedies that result from errors of calculation in warfare. It was hard, in those days, to find much right with our way of fighting the Japanese in the jungle.

Yet, in spite of the Owen-Stanley debacle and the costly Buna-Gona affair, the war did not seem to be going badly. The Japanese mistake at Milne Bay and the progress of American sea, land and air forces in the Solomons showed that strategic successes might be achieved even from a welter of tactical errors. The enemy, too, could blunder grievously.

During eight weeks of convalescence and another ten weeks awaiting accreditation to the United States Pacific fleet, I tried hard to sort out the lessons I had learned from nine months in New Guinea. Overshadowing everything else was an impression of the predicament of Australian and American soldiers campaigning against specialized coolie troops in terrain so rugged that machines, technological superiority, could give little help in the actual fighting.

It was an old story, a story as old as war between haves and have-nots. The legions of Caesar fighting the skulking Germani were in like case in the dank forests of the Rhine 2,000 years ago. Observers of other times might have watched the same factors at work when the English redcoats met France's Indian allies in the Canadian wars, or when the British line regiments fought the Americans during the Revolutionary War.

The primitive warrior always has the edge on the civilized

soldier if he can contrive equality of arms and the wilds for a battlefield. Against primitive warrior virtues, the soldier of civilization pits superior individual and group intelligence in combat, and a more accurate use of weapons. His margin of skill, intelligence, adaptability and initiative is an important factor in any single engagement, because it minimizes his combat casualty rate and increases the casualty rate of the enemy. But it does not necessarily constitute of itself a campaign-winning factor.

When I came out of New Guinea I knew that if we were to win the Pacific war, we would have to do better in the jungle than we had done. How? Was the answer a revolution in training methods, designed to build a *corps d'élite* of jungle fighters able to match the Japanese endurance of tropical campaigning conditions? I recalled the performance of the New Guinea Volunteer Rifles and their commando understudies – the only group of Allied troops who so far had outfought and outguessed the Japanese – and I thought they had the answer. But in time wider experience showed me that molding human material was by no means the complete answer. If it had been, then the outlook for the Allies would have been black. They would have had to debase their armies to a coolie standard of living and a coolie standard of endurance before they could hope to beat the Japanese. Overwhelming material strength, shrewdly directed, had defeated tough, primitive people many times before in history, and the conquerors had not had to 'go native' in the process. But the Japanese held an extra card in their hands in this war. Behind their armies of primitives were modern industries and technology. Their new empire stretched over thousands of miles of the earth's surfaces, with a multiplicity of resources.

Civilized ingenuity might reduce the price in flesh and blood which victory over such a people would cost. But there was a minimum price exacted by hand-to-hand fighting, which must be paid if the Occidental way of life was to survive. The problem was so complex, so vital, that it was intimidating. It was easier and happier to turn from consideration of it to the realm of the broader strategy.

216

Between September, 1942, and January, 1943, the Pacific war reached and passed its first great strategic crisis after the era of Pearl Harbor and Singapore. In these months the United States and to a lesser extent Australia were able to bring against the enemy just enough material strength – and just enough cleverness in the use of it – to contain further Japanese expansion. It was only a fraction of what was to be brought to bear in the future, and that meant the Japanese were henceforward to be permanently on the defensive. As conquerors in their own right, they had shot their bolt. From now on, they could expect to do no better than hang on.

The limitations of Japan's war potential were shown clearly in the nine months that followed the Pearl Harbor coup. That was the time when the enemy high command should have ensured geographical consolidation of its conquests by cutting the Pacific in two and eliminating Australia. Yet they were unable to bring more than four or five divisions against Allied defensive positions in the Central and South Pacific, and they could not undertake the final series of invasions that would have conquered Australia and fitted the keystone into the structure of their new empire.

Surely shortage of warships, troops or arms was not responsible for the failure. After the conquest of Burma and the Indies, the Japanese probably had some 35 or 40 fully equipped divisions available for service in the Pacific. Their fleet was then numerically the equal or superior of the United States Pacific fleet.

On the other hand, at no time in the first year of the war could the Allies have deployed more than 10 partly trained and equipped divisions (approximately eight Australian and two American) for the defense of the whole Australian continent; or have concentrated more than three or four divisions at any one threatened spot. It is doubtful whether more than four American and one New Zealand divisions could have been mustered to defend all the Pacific islands east of the 170th meridian. If the issue had depended upon land power, either alone or even supported by naval power, the garrisons of Australia and the South Pacific would have been overwhelmed.

217

Japan called a halt (1) because she had insufficient merchant shipping to carry and supply large bodies of troops farther afield, and at the same time exploit the resources of her East Indian conquests, (2) because she had underestimated the quality of American air power, which from the first was effective against the timidly used Japanese air force, and (3) because she did not possess the mechanical and technical equipment to consolidate fast and then move on fast.

Looking back on the Malayan, Philippine, East Indian and Papuan campaigns, the Allies could congratulate themselves only on the gallantry of their squandered soldiers. The Japanese could find even less reason for self-congratulation.

The vaunted Japanese navy and its air arm failed to follow up Pearl Harbor and complete the destruction of the United States Pacific battle fleet. By miscalculation and inferior tactics, it botched the Battle of the Coral Sea, the Battle of Midway, the supply of the Guadalcanal occupation force in the second battle of the Solomons in 1942, and supply of the garrisons at Lae and Salamaua in the Bismarck Sea battle early in 1943.

Although the Japanese Zero fighter outflew available Allied fighter types in 1942, the Japanese never managed to maintain enough Zeros on forward airfields to establish defensive air superiority or to use them as a decisive weapon of offense. With few exceptions, the performance of their high-level bombers was poor, probably through shortage or inferiority of bomb sights. The work of their torpedo and dive bombers was certainly accurate and resolute – but often so resolute that the losses sustained were a heavy price for achieving the objective. This was particularly true when the bitter lessons learned from the sinking of the *Prince of Wales* and the *Repulse* brought tactical and technical results, and proper provision was made for fighter escorts and antiaircraft protection of surface craft.

After their first brilliant but long-prepared surprise strokes against Pearl Harbor, the Philippines and Malaya, the Japanese air forces revealed themselves to be inelastic and unintelligent in their handling of tactical problems. They were unvigilant on the ground and were surprised time and again. Furthermore, the quality of their air crews deteriorated steadily as the veterans were killed off.

As a result of these failures, the Allies were able to establish an effective air defense with an absolute minimum of machines. In 1942 a handful of modern planes based on northern Australia, New Guinea and the islands of Oceania inflicted on Japanese shipping and bases an amount of damage quite incommensurate with their relative numerical strength. Early in 1943, when fighter types like the Grumman Hellcat, the Lockheed Lightning, the Spitfire and the Corsair began to operate in useful numbers, an almost unbelievable ratio of air victories over the Japanese was achieved. One American or British combat aircraft downed an average of four or five Japanese planes before it fell. Later the ratio was greater still.

After February, 1943, loss of air control took from Japan all but two hopes of winning the war. She could trust only in the success of her European partners, or else in her own ability to make the reconquest of the Indies and the ultimate reduction of Japan itself so costly that it would be unacceptable to the conscience of Western civilization. The first hope had vanished by the end of the year, but the second hope remained.

For the Allies, the establishment of a coherent defense in the South Pacific had been touch and go. Forced by the Pearl Harbor disaster and a desperate shortage of shipping to work on a shoestring, they had taken appalling risks.

Toward the middle of 1942, the Japanese had consolidated Rabaul and were ready to move down the Solomons chain, threatening the lifeline between the United States and Australia. Their occupation of bases on the Solomon Islands was not contested. The Americans had to content themselves with a counter-occupation in New Caledonia and the New Hebrides. A grim race to build up reserves and develop bases for the next push began. The Americans won – by a short nose.

Reviewing logistic problems of the first year of the Pacific war, a high-ranking naval staff officer at Noumea, then the base of the South Pacific fleet, told me that the American landing on Guadalcanal on August 7, 1942, had been a hazard so desperate that failure would have resulted in a complete collapse of Allied defense in the South Pacific. If consolidation of the landing and maintenance of supplies had proved impossible, the United States fleet would have been forced to withdraw from the Southwest Pacific, abandoning New Caledonia and the New Hebrides – possibly even New Zealand. Everything the United States could at that moment spare for the South Pacific was put into one blow against a vital spot – Guadalcanal.

When the Japanese made a fight on the island, the American fleet lacked tankers and fuel enough to undertake a major action at sea. There were not enough ships to supply the requirements of the hard-pressed Guadalcanal force, let alone build up defensive strength farther south. Losses of merchant tonnage were so high that the land and air forces were able to carry on only because of small, decisive cargoes brought in by transport planes flying from the New Hebrides to Henderson Field without fighter cover. Merchant ships that succeeded in running the gauntlet were stripped on arrival of every useful article of equipment and made the voyage home mere shells. Every small craft that could float and sail was mobilized to carry cargo and troops. Guadalcanal might not have been a battleground for continental-sized armies but it was a battleground upon which a very great crisis was resolved by the boldness and enterprise of the United States navy and by the gallantry of the marine division that seized and held the island.

Early in April, 1943, I presented my credentials at Admiral Halsey's fleet headquarters in Noumea, New Caledonia. The era of shortage was at an end. A squadron of capital ships and a heavy aircraft carrier were lying in harbor. The wharves were jammed with merchant shipping, much of it new and big, while other ships waited their turn for unloading at the roadsteads. Hundreds of acres of new iron-roofed storehouses gleamed in the morning sun. The air was full of the drone of planes. The cobbled streets of the little town roared with streams of jeeps and trucks that squirted exhaust fumes so virulent that the leaves of the shade trees were oily and wilting. The pavements were crowded with well fed, well-clothed

American soldiers, sailors, marines and airmen. The suburbs were grafted with canvas towns and satellite settlements of quonset huts.

The contrast between this panorama of plenty and the memory of the hungry frontline over New Guinea's mountains startled me. Looking back on the lean days at Moresby I wondered if these thousands of jeeps, trucks, tractors and cranes, these hundreds of ships and aircraft, these scores of acres of storehouses and tens of thousands of back area organizers, tradesmen, technicians, clerks and laborers, were necessary to maintain beyond the far horizon a phantom battlefront where a few battalions of combat troops were grimly digging out of their holes and killing a handful of jibbering Japanese entrenched in the forest. But that was how the new Pacific war was to be fought.

For a while I was quartered with other latecoming correspondents in a tumble-down hotel so dirty, uncomfortable and picturesque it might have been built and decayed to the specifications of Maugham or Conrad. The food was scanty, of poor quality, and execrably cooked. The place was infested with spiders, bedbugs, cockroaches and lazy Tonkinese servants. In short, it had preserved the status quo. No one but the island French much love or admire the island French.

Later, by dint of pressure and protest, we obtained a transfer to the administrative headquarters settlement a few miles out of town and there lived in great luxury, with lashings of drink, food that would have done credit to a first-class restaurant, ice, showerbaths, and beds with mattresses.

Here, the war might be compared to an iceberg. Only one tenth of it projected into a turbulent upper atmosphere of danger, suffering and privation. The rest lay deep in a calm element of industry and routine.

An opportunity existed here that was lacking in New Guinea. I could study the anatomy of a modern war, rather than the physiology of a jungle fight. Among those who contributed a great deal to my re-education were the staff supply officers for the South Pacific under Admiral Cobb. They quoted me fabulous figures of the quantity of gasoline, oil, machine parts, building materials, food, ammunition, clothing and other essentials necessary to police an ocean. The aeroamphibious war envisaged by the United States, they said, used 17 or 18 men in the services of supply to keep one man shooting at the enemy. Modern war was so expensive of material that subsistence cargoes – the food and clothing of the fighting men – were less than 5 per cent of the total supplies. The enemy subsisted on less than $2\frac{1}{2}$ per cent of his total supplies.

These men gave factual substance to my cloudy realization of the immensity and complexity of the battlefield. Their figures revealed the foundations that had to be laid before the defense against Japan could be stabilized and a counteroffensive planned. Cities had to be built in wildernesses, mountains leveled, swamps drained, ports equipped, airfields scooped out of jungles, thousands of miles of road pushed through unprofitable lands. The soldier with his man-killing machines was merely the cutting edge of the tool of conquest, a tool as complicated as the body of a mechanical civilization itself.

Because I had not yet seen what the machines can accomplish, I was disturbed by the boundless faith that Americans seemed to put in the machine – and in the weight of resources. They believed that the cost of waging war, in terms of human life and suffering, must always be kept to the irreducible minimum, regardless of the expenditure of time, material and industrial effort. They hoped by the development and use of machines to lessen the human cost of war.

Such is the ethical inheritance of nations that for generations have possessed the good things of the earth. They can afford such an inheritance. But in a war with nations that have not for generations possessed the good things, a code that sets a higher value upon individual human life and comfort than upon any material product of human society may be perilous, if enviable.

The Japanese value human life and comfort only in so far as they can contribute to the attainment of a racial objective – the domination of the Far East and the Pacific by Japan. The human being is no less, and no more, expendable than the machine. Both exist simply to perform a task. Where choice of preserving man or machine must be made, it falls logically upon whichever can contribute most to performance.

Unfortunately the realities of conquest are not influenced by ethics. It might as well be admitted frankly that any nation that wages war and at the same time observes the ethics of a prosperous democracy is necessarily fighting under a material, if not a moral, handicap.

Too much preoccupation with humanity can defeat its own ends. By contrast with Australian troops, Americans in the South Pacific were luxuriously fed, clothed, housed, equipped and doctored. One envied them, and the wealth of a nation that could do so much for the comfort of its fighting men even when the supply position was critical. But one could not envy the lot of American fighting men who would eventually have to plow through stinking swamps and jungles, and prod the enemy out of his holes at bayonet point. For in spite of all that machines might do to 'soften' the enemy, they could not harden American men to the filth, hunger, tension and unutterable discomfort of warfare in the tropics.

Part Four

PATTERN FOR VICTORY

THE costly defensive success won by Australian and American troops in New Guinea toward the end of 1942 and at the beginning of 1943 proved that, as a general rule, white armies were not and could never be the man-to-man equal of the Japanese in prolonged jungle campaigning. If Japan was to be defeated, some grand strategy must be evolved wherein jungle campaigning would be reduced to a minimum. Victory in Guadalcanal had given a clue to what could be achieved in the Pacific by combined operations. A plan was born, and its first postulate was selective concentration of overwhelming material strength against the enemy in his key island strongholds. On a modest scale, elements of the United States army, navy and marines tried out this plan in the New Georgia group in July, 1943. It came within an ace of failure because once again the human element had not been trained to fight the jungle as well as it had been trained to fight the Jap. But for all that, the New Georgia campaign was the beginning of Pacific victory. The cruel, experimental phase of the war was done. In the next year United States forces swept through the Gilberts, the Marshalls and the Marianas, and Japan came within range of the most deadly aerial weapon ever devised – the Boeing Super Fortress. Far to the south, Japanese armies, isolated by man's mechanical conquest of geography, were left to rot behind the disjointed fragments of the green armor that had been our protection and their undoing.

CHAPTER 18

PASSAGE TO GUADALCANAL

EXPLORATION of the labyrinthine foundations of a war that obviously could not take a decisive turn for a year or more left me with many undigested facts and uneliminated fallacies. When in Noumea I attended the movies every night in the marine camp below the headquarters settlement. It helped me to forget the reality of steam shovels liquidating mountains, planes crossing oceans on schedules that read like rural train services, and tonnages with strings of ciphers that made the imagination giddy. But even at the movies one was not entirely free from feeling of being present at the birth of a juggernaut destined, before its life was done, to crush half the Orient.

The shows began at nightfall. The audience sat in rows on a gentle hillside above the bay beach. Soon after dark, the sound of a powerful motor approached from seaward. If one peered hard, one could see through the new night a fantastic and horrible shape wallowing into the shallows from deep water. It would rear itself up, splutter, cough, and start roaring again in a different key. Then it would crawl across the beach and mount the slope, showing itself to be an amphibious tank. The great machine would roll on until it reached a vantage point directly in front of the screen. It would there stop. Five heads would emerge from the superstructure, five behinds wriggle themselves into positions of comfort, and five nonchalant young men yield themselves for two blissful hours to shadowy allure.

The tank that attended the movies started by stimulating my imagination, and ended by haunting my dreams. In the end I transferred to another show three miles away and took my doses of escapism without distraction.

The South Pacific war was in the doldrums. More than three months before, the Americans had mopped up the Japs on Guadalcanal, the Australians and Americans had fumigated the last foxhole in northern Papua, the 17th Brigade of the Australian Imperial Force had written an end in sweat, blood and resolution to the Bulolo valley defense. Lastly, American and Australian air forces, now at adequate numerical strength, had annihilated the great convoy bound for Lae in the Battle of the Bismarck Sea.

November to February had been good months. If the tide had not yet turned, it was at least slack water. The balance sheet showed a satisfactory credit. General MacArthur claimed that 15,000 Japanese had been wiped out in the Owen-Stanleys and in the siege of the Buna forts. Another 3,000 or 4,000 had been accounted for in the push from Wau over the Kupers. Three thousand Japanese bodies had been buried at Milne Bay. The Bismarck Sea cost the enemy 30,000 drowned, and the Second Battle of the Solomons another 30,000. Japanese casualties in Guadalcanal land fighting were about 35,000.

The most cautious assessment indicated that 100,000 Japanese had perished from Allied operations which were, in a strategic sense, only local counterattacks. No announcements of Allied casualties were made, but they were probably not more than 15,000 killed and wounded in the whole series of battles, although a large number of sick had to be added to this figure.

Against any enemy but the Japanese, this ratio of manpower loss would have been significant. But the Japanese had said, and I believe they meant it, that they were prepared to lose 10,000,000 men to win their war. At this rate, 1,500,000 Americans and Australians must be killed or maimed to cover the enemy's stake.

It was no use looking in the blood ledger for war-winning figures. It never was, and probably never will be. The real signs were in the tallies for sea and air. The campaigns in

New Guinea and the Solomons had cost the Japanese at this stage at least 1,500 bombers and fighters, exclusive of operational losses which are always high on island airfields and long ocean flights. We had lost not more than 200 machines in combat.

At sea, the figures were less reassuring. In naval operations directly connected with the Solomons campaign the Americans claimed to have sunk 2 Japanese battleships, 12 cruisers and 26 destroyers, and to have sent to the bottom 100,000 tons of merchant shipping. They admitted the loss of 2 aircraft carriers, 13 cruisers and 15 destroyers. No figures of merchant shipping losses were given.

Even cursory analysis of the actions in which all this damage was inflicted and sustained revealed air power as the Allies' potent weapon – air power based on technical superiority of planes, pilots and ground organization. If the Japanese had had technical air parity in New Guinea, we could not have taken our troops over the Owen-Stanley range by air or sneaked them up the coast in small craft. We could not have recaptured Buna or developed any campaign on the north coast. The Japanese holding forces would have received substantial relief. They would not have been starving and decimated by disease when their last elements fled.

If the Japanese had been able to deploy enough fighters, the 17th Brigade could never have landed on Wau airfield and thereafter been supplied mainly by plane transport. If the prodigiously gallant marine and navy fliers whose planes were based on Henderson Field had not been able to shoot down four or five Japanese planes for every one they lost themselves, the United States marines and the infantry regiments that reinforced them on Guadalcanal might have been pushed back into the sea or starved out.

Aircraft alone blasted the Bismarck Sea armada. Aircraft inflicted by far the greater proportion of damage on enemy surface craft in the series of air-sea engagements that finally smashed the 'Tokyo Express' bringing reinforcements and supplies from Bougainville to Guadalcanal. Only in the Second Battle of the Solomons had the warship re-established its value as a fighting machine – and even then planes had to finish the job the cruisers began. The airman had had the honors in the past, and his uses in strategy pointed the way for the future. One wondered what air power could not do, and whether it would be as decisive on the offensive as it had been on the defensive.

There were signs. Every now and then the battle fleet would put to sea, at about an hour's notice, 'on information received.' Sometimes correspondents accompanied it, feeling extremely expendable at their battle stations on the searchlight platforms of battleships and cruisers – or underfoot on the bridges of destroyers. Nothing happened except abortive submarine alarms or reports of prowling enemy aircraft. I was reminded of the aphorism that when strategy fails, naval battles ensue. The trips were interesting but provided no headlines. The naval correspondents' theme song for the first six months of 1943 might well have been: 'And what did we see? We saw the sea!'

There was more profit in watching the sky. The Japanese had whistled up air reinforcements to Rabaul – either preparing to resume the offensive or in expectation that we would assume it. In close succession they had staged two raids employing 100 bombers each, one on Port Moresby and one on a concentration of American shipping off Koli Point, Guadalcanal.

More and more reports came in of raids by Allied aircraft on the Japanese bases of Vila on Kolombangara Island and of Munda on New Georgia. Hundred-plane raids and concentrations of shipping do not just happen by chance. Nor are bases bombed as frequently as Vila and Munda without reason.

Several of us decided it might be wise to move north and leave the battle fleet to its heavy contrapuntal maneuvers. However, before anything came of the decision, the South Pacific command passed the word – 'We're going into *New Georgia.*' 'Confidentially,' said the very high staff officer who broke the news to the daily press conference, 'we don't expect a great deal of trouble. The Japs must be pretty bomb happy already, and the navy will prepare the way. Still, you never can tell.'

Trouble or no trouble, an invasion of New Georgia was a very significant move. First, it was the initial step in some sort of counteroffensive. There was no defensive compulsion about moving on New Georgia.

Second, it was at least a partial committal to the so-called island-hopping strategy. At that time the public of both the United States and Australia was very concerned about 'island hopping'. The prospect of a long hard war, with territory gradually regained and a stubborn enemy gradually weakened, held little attraction for peoples who had only recently seen a round won for the first time. They were in better mood for a slapdash raid on Tokyo than a limited operation that would cost the Japanese 100 times as much damage. The expediences of democratic politics and of global strategy are uneasy bed-fellows.

Third, it was clear that enough troops and equipment were available to make an invasion of New Georgia something of a test case. There had been time to make the weight of growing air ascendancy tell against limited objectives. If, from the bitter experiences of Papua and Guadalcanal, the Allied command had evolved a basic formula for dealing with the Japanese concept of defense, New Georgia was as good a place as any to try it out.

I was determined to see this vitally important experiment on New Georgia and obtained permission to travel on one of the destroyers escorting a convoy to the operational base on Guadalcanal. I drew a 'gold-plater,' one of the new, extremely lethal ships designed for Pacific service. It was good to get aboard and exchange the atmosphere of ponderous administrative dignity that pervaded fleet headquarters for the simple courtesy and good fellowship that seem to flourish best among men who are not too important to be shot at.

Passengers on a destroyer are damnable pests both to themselves and the ship, but I enjoyed my ride to Guadalcanal with a company of deepwater men. Until the third day the passage was uneventful. There were a couple of submarine alarms that came to nothing, and the familiar report that enemy long-range reconnaissance planes were out.

When I came on deck the third morning, the feeling was different. The ships were running into the 'bad air' south of the Solomons. Additional warships – one of them an auxiliary aircraft carrier – were cruising in formation far astern, barely visible in the powder-blue haze that veiled the edges of a calm sea. The transports and freighters pounded along majestically in two columns, their wakes boiling white. From the destroyer's decks they looked like floating castles of steel washed by the sea. They were tall and alarmingly conspicuous among the thin, vicious little ships that shepherded them.

By midmorning the few friendly reconnaissance planes that had accompanied us most of the way were joined by flights of stubby winged Grumman fighters that wheeled, climbed and dived with the aimless industry of bluebottle flies. The weather was still and humid, and a faint breeze was blowing from the northwest. Just before midday the ship's buzzers sounded general quarters – a flat, harrying noise broadcast by amplifiers.

The sailors in blue dungarees went without apparent haste to the guns and torpedo tubes. The turret guns fore and aft slewed skyward and started a slow, restless swinging. There is something singularly inexorable and terrifying about naval guns ranging. They look more merciless than any other weapon. A Filipino boy with a soft, slurred voice came up to me and said: 'Cap'n's compliments, sir, and would you care to step up to the bridge and watch?'

The ship had been cruising her zigzag course at a steady 15 knots. Suddenly, speed was rung. The stern sank down as if to get a firmer grip on the water. She leaped forward, heeling over as she turned. Two wide bow waves feathered out over the blue-green swell.

Enemy planes were reported astern at 5,000 feet. There was a cloudbank to shield us. A dense puff of white smoke shot from the destroyer's forward stack. The captain's heels left the deck.

'White smoke from Number 1,' he roared. 'Stop it at once!'

232

The offending stack gurgled and subsided. The smoke dissolved.

I watched the second hand of my wrist watch. Two minutes passed . . . three, four, five. Telescopes and binoculars were trained aft. The face of the cloudbank remained featureless. Then – so far off that the sound was hardly distinguishable from the thin voice of the wind against the ship's structure – came the tapping of machine-gun and cannon fire in the sky. Tension eased.

Quarter of an hour passed. A yeoman of signals handed the captain a message from the radio room. He glanced at it, scribbled his initials and smiled tightly.

'Carrier's fighters got four of the little sons of bitches,' he said. 'The others have scattered.'

The destroyer resumed her place as wing ship of the escort. The signal lamps chattered from bridge to bridge. I went down to lunch – well-cooked cold meats, salad, fruit pie and coffee. Most of the time, it seemed, war at sea was a decently civilized business.

All afternoon enemy aircraft searched for the convoy. On deck the glare hurt the eyes and the heat was oppressive. After an hour of expectant watching I went below, took off my clothes, and flipped a book out of the skipper's shelf without noticing the title. It was named *Dangerous Water*!

A second call to general quarters came at sunset, just as we were finishing dinner in the wardroom. The gunnery officer, a fresh-faced, happily plump lad, was inordinately fond of ice cream. He magically crammed down the last spoonfuls of a double serving, wiped his chin and complained: 'God, how I hate night torpedo attacks! You don't know what the hell is going on. The God damned transports get all over the place. After 10 minutes, your eyes stick out like a lobster's, and nobody ever hits anybody else!'

It was a beautiful, quiet evening. A new moon was hanging half up the sky, and just below it Venus was big as a lamp. The destroyer screen huddled so close to the transports you could see the waves slapping their sides. Darkness was very near and the last of our fighters buzzed for home. Only one or two cumbersome flying boats, scudding low over the waves, were discernible in the failing light.

'Four to six enemy planes, bearing two-two-zero, range four miles and closing,' said the yeoman of signals.

The vibration of the engines grew until every part of the ship trembled in eager unison. Making a turn to starboard, she heeled so far over that the dark water hissed level with the scuppers. It was a strange sensation at top speed – 40 knots or better. As we turned, the transports seemed to gyrate on the horizon. A destroyer on the other wing opened fire with her heavy guns. Others joined in. The bulk of the transports was silhouetted against the yellow flashes from the gun muzzles. High in the sky behind the ships, bursting shells made little shining pips that dulled the brilliance of the early stars.

The 20-millimeters opened up and tracer began to bound and spurt. Each glowing slug had the appearance of a red ember. There was still a little light left and the tracers crossed it in an arching shower. Suddenly an aircraft sped across the bows of the destroyer, flying very low. One could just see it against the junction of sky and water. It was a big machine, doped for night flying. One moment it was there, the next it had vanished in a confusing twilight. The Bofors astern barked angrily and the ship turned on her heel.

'Jap!' said the man who lurched against me. 'Going like a bat out of hell, the dirty little bitch!'

It was no new simile, but it served. The plane had sped in a ponderous yet airy haste – exactly as a bat might fly through the twilight of abysmal spaces.

Someone said: 'I guess that'll be all for an hour or so. Guadalcanal says to expect another attack at about 8:30. They didn't do so good that time.'

Below, the ship's lights had been switched onto the battle circuit. The lanterns on the bulkheads reflected a cold and beautiful blue which gave only enough illumination for one to move without groping.

I watched the men going about the ship's work. All wore steel helmets and carried knives in their belts to cut the raft lashings free. Some had put on bulky life jackets. Some had plugged their ears with cotton waste against gun blast.

Before this, they had been individual men, with individual faces and individual expressions. But when the guns opened up they seemed to lose entity, to be fused together in thoughtful gravity and concentration upon the parts of a common task. For all their activity, there was an uncanny stillness of spirit about them. They spoke quietly, and their voices were sibilant, in tune with the sea.

At 8.34 the firing began again. This time I stood astern to watch the gun crews. Our flank of the destroyer screen opened up together on the first flight of five torpedo planes. The sky was spangled with flak. The cannonade spread until every ship of the convoy was in action. The transports' gunners pumped it up like madmen. The reports blended into one continuous pulsing crash, and the flashes into a continuous sheet of yellow flame.

Sprays of tracer curved over us, and little pieces of shrapnel and spent bullets rattled on the steel decks. The crews waiting for a target flinched and bent their bodies away from the fury of sound and light. They were revealed against the brilliance like figures in a grotesque woodcut. Then the fleet ceased fire.

'Made it too hot for the little suckers,' said a machine gunner, blowing on his hands. 'The captain'll give 'em the slip now. You see. He's an old hand at this.'

The destroyer lost speed, wheeled 180 degrees. Eyes strained could just discern the shapes of the transports veering away on a new course at reduced speed. Our own wake, when the bomber planes were making their fruitless run, had been bubbling white and luminous. Now it was hardly visible. The ship seemed to hold her breath and go on tiptoe, seeking to hide in the emptiness of the ocean. The bright moon slipped suddenly behind a long, ragged cloud. Never was dark a better shield. Ten minutes passed. Twenty.

Away to the northwest the enemy planes dropped three flares, either to rally their own flak-scattered formations or as a bait for some overeager gunnery officer to fire and reveal the convoy's new course. The flares floated down from the clouds, all green and sickly. Then they stripped off and fell in fiery, oily pieces into the sea. Thirteen minutes, counted off on a watch.

'Four to six bogies – six miles – opening.' Six thousand yards astern a destroyer acting as a decoy fired briefly. That was the end of the action.

The ship stayed at general quarters until midnight. Then I went below and drank coffee in the galley. The ventilation blowers had been cut off when we went into action. The wall thermometer stood at 120 degrees.

One by one the ship's officers came down, drank their coffee and went back to duty. They were a little pale with tension and the sweat glittered on their faces, but the night's work was just beginning. It was pitch dark now and the convoy must be brought on its crazy, evasive course through narrow reef waters. I slept, lying naked and wet under the skipper's electric fan.

The convoy was off Koli Point, Guadalcanal, just after daylight. The ships came to anchorage in an almost dead flat calm. Barges began plying industriously to and from the shore before the rattle of the anchor chains had died away. It was still considered unhealthy to stay offshore at Guadalcanal longer than was absolutely necessary.

The sea between Guadalcanal and the precipitous shores of Florida Island over the strait was a soft greenish-blue and the sky yellow with sunrise. All the destroyers in the Pacific seemed to be pacing up and down the channel like chained watchdogs, restless and vigilant, while the clumsy big ships disgorged men and guns in dun-green streams from hatches to barges. Security patrols of fighters were up. A formation of dive bombers winged its way west into the Slot – a narrow gut of water between the double chain of reefs and islands that run all the way from San Cristobal to the Shortlands.

I looked hard at Guadalcanal. Its far-off mountains were high and noble and mysterious, softly clothed in forest. The spacious morning was all about them in airy colors and mild moistness. The palms of the coastal plantations stood in ranks as far as the eye could see, bowing politely over the beaches.

Here and there, a blight had got into them. Through glasses

I could see stretches of trees that had no fronds, but stood an acre or more of ragged sticks.

Shellfire and bombing had blasted the life out of them. The battle here had been very different from the battles in New Guinea. It had not spread over great areas, but was held within the flat coastal belt on the north side of the island. For both Americans and Japanese the problem of supply had been maritime, centred about ships plying in narrow waters under menace of enemy air action. On Guadalcanal, cargoes were unloaded on the beaches within range of Japanese machine guns.

Compared with New Guinea, no land supply problem existed at all. Seldom were the most advanced troops more than a few miles from a beachhead. They did not fight in terrain of difficulty comparable with that of Salamaua or Sanananda or Kokoda. There was certainly some broken ground laced by deep rivers, a few patches of rain forest, and hills toward Cape Esperance – but there was nothing even remotely resembling the Mubo Gorge, the valley of the Kumusi River, or the Gap trail.

In consequence, the intensity of the fighting had been greater than any in New Guinea. Maneuver had been less important, and each side had been able to bring heavier weight of arms against the other.

Engagements in the coconut plantations about Henderson Field were modern battles in which artillery, automatic weapons and, to a lesser extent, armor had played a visible and audible part. The tactics of attack and defense had been the tactics of modern counterpositional warfare, in an area where the terrain had kept troops closely concentrated. Against the creeping, whispering, diluted conflicts of New Guinea, this kind of war had been honestly noisy, bloody and decisive.

The land, sea and air within 50 miles of Henderson Field are historic. Here the United States discovered a method of beating the Japanese in the Pacific – the method of selective, aero-amphibious attack. Here, in a critical series of interrelated actions between naval, air and land forces, American leaders learned the basic truth that Japan could not be beaten if she were allowed to choose her own weapons and use them her own way, minimizing her inferiority in technology and resources. They saw that a successful counteroffensive in the Pacific must be directed against key localities in order of accessibility, rather than diffused among key zones in order of political importance. Moreover, a counteroffensive must develop through three stages: (1) air superiority above the objective and along lines of supply, (2) blockade of the enemy and his consequent attrition, and (3) destruction of the enemy by eventual assault. The third stage would usually involve difficult large-scale landings close to the blockaded enemy base, and casualties in proportion to the urgency of the schedule.

This clear conception of Pacific tactics emerged after more than a year of war against the Japanese, and was based mainly on lessons of the Guadalcanal and New Guinea campaigns. The Guadalcanal affair had indicated what *could* be done against the Japanese, whereas New Guinea fighting had given evidence of what could *not* be done.

The land fighting had finished three months before. The battle-fields of the Tenaru and Matanakau rivers had been given back to silence. Undergrowth was healing the earth, so wounded by bombardment. Foxholes of Japanese and Americans alike were unplotted pits in the forest floor, and the stench of death and explosion had merged into the muskiness of jungle mold. The battalions of the American dead were on parade, rank upon rank on flats and hillsides, each bearing a cross or simple stake as his last banner. All about them the ilimos and myrtles flung up their vine-draped arms in the gestures of age-old struggle.

After the eviction of the Japanese from Guadalcanal, a brisk and rather one-sided aerial war went on for several months. American bombers and fighters were beginning the first phase of an offensive by blockading the Central Solomons, harassing the enemy rear end and, at the same time, maintaining defensive superiority over their own bases.

Henderson Field with its miles of steel-matting runways, sandbagged revetments and deep dugouts was worth watching at any hour of the day or night. Hurricanes of yellow dust swept over it as bombers and fighters took off, not in the paltry threes and fours I had known at Moresby, but in scores. The miles of shabby coconut groves about it sheltered cities of tents and acres of dumps, deep in the island mud which even machines could not conquer.

From Koli Point to Kokumbona Beach and far inland, a network of new roads carried heavy traffic between airfield and airfield and camp and camp. Whenever one went to the shore, one saw destroyers prowling in the channel, and cargo ships unloading into barges and lighters that slapped merrily about in the trade-wind chop.

The Japanese could do very little about it. They must have been aware that the Americans were building up for another stroke, but the air above Guadalcanal was deadly. Nearly every night they sent over groups of four or five bombers, which kept weary workmen out of bed but never hit anything. The antiaircraft guns would bark for a time, the searchlights finger the sky, and a night fighter or two worry about pursuit. The bombs would rumble distantly among the coconuts or in the bush.

Between April 7 and June 16, the enemy made only two sizable attacks upon Gaudalcanal. The first was aimed at shipping off Koli Point, and sank an American destroyer, a tanker and an escort vessel of the Royal New Zealand Navy. It cost the enemy 39 planes out of an attacking force of 100, but it was probably worth it.

For the second attack, the Japanese sent the largest number of planes used in any one operation since Pearl Harbor. Their formations of more than 120 fighters, torpedo planes and dive bombers suffered a defeat which up to that time was unprecedented in Pacific air fighting.

They came soon after two o'clock on the afternoon of June 6. I had just left air intelligence headquarters and was walking past Admiral Mark Mitscher's office when the sirens sounded Condition Yellow – enemy planes approaching. The admiral came to the door and looked reflectively at the weather.

'You'd better get down to the beach,' he told me. 'They say it's going to be a big one. The air-watching stations up the line report more than 100 planes. If they get through, most likely they'll go for the ships off Kokum or Lunga.'

I dived for a jeep.

The fields were roaring with activity. Undispersed bombers were taking off, and formations of American Corsairs and Lightnings were circling for altitude. Beneath them the New Zealanders' P-40's scurried in packs up and down the channel. At a coast-defense gunpit opposite the anchorage, a team of sunburned .50-caliber antiaircraft gunners were fondling their weapons with oily rags and checking belts of ammunition. I thought it would be a good place for seeing the show.

Offshore the ships were under way, zigzagging for sea room. Three destroyers patrolling half a mile from the beach swung their guns anxiously. There was a faint, concealing yellow haze at about 10,000 feet. The sky looked windy and the sea was marked by big slicks of oil pumped out of bilges.

It was stiflingly hot in the gunpit under the camouflage net. But we hadn't long to wait. The heavy antiaircraft at Henderson Field went into action briefly – pointing. The noise of aircraft grew from a mutter to a roar. There were slaps of machine-gun and cannon fire somewhere above the haze. A spent bullet whispered.

The ships had made a fast getaway. Still in sight were only two tank landing ships, the three destroyers, one Liberty ship, and a small freighter loaded with oil drums. The rest had vanished, either in the direction of Tulagi or eastward along the coast.

Suddenly I saw planes, high up and coming out of the sun – a formation of 20 Japanese torpedo and dive bombers. They started to peel off and plummet down on the Liberty ship and the destroyers. The sky blackened with shellbursts. The wakes of the destroyers boiled. The attack swept closer.

One Japanese torpedo bomber was struck by a shell. It burst amidship, split apart by lurid red flame. The two halves rolled soddenly and began to fall, spurting gasoline and smoke. Two dive bombers did not level out. They kept on going and lifted towering columns of white foam from the sea. Another dive bomber unloaded on the stern of the Liberty ship.

Smoke and flames shrouded her. The sea erupted with misses from the rest of the attacking flight.

Then something got the freighter. There was a tremendous explosion in her after hold. Drums of oil and gasoline hurtled high into the air, and the shore and sea were sprayed with burning liquid.

It was too close for comfort and I put my head down. Spent flak was pattering like hailstones. In the fog of smoke, you could see nothing but meaningless gobbets of fire and debris. Then the fighters came squealing down.

When I looked again, the wind had blown most of the smoke away and the battle had diffused. Fighters were chasing the enemy bombers in the direction of Tulagi, where a terrific barrage opened up. I yelled at a gunner: 'Look at those shell splashes!'

'Shell splashes hell!' he said, glued to his spotting glasses. 'Those are planes going into the drink, son!'

It looked like a salvo falling into the water. The planes came down the sky like rain. The fighters were among them, all right. But it was too far off to see. The battling aircraft were dark specks on a dazzling field of sunlit sky.

The Liberty ship staggered toward the beach with smoke and fire spouting from her stern. One of the tank landing ships had been hit, too, and was smoldering with her nose on the beach. The little freighter burned furiously. It was all over. There was nothing to do but go back and await the accounting.

On an open patch of lalang grass beside the road, a Japanese dive bomber had crashed. There was very little left – a few fire-bleached ribs, crumpled rags of metal, and a big charred patch where the debris had burned.

A dozen tall young Americans were gazing down at the splash of neutral-colored clothing, blood and featureless flesh that had been the rear gunner. The men seemed to be neither thinking nor even feeling. They were deep in the hypnotic spell that the spectacle of violent death casts over the living. Their faces were as expressionless as dough. One with full red lips turned to me and parted them narrowly. 'For Christ's sake,' he said out of the slit. 'Will you look at the little son of a bitch? I ain't never seen anything like it!'

Late that night, little Colonel C. looked up from the sheaf of reports on the desk in front of him. His face was drawn with the strain of prolonged concentration and was finely beaded with sweat, but his tired brown eyes were alive and bright.

'I've checked it all ways and canned every claim not confirmed,' he said. 'Without counting the ack-ack score, the fighters brought down 77 out of 123 planes. Twelve to fifteen are probables. Our losses are nine planes. I can't believe it, but it's true!'

Forty-eight hours later, the score had risen to 94 certainties and 16 probables. Our losses remained at nine planes. 'They can't take it,' I told myself. 'Not even Japs can take such a licking. Maybe they can conceal it from their people at home, but they can't conceal it from their fighting men. I wonder what it's like when 123 pilots come into mess for breakfast, and only 20 come for dinner. Not even the Japs can take that for long.'

CHAPTER 19

THE SECRET INVADERS

AIR crews in the South Pacific had no monopoly on colorful heroism and adventure. There were fighting men, key fighting men, who sported neither bars nor stars, and very little gold braid. They were an aristocracy unrecognized by the rank and file but received with deference by generals and admirals.

Half a dozen of these men were quartered on Gaudalcanal near Correspondents' Row at Camp Crocodile, the establishment of the Commander, South Pacific Amphibious Force. They were reticent, rather overpowered by the formality of a navy camp. The most personable was a tall, thin, neatly mustached youngster who labored under none of the social disabilities of his companions and who had been rewarded for it with a majority in the New Zealand army. The rest were nondescripts – arbitrarily absorbed in the New Zealand or Australian armed forces – blotchy-complexioned men on the wrong slope of middle age. They looked uncomfortable even in tropical uniform and were silent, hasty feeders in a corner of the mess. Yet they had one thing in common – a 'salted' look. And it was noticeable that when one of them crossed the compound in the lazy hours of early afternoon, he had a galvanic effect upon any natives who might have come in to trade carved canoes for packets of American cigarettes. These were the Solomon Islands old-timers, the secret invaders in the new war that had engulfed their dreamy tropic world.

One of the Allies' greatest handicaps in planning counter-offensives against the Japanese in the western Pacific was the scarcity of men with detailed knowledge of the terrain. Maps or written data prepared before the war gave little help. New

Guinea and the Solomons had been the province of British administrations for decades, but before 1941 the only good military maps of them were confined to areas about administrative centers and harbors. Hydrographic data were equally incomplete and sketchy. Of inshore waters, only main channels were adequately charted. Aerial photography to some extent offset the lack of information about reefs, streams, shoals, beaches and heights – but it could not supply many essential details.

Before the war the white population of many islands and districts strongly garrisoned by the Japanese after their invasion numbered a few score at most, and not many of them really knew the physical features of the districts where they lived. Allied commanders wanted such information badly. The few men who possessed it were milked of everything they knew in their conscious minds – and their subconscious was raked over for more. They were consulted, questioned, cross-examined, checked and wafted from place to place interminably when any new operation was in the wind.

They entered into the spirit of the business and usually took quiet enjoyment in being persons of consequence for the first time in their lives. Almost without exception they had been minor government officials or small independent planters who had had to move about and study the country. They had been small men, and they proved to have the small man's quality of heroism in crisis. They did more than tell what they knew. Many volunteered for a type of service requiring more cold-blooded courage than is asked of any commando. They went back to islands occupied by the Japanese, sometimes alone, sometimes with picked reconnaissancers, to observe the enemy's fortifications, numbers and dispositions, or to find some link missing in the chain of knowledge forged by the invasion planners. They instructed the leaders of special missions in the lore of forgotten jungle trails, caves, streams and entrances.

They landed on Guadalcanal long before the invasion of August 7, 1942. They lurked on New Georgia, Vangunu, Rendova, Kolombangara and Bougainville weeks or months before the beachheads were taken by storm. When a Japanese patrol moved into some abandoned plantation house, they would move out. When the Japanese departed, they would move in again. Their influence kept the natives of occupied territories loyal to the old order.

Their daring and unshakable nerve was legendary among the fighting men of the South Pacific. The Japanese hunted them relentlessly, but caught up with very few. They had narrow escapes. They slept with fear for a bedfellow – the fear of capture, torture and death. Their own hard life tramping jungle trails, stewing in little beachside trade stores, piloting cutters among the world's most treacherous reefs had given them a hard self-confidence. They said contemptuously that the Jap was no bushman and as waterman he was overrated. The Jap cerebrated slowly. He could not make quick, intuitive decisions in a tight spot.

It would be difficult to overestimate the importance of the part played by these island veterans in the planning and execution of the Solomons campaign, and the many subsequent campaigns. Upon their recollection of conditions, places, distances, and upon their judgment of probabilities, the tactical details of the landings and assaults were based. They were not infallible, of course, but their information was rarely inaccurate and they would risk their own skins to put it to the proof.

More than one ranking naval officer frankly admitted to correspondents that if the staff had lacked the local knowledge of the old-timers, it would have hesitated to bring small craft against defended positions in New Georgia. Munda Point itself was classed among the world's most naturally impregnable spots – girded on three sides by very nearly impenetrable reefs and shallows, and on the fourth by densest jungle. Yet many thousands of men slipped through its geographic defenses before the enemy even discovered their presence.

The reconnaissance that must precede any assault upon Japanese-held islands is probably the most delicate and nerve-racking part of the operation. Old campaigners will tell you that the worst of war is that hour of unnatural quiet that comes before the opening of a great battle. Reconnaissance hundreds of miles deep in enemy-held territory is like an illimitable number of such hours. Its suspense cannot be measured by the creeping second hand of a watch, for there is no end to it until the job is finished.

Weeks before the Americans landed in force on islands of the New Georgia group, parties of reconnaissancers led by local men were spying out the ground.

On June 21, a transport destroyer was sent to pick up a party of marine corps officers and men returning with final reports for Amphibious Force headquarters, Guadalcanal. I was allowed to make the trip, and to this day count it one of my most humbling experiences of war.

The destroyer, an aged four-stacker with two firerooms removed and converted for troop carrying, left Koli Point in the midafternoon for the 300-mile dash into the heart of enemy country. She was one of the little ships that had done so splendidly in the early days of the Guadalcanal fighting – strictly expendable, stripped in armament and equipment to barest essentials, camouflaged in splotchy greens to blend with the jungle-clad foreshores, her masts and stacks sawed off to reduce her silhouette.

The man who skippered her was one of the few daredevils I have ever met who looked his part – a chunky, square-jawed, square-skulled New Englander with the sea in his eyes and with clear, weathered skin stretched tight over the bones of his face. His every word and gesture betokened ability to make split-second decisions and the guts to stick by them to the finish. His crew had nicknamed him Iron Mike.

Iron Mike himself drove me down to the beach from Camp Crocodile at a breakneck pace, genially enraged that the hospitality of the admiral had delayed his sailing by half an hour. Iron Mike loved his ship. You could see it in his eyes as they flicked over the decks when he came aboard from the Higgins boat and the bosun's whistle trilled. Even the gold-plater skippers didn't look at their ships like that – the sort of look Dick Turpin might have given Black Bess, a look that remembered adventures shared and hoped for adventures to come.

The transport destroyers – the APD's – are the commandos of the sea, even more than the flashy motor torpedo boats. They are not part of the fleet's strategic strength. When a job is too risky for a gold-plater, when ships must carry troops or cargo and take their chance of return, then the APD's are assigned. No channels are too tortuous for them to venture, no shallows too poorly charted, no waters too dominated by enemy bombers.

Iron Mike called a conference of his officers in the ward-room as soon as the ship was under way. Even with the blowers roaring, the wall thermometer stood at 115 degrees. The Negro mess boys, their faces a shining wet ebony, served cups of steaming coffee all round. Iron Mike sat at the head of the table with a sheaf of charts in front of him and the bridge telephone at his right hand. In nasal monosyllables he explained the mission and its purpose, tracing positions and courses on the chart with a square-nailed forefinger.

The ship would proceed through Blanche Channel, *thus*, to a point off Segi reefs, *here*. Air interference would not be encountered until the Russell Islands were astern. North and west of *this* line must be regarded as enemy territory. Aircraft or ships sighted would be hostile. The mission, how-ever, was not to fight. The mission was to keep a rendezvous with a party of marine raiders and scouts on an unnamed island situated approximately *here*. However, if fighting were un-avoidable, the ship would fight.

The time set for the rendezvous was midnight. The ship could not approach the island of the rendezvous closer than three miles because of the shallows and uncharted reefs. It would lay to *here* and launch two Higgins boats which would proceed at full speed inshore. When they were within 100 yards of the island they would identify themselves with two red lights. Shore would reply with three green lights.

The Higgins boat commanded by Mr S. would then run up the beach if the surf was not too heavy and embark such

247

personnel as the officer in charge of the raider party would indicate. If the surf was too heavy the Higgins boat commanded by Mr S. would launch a rubber raft and float it ashore on a line. The personnel to be embarked would come out four at a time on the raft. The operation must be completed before moonrise, which was approximately 0100 hours. The Japanese were known to be moving considerable numbers of troops by armored barges along this shore at night; consequently any other small craft sighted must be considered as enemy. The Higgins boat would avoid encounters, but if fired on would return the fire and get back to the ship as quickly as possible.

The boat commanded by Mr J. would not land unless necessary. It would stand offshore giving cover with its machine guns while the embarkation was in progress. Its use, however, would be left to the discretion of the boat officer.

It was unnecessary to emphasize the importance of completing the operation and escaping from confined waters by moonrise. Once the reconnaissance party was aboard, the ship would promptly perform the classical naval operation of hauling its arse out of bad water as quickly as its screws could take it. That, gentlemen, was all. Was everything clearly understood?

The two boat officers had a few questions. Iron Mike answered them succinctly. At half-minute intervals during the briefing, the bridge telephone rang. His hand lifted it automatically, and he would stop in the middle of a sentence to say out of the corner of his mouth, 'Shoot!' Having heard, he would acknowledge with 'Okay!' and continue his sentence.

The officers rose.

'Oh, one thing, gentlemen,' said Iron Mike with a tigerish grin. 'I forgot to mention. Just before I came aboard, the flagship received a message that seven Japanese destroyers are known to be cruising off New Georgia tonight. Our planes spotted them steaming south from Vella Lavella at midday. No doubt the enemy has got wind of troop movements and is hoping to intercept us. A force of our own cans is out, looking for a little fight for themselves, but they won't come anywhere near us. I just thought you'd like to know.'

248

Topside it was almost cold after the wardroom oven. 'God, these are hot ships,' I said unguardedly.

Iron Mike grinned again. 'Thought it quite a pleasant day myself,' he said. 'You must have a look over our firerooms.'

Cape Esperance was spinning past on the port beam – precipitous, grassy hills with deep-blue shadows in the valleys. The grave of more than 6,000 Japanese dead. Some living, they said, were still in the hills, hiding, starving, dying of disease. The mountains behind the hills were wild with jungle, topped by cloud. The palms of the beaches slid by. There were rust-red shells of ships, wreck after wreck, noses thrust into the green. 'Graveyard of ships' was right.

Twenty-five knots. The ship had set her stern into the water and was thrumming. Her bow cut great furrows in the sea. The blowers roared and drowned the sound of the wind. Gray-green decks, and men leaning against the wind. A squadron of Lightnings scudded west.

'Condition red on Russell Islands,' someone said.

The general quarters buzzer sounded. A sailor gave me a kapok life jacket and a steel helmet. I went forward to Number 1 gun. The crew squatted in the shelter of the circular shield.

'We'll stay at general quarters all night now, God damn it.'

A transport plane from the landing strip on Pavuvu hurried along, only 50 feet from the sea. The afternoon was gold and blue, but its colors were deepening. A purple squall passed like a shadow off Visale. Savo was a rounded mountain-top. The sea there was very deep. Down in the tideless chasms lay the broken, corroding bones of the cruisers sunken in the night battle of October 26, and the sea-changed dead. A merciless deep covered by frolic waves. I looked, and shivered.

To the west, war was visible. A pillar of smoke rose above the horizon and mushroomed at 1,000 feet. Only a huge fire could make that.

'Must have hit a fuel dump.'

The gun crew stood up and stared with narrowing eyes.

'It's all clear on Russell Islands.'

A palm tree grew out of the sea. A clump of stilted man-groves. The destroyer heeled to the west.

249

'Give them a wide berth.'

I looked up at the chartroom windows winking in the late-afternoon sun. A steel-helmeted officer was studying the column of smoke with a telescope.

'Stand by . . . enemy aircraft!'

The gun layer settled his helmet. I moved aft behind the superstructure, staring up at the sky, and could see nothing.

'Four of them, over there, opening.'

But I could see nothing. The destroyer still sped west. I thought the enemy aircraft would report her course. The sea was very enmpty now. Even the palm tree had sunk below the horizon, marked by heavy edged clouds. The sun was low and blinding, and a mild wind carried the smell of reefs. Flying fish cascaded from the crest of the bow waves in silvery showers. The short evening was coming.

'Now is the time, if we're going to get it. Their evening patrols . . . '

The column of smoke fell far astern. It marked the boundary of the friendly world. This was enemy water. Jap water. No man's land was behind, a long way behind.

An extra knot or two. The shivering of the ship quickened, and the roar of the blowers grew louder. The ball of the sun dipped and touched the sea, sank. There were long ribbons of scarlet and turquoise and amber in the sky. They had a hard brilliance, but in a moment they were pastel, and then gone in a diffuse golden glow.

An island rose up. The surf slapped flake-white on its guano-streaked base. That, I told myself, is a Jap island. That island is in the New Georgia group. Strange!

Then darkness came. The walls of the wardroom hummed and trembled. The blue battle lights gleamed.

Black coffee.

The surgeon and I played chess. What he was thinking I do not know. I thought maybe he was used to this expectancy of the unknown, this leaden conviction that the future was so unalterable that fear, anxiety, anticipation were no part of living. I listened for the sound of a gun, for the sound of an explosion.

The executive officer came down. 'You might as well step up now, White,' he said. 'They're standing to the boats from 10 o'clock – in an hour. I'm glad you're going with the boats. It'll give you an idea of what this run is like . . . the difficulty of it. You are going with Mr S. It's fixed for you to land on the raft if there's no other way of speaking to the officer in charge of the raiders. But you'd better take what you want with you, in case of trouble getting back. We mightn't have time to pick up everybody.'

A tail of greenish fire, the wake, curved into the darkness. Beyond that, one could at first see nothing, not even the bulk of the ship. I held a hand before my eyes, with extended fingers. Nothing. The ship was like a comet speeding through space beyond the farthest suns. All that remained of a world one knew was the deep beat of her turbines and the roaring blowers.

By sense of touch I found my way to the boat hoists and the steel ladder up the superstructure. I brushed against something damp and yielding – an oiled life jacket. A horny hand steadied me.

'Over here, sir. Look!'

A flicker of brilliant yellow flame ran along the edge of the sea. I saw a dark, racing shape down in the water. My stomach screwed up into a hot ball and turned over.

'Christ!' I said, 'it's a can opening up!' and crouched down and listened for the scream of the shells.

The man beside me laughed. 'That's what we all thought at first. Summer lightning behind atolls, that's all, sir. There's a long string of islands there. With the lightning behind them, they look just like cans steaming in line ahead. Scared the bridge, too, the first few times. The lookouts called enemy ships.'

After awhile the sky became distinguishable from the sea. There was a tear in the overcast and half a dozen lamplike stars shone out. The lightning kept flickering behind the islets, and in profile the shapes were uncannily the shapes of destroyers. I could not quite convince myself of illusion until they had passed astern and a mountain was silhouetted.

'What island is that?'

'That would be Vangunu, sir. Plenty of Japs there.'

Vangunu. Yes. There was a Jap garrison there. I could imagine the sentries on the beach, looking out to sea . . .

Half an hour passed. The bridge called: 'Stand by the boats!'

I groped to the Higgins boat.

'Here, come aboard.'

Mr S.'s voice gave orders to the coxswain. There was a movement of invisible bodies. The hum of the ship changed pitch. Speed was slackening and she heeled slightly on an alteration of course. One could hear the hiss of water. Iron Mike shouted over the after bridge rail: 'Get those boats slung out, there. Be ready to launch as the way comes off her. Are you ready?'

'Aye, aye, sir.'

There was the blanketed sound of the engine-room telegraph. The blowers' roar died away and the hiss of water was loud. The hoists squealed and I could feel the rough plates of the barge bottom stir. Suddenly I could see the bulk of the ship slipping away. Her stumpy mast and flat stacks climbed against the differing darkness of the sky.

'This is as far as I can bring her,' Iron Mike said from the after bridge rail. 'Take a bearing from the bows and check. Remember, no shooting. Two 30 calibers against a barge is bad business. But you've got to find that island. Get it?'

'Aye, aye, sir.'

'All right, then. If there's trouble, I'll do what I can, but this ship must be out of here by moonrise. Good luck to you.'

'Good luck to *you*, sir.'

The barge bottom slapped the water. Silver chips of phosphorescence flew up.

'Cast off, there!'

The motor kicked, roared into life.

'Man those machine guns!'

'Aye, aye, sir.'

There was a flash of lightning behind the peaks. In its brief ghastliness, I saw the destroyer bow on, in a silky calm sea, and two life-jacketed sailors just aft of the ramp, swinging the twin barreled machine guns on their circular metal mounts. The Higgins boat's stern settled down and she moved away.

I stared forward, straining to hear sounds above the muffled beating of the underwater exhausts. Somewhere out there the Jap barges were plying. Then our motor died sickly, and there was a flash of white abeam. The second Higgins boat shot past and turned, her wake luminescent.

'What's wrong?'

'The bitch won't pull.'

'Check your course, coxon.'

'Oh, hell, that *would* happen!'

'Try her with the exhausts cut out.'

'Aye, aye, sir.'

The noise was deafening, but our boat leaped forward.

'They'll hear that.'

'So will Abe Lincoln, b'Jesus.'

'Check your course, coxon.'

'One-four-zero.'

Behind the mountain, a yellow ray swept leisurely across the clouds.

'What's that?'

'Don't know.'

'A Jap searchlight!'

'Ah-ah.'

'Hear anything?'

'Pipe down.'

'How long have we been traveling?'

'Seventeen minutes.'

'Look – there's an island.'

It was lightning again. It shone on a reef. Sandpits and islets and shallows were a polished sheeny blue. A tree was reflected in them.

'Which island?'

'Starboard 20.'

'Stop your engine.'

'Aye, aye, sir.'

When the noise faded, one became aware of the surf's voice – a voice like the voice of gargantuan wooden drums. The surface of the sea was smooth, but rollers 15 feet high were pounding the coral. I remembered a chart of this coast and the marking in fine red print, *Very heavy surf*. No boat, not even a Higgins boat, could land through that. Perhaps a rubber raft could land, but it could never come out again through those smooth, mighty rollers.

'It can't be the island.'

The boat officer was silent.

'They were to show lights, weren't they?'

'It *can't* be the island.'

The boat officer said: 'Show two red lights.'

We stared, conscious of the very veins of our eyeballs. The searchlight cut its great deliberate arc.

'*What's that?*'

A motor. Somewhere in the dark a motor was thrumming.

'Get going. Give it hell, sailor.'

The men at the machine gun moved. I looked at my wrist watch. Eleven fifty-three.

'The raiders can't be on the island – not there. They *couldn't* have landed through that surf.'

Where was the destroyer? We ran for 15 minutes. Every muscle and nerve in me was aching with an awareness that stretched the seconds to snapping point. Nice thing to pile up on a reef and wait for dawn and the Japs. Maybe the Dumbos would get us if we did. Maybe not. Suppose we *couldn't* find the destroyer? No trace of her, and we'd been running 15 minutes. Here on the sea, with the dawn coming up!

Lightning again. Then we saw the ship. The ship! Over there, lean and hungry and waiting. The Higgins boat swept under her side. Thank God for that, anyway. Thank God for the musty heat of the wardroom and the comforting sound of haste.

The boat officer called up: 'No sign of them on the island, sir. I don't think they could have landed. Nothing could get through the surf.'

Iron Mike answered: 'If they're not on the island, they'll be near it, Mr S. We've got to get them. You have an hour to moonrise.'

I wanted to scream like a child, 'Take me aboard, I'm sick

of it. If something doesn't happen, I'll go mad!' But I hadn't the nerve. In that quiet, the blast of Jap heavies from an armored barge would have been heavenly release. The Higgins boat turned away. This time no one spoke.

What was time? An eternity spaced by the sweep of a searchlight and the senseless play of lightning among clouds? There was the island again – the same silly damned island. Who cared?

Something dark was floating on the water near at hand. The Higgins boat lifted sluggishly to the swell. Listen – *voices.*

'Careful, careful!'

'Ready the guns!'

The man beside me moved.

'Call them and stand by,' the boat officer whispered.

Our engine coughed.

'Ahoy, there!'

'Ahoy!'

A dark shape drifted by. Mutter of voices.

'For the love of Christ!' A man near me said it like a prayer.

'Steady.'

'Who are you?'

Mutter of voices again.

A machine gunner moved.

'Hold it. No shooting yet.'

'Ahoy there, show your lights!'

The feeble flash of a torch across the water.

'Wrong light!'

'Hold it, you scatty son of a bitch. Hold it, I say!'

Then the boat officer said: 'Shine the lights on your faces.' For a moment nothing happened. The officer's voice broke, shrilled in a childish tremble.

'Shine the lights on your faces, God damn you, or by Jesus, we'll let you have it. *On your faces,* I say.'

A hand-shielded flashlight glowed on a pale, stubbled face, grinning up at us. I glimpsed a muddy, spotted camouflage suit; the muzzles of tommy guns, trained and steady; the high prow of a canoe carved like the head of a bird with ruffled neck feathers; the smooth oily backs of kanakas.

'Ah-h-h. Right, coxon. Take her alongside the canoe.'

'Thought you was Japs.'

'Same to you, bud.'

'They're out tonight, scads of them – we heard the barges.'

'Are they?'

'Where is your officer?'

'Here,' said a man in the canoe. 'Sorry we couldn't make the island. Couldn't get through the surf. Was it you who turned back 40 minutes ago – you or a Jap?'

'Us.'

'Thought so. We were worried.'

'We showed lights,' said the boat officer.

'Sorry – didn't see them.'

'Well, no damage. Whoever's coming had better get aboard. Skipper wants to clear out before moonrise.'

'Okay, get aboard. Look lively, you men.'

They stank like goats. For 27 days they had been living like wild beasts in the jungle.

The rendezvous was kept. I will never forget it – the pale stubbled face grinning, or the prow of the canoe, or the backs of the kanakas, or the talk. No moment of action in my life has ever surpassed for drama that moment when the boat officer's voice broke and he said: *'Shine the lights on your faces . . . '*

CHAPTER 20

PLAN AND ITS TESTING

THE attack upon the New Georgia group was to be the first fullscale test of the ways of war evolved from New Guinea's failures and Guadalcanal's hair's breadth success. Method was indicated, material now assembled.

Guadalcanal now had five excellent airfields. Based on them were 600 or 700 combat aircraft – heavy, medium, torpedo and dive bombers, and Wildcat, Lightning, Corsair and Warhawk fighters. The force was formidable in offense and adequate to support a move against limited objectives. Although it suffered from a proportionate shortage of fighters, this was partly compensated by the superior performance of our fighters.

At sea, the picture was just as satisfactory. The merchant-shipping position in the Pacific had improved very much since the beginning of the year, and there were enough small invasion craft – tank and infantry landing craft, transport destroyers, motor torpedo boats and barges – to give proper balance to the modestly conceived offensives against Munda and Vila. Powerfully reinforced cruiser task forces, with battle-fleet support, were ready to meet Japanese reaction if – as the navy undoubtedly hoped – it proved more violent than the strategic occasion warranted.

At least two divisions of typical American troops, approximately 30,000 men, had completed training schedules intended to meet in full the requirements of the operation. They were splendidly equipped with a high proportion of the latest automatic arms, camouflaged uniforms, and a plethora of tropical campaigning gadgets that ranged from waterproofed miniature electric flashlights to hammocks with built-in mosquito nets and rainproof canopies. They had in support one regiment of marine raiders, briefed to clean up pockets of resistance threatening supply, and reconnaissance units of Pacific island scouts led by New Zealand officers familiar with New Georgia.

The planning of the operation against the New Georgia group, and the balancing and equipment of the forces, was a precision job. In due course we correspondents, who now numbered more than a score, were bidden to a conference at which the invasion details and schedules were most frankly discussed by Admiral Turner, then commanding the Allied Amphibious Force in the South Pacific.

The plan he outlined was this:

At dawn on June 30, at least three infantry regiments, with the support of heavy and medium artillery, were to land from five large transports and numerous small craft at Rendova Harbor, six miles across the narrow strip of water separating Rendova Island from Munda Point on New Georgia proper. The landing was to be preceded by heavy air bombardment of Munda Point. While the ships were unloading, destroyers would shell coast and anti-aircraft gun positions on New Georgia.

Heavy and medium artillery was to be emplaced on the beaches of Rendova and on islands offshore, and an immediate attempt made to establish beachheads on New Georgia Island, six or eight miles from Munda Point. These beachheads would be supplied by barge and shallow-draft landing craft from the base to be established at Rendova Harbor. A force of not less than two infantry regiments, with cover of flanking artillery and dive bombers, was to advance from the beachheads due west, parallel with each other and the coast, against the core of Japanese resistance about Munda airstrip. One heavy naval bombardment, or a series, would precede the final assault on the strip, which was scheduled to begin seven to nine days after the Rendova landing.

The establishment of a secure beachhead on Rendova was the most important phase of the whole operation. Simultaneously, however, smaller expeditions were to deal with Japanese outposts on Vangunu Island and at Viru Harbor and Segi plantation on the west coast of New Georgia fronting Blanche Channel. It was proposed to build a fighter strip at Segi in record time, beginning work immediately the Japanese were ousted.

The recapture of Munda airfield was merely the first step in the recapture of the whole New Georgia group. The Japanese were also firmly established on Kolombangara Island, just north of New Georgia, with its airfield at Vila. Until they were thrown out, the conquest of the Central Solomons would be incomplete. While the Munda attack was developing, preparation was to be made for assault on Vila. Mixed marine and army elements would land at Rice Anchorage, on the northern coast of New Georgia, obliquely opposite Vila across Kula Gulf, and would assist the Munda operation by cutting the supply trail between Munda and Bairoko Harbor, almost directly opposite Vila. At the same time, the force would assure control of all anchorages and landing places on New Georgia for the eventual amphibious move against Kolombangara.

Such was the model plan of assault upon a Japanese island stronghold. The Central Solomons posed, on a small scale, every problem likely to be met in an advance through the western Pacific as far as the Philippines. The operation would involve provision of leakproof air cover at the extreme limit of fighter range, overwhelming superiority of bombers, both tactical and stategic deployment of naval forces, navigation of large convoys including swarms of small craft through difficult and indifferently charted waters, and organization and use of amphibious forces against defended and undefended localities alike. Anticipation, speed, precision and split-second timing were prerequisites of success. Success would blueprint a design for victory effective against any enemy island base from Guam to the Netherlands Indies.

Most of the correspondents, I think, came away from the conference with the feeling that the strike against the Central Solomons was of much greater ultimate importance than its territorial objectives. We certainly needed its air bases to hit at the series of airfields, anchorages and fortified zones on Bougainville Island, which was then the western bastion of Rabaul's defenses. But even an advance of 170 miles would not be the major gain of the operation. We envisaged the dim and stirring future when not 5 but 50 large transports would be used, not 600 planes but 6,000, not two divisions but 20. Tarawa, Eniwetok, Saipan were victories yet to be planned and won.

Personally, I was most impressed by the command's intention to confine the main attack to nine days and to eliminate attenuated land communications. I wondered, too, how Japanese morale would react to a rain of naval shells and aerial bombing heavier than anything so far experienced by him in the Pacific.

I was a little jumpy and overeager from hard work – from air reconnaissance trips up the Slot, a bombing mission on Munda, a night prowl with the PT boats. I had now done enough and seen enough to have a fervid, if mistaken, sense of participation in what was going on. But never again, after the martial enthusiasm stirred by the 21st Brigade in Moresby, could I commit the sin of incaution in dispatches.

I wrote: *'American generalship is facing its crucial test. Has it perfected tactics, trained troops, and devised equipment good enough to beat both the Japs and what was once our, but is now their, help – the terrain? This war is as much a battle of wits as it is a battle of guns, planes and warships. We need more than mechanical means to deliver explosive on the enemy – we need men to beat the forests and swamps and mountains and seas behind which he has entrenched himself. We need boatmen and pilots with genius, bushmen and guides with genius, divisions of fighters sharing a corporate genius. But above all we need generalship such as has not yet been seen in the Pacific war.'*

Nothing in this war is certain – least of all a master plan. I knew that. Three or six months ahead, the New Georgia campaign would perhaps be forgotten, eclipsed by bloodier and more spectacular battles than the extermination of 10,000 or 12,000 Japanese who had long been virtually cut off and who were probably ragged with constant bombing. But its real significance would not diminish. It would prove something – how much down-to-earth combat cunning had been learned by the people who were chiefly fighting the Japanese, the Americans, in the 18 months that followed Pearl Harbor.

All morning the bombers thundered away from Henderson Field. It was a gusty, yellow day again. The sea was choppy. There was no visible concentration of shipping – only destroyers roving in the channel with the wind whipping mare's-tails from their stacks, and two transports embarking the last troops for the Rendova landing.

The men were clad in leopard suits, weighted down under arms and equipment. They went into the barges speedily and silently. From an escort destroyer, I watched them swarm on gangways and decks, and disappear below. The ships swung sluggishly on their anchor chains. The winches clanked. The screws turned. The gunners stood by their guns.

What had once seemed an operation of great complexity was now simple. A thousand tributaries of purpose had come together into one stream of action. These ships must pass west for 170 miles. The men they carried must be landed by tomorrow's dawn on Vangunu, Rendova and New Georgia. There they must be kept.

From a score of dispersal points the invasion fleet came to its rendezvous at sea. It formed into columns, steamed toward the setting sun with the destroyers herding it. Squadrons of fighters slid, circled and darted in the sky. The signal lamps flickered on the dark wings of bridges. *This was the hour . . .* the little D-day of the Pacific.

Unblinking eyes strained at the sky. Restless eyes searched the water, pausing suspiciously at each feather of white and each shadow on distant waves.

In the humming gloom within the ships, the invaders sat on iron decks with their legs outstretched, listening. Some played cards, some read. Some went to church services. Some slept. Some talked and laughed. At dawn the big lottery would be drawn. But each in his heart of hearts said: '*It won't be me.*' There was a sameness in their faces, whatever they did.

The lightning darted behind the islets. The blue battle lights gleamed in the 'tween decks. The night was dark and warm, and the wind damp. No sound of gunfire disturbed the wind's sighing. The minutes dragged into hours, hours toward the edges of night.

There was the mass of a tall mountain to the left, a gloomy line of jungle on the water. The hum of engines was pitched in a lower key now. Was this *it*?

The dark before dawn and disembarkation stations. The orders boomed through the speakers and the ships seethed in their bowels. Bells clanged and thousands of feet shuffled on greasy steel decks.

Disembarkation stations.

The landing craft were deploying in a long line inshore. The water was still as melted grease. The motor of a barge roared, then others in quickening succession. With blunt noses high and sterns down, they cut curving paths of foam across the track of the big ships. Then they swung into line and sped for the unseen coast. The men in leopard skins huddled in them, leaning forward, helmet straps denting the bunched muscles of their cheeks.

The bombarding destroyer force had approached from the west. Now they were steaming down the narrows between Kororana Island and Munda Point. They passed like painted ships. Smoke belched out of them and the guns spoke, tracer cascading down the gray predawn.

So . . . this was it. What now? There was a roar as the salvo burst. The guns settled down to a steady drumming. Brilliant flashes from the enemy guns ran along the shore of New Georgia.

But on Rendova Island there was no sound. The Higgins boats played follow-the-leader, charging the gaps in the reefs at 20 knots. Inside the last obstacle of hidden coral heads they fanned out and raced for the beach.

A tumble-down plantation house and copra sheds stood near the water – headquarters of the enemy's defense company. The boats grounded 30 feet from the tidemark and the first wave of troops hurled themselves through knee-deep water for the cover of the palm trunks.

Far off to the left a tommy gunner fired on a Japanese who had sighted the barges and run to give warning. In the half light, knots of startled little Japanese soldiers were seen to scuttle for their arms. Through the noise of automatic arms their squealing was loud and horrible. An officer pranced out of a shed, waving a sword. Bullets eviscerated him. His bowels ran out of his uniform like sawdust from a torn rag doll.

The Americans advanced slowly through the coconut groves in open order, blasting at every movement in undergrowth, every fleeting figure half seen. Sometimes a rifleman would pause to prod with his boot the shapelessness of a corpse. *Make sure*, the book of words said. *Japs fox dead and shoot you in the back.* That was to be remembered.

It began to rain. The big drops spat and hissed. When day came, the virulent green centrosema and grass beneath the palms were flattened by wet.

Nothing to it, buddy . . . A piece of cake . . .

The tin cans were still blasting Munda Point and the firing of the tommy guns grew fainter as the enemy ran into the jungle. The beachhead on Rendova was secure.

Far out in the channel, the big transports were unloading. Trucks and tractors and jeeps came out of the holds and into the barges, drivers at wheel and engines running.

The bombarding destroyers hauled out of the narrow water before full light. One had been hit. A few Jap three-inch batteries still popped on Munda Point, and water spouts from the shells rose lazily. Before noon, a regiment was established – its tent poles, its cookhouses, its officers' bedrolls, all shipshape.

The first medium batteries were emplaced on Bau and Kororana islands to the north, and the first heavies behind East Beach in Rendova Harbor.

By 2.30 p.m. the heavy transports had disgorged and were on their way home. Two hours later, the first wave of Japanese torpedo and dive bombers appeared abreast the cone of Rendova Mountain, and slid down the timbered slopes upon the retiring invasion fleet. The flagship *McCawley*, a 14,000-ton

transport, was twice hit amidship and taken in tow. But by sunset, the Japanese air command was scraping the bottom of the dish. Our fighter patrols and intense antiaircraft fire had destroyed or disabled practically every enemy squadron that was at hand for the primary defense of the Central Solomons. It was a great victory.

In a last desperate kick, the enemy sent 23 cumbersome seaplanes against the fleet. That kind of suicidal stupidity makes opponents doubt if the Jap is quite human. The clumsy 'ducks' were sitting shots for the Bofors 40's and the 20 millimeters. Nineteen of them were blown apart in the air without one bomb finding its mark. At midnight, however, the *McCawley* sank after an explosion amidship, attributed 'officially' to a torpedo from an enemy submarine.

By noon next day, the remaining big ships were dispersed in safe anchorages and the supply of invasion points was taken over by transport destroyers and tank and infantry landing craft. So far, the operation had gone like clockwork. Ship losses were below estimate, control of the air was assured.

Enough troops and material to sustain an attack on Munda Point had been landed with trivial losses and exactly on schedule. Heavy and medium artillery was placed to bring the enemy's garrison area on Munda under continuous fire. The air arm was cooperating with split-second precision in bombing, reconnaissance and strafing.

Lines of communication were also secure. Enemy resistance at Segi had been negligible, although small bodies of Japanese marines had been met at Viru Harbor and at Wickham Anchorage on Vangunu Island. Marine raider detachments, following 48 hours of heavy air and naval bombardment, took care of them. At no time were the enemy garrisons on the flank of the channel any real menace to the supply of troops deploying against Munda. The important amphibious phase of the campaign – its most complicated and tricky chapter – was completed with 100 per cent success.

The problem now was to maintain full air cover of both the forward areas and the lines of supply. The sea blockade of New Georgia and Kolombangara must be held tight against

Japanese efforts from their bases on Bougainville Island.

Fighter squadrons stationed on Guadalcanal and the Russell Islands kept unbroken dawn-to-dawn patrols over Rendova, breaking up repeated attempts by Japanese heavy and dive bombers to paste the beachheads. American heavy bombers pounded the Bougainville airfields without cease.

In that critical week of the consolidation of Rendova, the Japanese only twice succeeded in putting through considerable bomber forces. On July 2, between 20 and 30 dive bombers caught headquarters elements of two regiments undispersed behind East Beach and inflicted several hundred casualties. Two days later, dumps on the beach itself were hit. The two attacks taught an inexperienced army command the value of prompt dispersal, but they did not do enough damage to delay or cripple the initial development of the movement against Munda Point.

Within 24 hours of the Rendova landings, beachheads had been seized and consolidated on New Georgia within six miles of the airfield. In spite of the narrow and difficult reef channels in Roviana lagoon, supplies and reinforcements were ferried across it by Higgins boat and tank and infantry landing craft. They suffered little or no interference from the Japanese.

One contingency was not resolved. Would the Japanese bring heavy fleet units south to batter the American naval blockade? If so, the most vital aspect of the campaign was yet to come. In readiness, I concentrated after the landings on keeping in touch with the work of the bomber and fighter squadrons based on Guadalcanal, and of the two cruiser task forces charged with smashing any attempts to restart a 'Tokyo Express' to reinforce Vila Habor on Kolombangara Island.

As it happened, the Japanese chose not to use their heavy fleet units. Instead, on the night of July 5–6, they dispatched from the Shortland Islands, some 100 miles to the northwest, a force of 19 ships – light cruisers, destroyers and transports – to run men and supplies into Kolombangara or Bairoko on the north coast of New Georgia.

The American cruiser task force on duty followed the Jap

fleet boldly into Kula Gulf and in a remarkable night engagement destroyed three quarters of the enemy force. American losses were the cruiser *Helena*, hit by a chance torpedo, and one destroyer. The engagement was remarkable in that only one Japanese vessel, a destroyer, was visually sighted by any ship of the intercepting force.

From above, the Kula Gulf battle was an extraordinary spectacle. I had an owl's-eye view of it from the hull of a Catalina flying boat. The night was black and moonless, the sea scarcely distinguishable from the mass of the land. The wakes of maneuvering ships appeared as fine white scratches on the smoky glass of the gulf waters.

Now and then gun flashes would briefly illuminate the shape of ships as small as toys 12,000 feet below. Tracer showers curved through the darkness at queer angles – flights of lazy yellow and red comets chasing one another in a strange silence.

Then, in the unheard hell of gunfire and churned water below, a salvo would strike a Japanese ship. It would expand, rather than explode, into a glowing sun of fire that grew redder and deeper until it was extinguished forever in the sea. One by one the cruisers remorselessly ran down the ships of the now fugitive Japanese force. One by one they died in a blaze of infernal beauty.

It was a pageant of remote conflict never to be forgotten . . . a pageant of light and darkness in such designs as God might idly have fashioned when He first called light and darkness from the void of uncreation. Only the heart recalled that in each blossoming of flame were the macerated sinews and bones of men, and all the sorrow of self-tortured humankind.

Rendova. The blockade was still held. On July 9, the two regiments sent across Roviana lagoon for the attack against Lambeti plantation and Munda point on New Georgia, reached their line of departure after brisk skirmishes. The troops were advancing at the rate of 1,000 yards a day.

No blitz, I thought. Perhaps a clue to the slow rate of progress lay in the now paralyzing mud of Rendova. I had seen a good deal of mud – island, monsoon mud – but Rendova mud was the worst yet from the military point of view. It was clayey and it clung. Even the machine-loving Americans had stopped trying to use motor transport. Even the jeeps squatted disconsolately on their axles, beaten. Sometimes a three-tonner made the 600-yard trip from the beach, by dint of hauling itself from palm trunk to palm trunk on its own windlass. It was less labor to carry by hand anything that could be carried.

The coastal strip behind Rendova Harbor was only a few hundred yards wide. The slopes of the mountain that dominates the northern end of the island swept down almost to the water. The jungle – deep, cool-green and invitingly clean – ended where the drab coconuts began.

Hundreds of brown tents were set up under the palms. Each tent had its foxhole. There was an air-raid siren up the slope. Very seldom during the day did it blare forth its chilling wails, but it worked hard at night. Japanese nuisance raiders came with the darkness. 'Condition Red! Condition Red!' the watchers would call from their steel towers on the hillside.

The troops would go to ground in a foot of stinking water or mud.

Our antiaircraft, which was increasing in strength day by day, would put up a hellish barrage, and the shrapnel patter down. In the watchtower I often felt the concussion of the discharges flutter the damp shirt on my back like a breeze.

Although the indiscriminate bombing of the sneak raiders rarely found a target in the bivouac area, the nights were a misery of noise and nerviness – a misery aggravated by perpetual dampness, and by the countless thousands of small black millepedes that infested the earth and undergrowth all around us.

For the first few days I was alone in the tent allotted correspondents at divisional headquarters. Then I was invited to share the shelter of my next-door neighbors, the G2's orderlies. They were steady, taciturn lads – typical products of New England small towns. I was impressed because they never grouched or cursed at officers or became fractious, as most Australian troops would have done in similar conditions. But

268

one night, the quietest of them said in a conversational voice: 'Everything about this place is a nightmare. Sometimes I can't believe it's real. The noise of the guns, the bombs, the dirt – the suffering and dying . . . We always knew war was horrible, but I don't think any of us realized war was as horrible as this.'

That started me into a priggishness. I said, jerking a thumb across the straits at Munda: 'It's worse over there!'

'I know that,' the youngster said softly. 'It must be so bad I wonder they don't go mad.'

Our second full-scale naval bombardment of Munda Point on July 11 was to have coincided with the final land push against the tactical objective – the airfield; but Japanese resistance and American supply difficulties were seriously holding up this advance on New Georgia. It had faltered at a point on the coast about five miles from the edges of Lambeti plantation. The perfect schedule was showing signs of breaking down.

Throughout the day on July 11, the field artillery, the 155's and 105's, pumped salvos at the Japanese hidden in the bush. The flights of shells passed overhead with a noise like electric trains rushing out of tunnels.

I had never before heard a big artillery preparation. The barking 25-pounders on Moresby's perimeter had been popguns compared with this. That night I slept at the observation tower. The cruisers and destroyers were due to bombard from three until four o'clock in the morning.

There was a raid by a small group of Jap Type 97's and Kawanisis just after sunset. The antiaircraft fire was even fiercer than usual and one plane exploded over Roviana, showering the sea with burning oil.

The men on watch woke me at 2.50. It was very dark. I climbed onto the shaky platform of the tower with a pair of field glasses. As the second hand of my watch touched the hour, the first broadside from the American cruisers and destroyers went away in a sheet of lemon-yellow flame and a cloud of luminous, bluish smoke.

The narrow gut of the channel was a polished calm. The ships cruised in line, their silhouettes revealed by the gun flashes – lethal monsters swimming in the mild shallows. Shower after shower of red, yellow, green and blue embers arched away from them. The guns made a tumbling sound over the taut skin of the sea. The shellbursts were mere points of light, pricking the dark mass of Munda's coast. 'God, but they're getting hell!' exclaimed the man beside me.

Then a Jap dump exploded. The sky was lit up. For perhaps the fifth of a second I saw Munda Point as it really was – a barren, steel-swept, deathly desert. The coconuts had been shredded by blast of every vestige of foliage. The sturdy trunks whipped like canes in the wind of explosion. It was inconceivable that anything could continue to live on land raked by such fire.

At four o'clock the ships withdrew to the northwest, spurting antiaircraft fire against a single enemy patrol plane.

At dawn American dive bombers started to arrive from Guadalcanal. In squadrons they circled for position, then tipped and plummeted down on Munda Point through desultory flak from the Japanese dual-purpose three-inch guns. It surprised me that any guns remained in action at all after the shelling.

Two hundred planes dived on the core of the Japanese positions on Munda that morning. I thought it was surely the beginning of the end, and obtained orders to go up the line immediately. General H.'s Higgins boat was making regular runs between divisional headquarters on Rendova and the Zanana beachhead on New Georgia.

It was cloudless, windless weather again after a week of rain. Roviana lagoon, the old-timers had told me, was the most beautiful place in all the South Seas. Now I believed them. The clear water was studded with a multitude of verdant islands where the jungle came down to the sea margins. Its vine flowers and exotic palms were reflected in depths tinted with the pink and heliotrope and creamy white of coral ledges. Fish schools darted in angular showers through the sinuous corridors of the reef.

There was a red alert as the boat passed between Bau and

Kororana Island, but it could not quite distract me from the beauty of the lagoon. It took the American 105 batteries to do that. The halcyon island in the strait was riddled with our gun positions, and the gunners seemed to take malicious delight in firing just as a boat traveled under the muzzles of their concealed batteries.

To the west, the Japanese were doing a little counterbattery work at about a 7,000-yard range, but generally their aim was erratic and the shells as often as not fell short into the water. This time it was different. The moment we reached the narrowest part of the channel – a bare 12 feet from marker buoy to marker buoy – a Jap gun started to range on the gap. The boat was going dead slow and the shell splashes drenched us.

Being shelled in a Higgins boat is an experience that makes the toughest man feel like a hermit crab that has lost its shell – revoltingly tender, and naked down to the very skin of his soul. I was almost tearfully grateful when the coxswain ran under the lee of a small island and hit Zanana at speed.

As a beach it wasn't much to look at – a strip of coarse sand and coral fragments hardly 10 yards wide. Behind it was a patch of deep and gloomy jungle that concealed the beachhead installations from enemy reconnaissance planes. Great quantities of food, ammunition and material were fed through here to the front, out of a series of untidy, ill-dispersed dumps. Zanana beachhead bore evidence of the truism that organizational theory and operational practice are by no means interchangeable terms.

But the engineers had built a jeep road running westward roughly parallel with the coast and had managed to keep abreast of the combat troops' advance. The regimental command post was 6,000 yards west.

At headquarters it was clear that the push was not going according to plan. That took me aback, but in such cases you don't ask questions. You keep your ears open. Nights, it seemed, were the trouble. The Japs had the edge on us in night fighting. The troops were getting no rest. A number of wounded were coming down the line.

'How are you doing, bud?'

'You can't see the little suckers! Haven't seen one yet.'

These men were showing strain. They were showing strain worse, even, than the 2nd/16th Battalion of Australians after they had been cut to pieces trying to hold Isurava and Eora Creek ridges. But it was not the strain of the prolonged jungle campaigning. They had been in the line only a week. It was the strain of jungle fighting for which, in spite of all their training maneuvers, they had not been really prepared. It was the strain of blind fighting, of firing at sound, of endless listening in a blackness terrible with mysterious sounds.

'You can't see the little suckers!'

The men were still in good condition. They had not had time to sweat off their good food. But their eyes were hollow with sleeplessness and their lips slack with exhaustion. Their leopard uniforms were already stiff with mud and stinking with jungle mold. Many of them had knife wounds – not inflicted by the Japanese, but by their own nerve-racked comrades in frontline foxholes who had mistaken them for the enemy in the darkness.

By day the troops had been making steady, if unspectacular, progress clearing the outer system of enemy defenses. It was hard, unfamiliar, perilous work. The underbrush was very dense – so dense that it was rarely possible to see more than 30 feet ahead. The Japanese were strongly entrenched. They had dug or blasted out deep machine-gun pits in the shallow earth and underlying coral. They had roofed them with tree trunks, sometimes three layers thick, covered them with coral and earth, and camouflaged them cunningly. Apart from the concealed entrances, the only apertures in these roofed pits were narrow slits that gave the machine guns limited play, but the whole system was so well planned that every obvious approach was covered by interlocking fields of fire.

Such a defense system could not be broken by frontal assault while the Japanese ammunition lasted. Artillery preparation was not wholly effective. Many of the earthworks were so solidly constructed they could withstand even a direct hit by 105's – and direct hits were few, because accurate observation of fire was almost impossible in dense undergrowth beneath a jungletop.

Dive bombing against infantry positions in the jungle was useless, except as a morale breaker. Target areas could be only roughly defined and where American troops were operating close in, the bombs were as much danger to them as the enemy. The only way to crack the Japs was by patiently probing out the weaknesses of their interlocking system of defenses. When a corridor not swept by bullets was found, each foxhole could be reduced with grenades and bayonets.

But this type of warfare was excessively hard on troops not intensively or realistically trained for bush fighting. That was particularly true at night. Our men were at a distinct disadvantage in night fighting. At three o'clock every afternoon they began digging in.

At the first dark, the Japanese came cockily out of their holes. They were practiced night fighters. All the emphasis of their preparation for war had been on the art of maneuver, confidence and co-ordinated action in heavy cover and in darkness. They swarmed in the trees overlooking the shallow shelters scooped by the exhausted Americans. They sniped at every projecting head, tossed grenades at every position they could locate, howled, catcalled, jibed.

Because the Americans were unfamiliar with the jungle – because they had not learned the art of silent movement, or how to distinguish the normal sounds of the forest from the abnormal sounds, because they had no confidence in the cover given by jungle to men who understand it – they lay immobilized all through the hours of darkness.

The Japanese kept them awake and on the *qui vive*. When they learned that our men were upset by their tactics, they were emboldened. Some fanatical seekers after immortality walked among our foxholes throwing grenades or jumping in with knives.

The nights had been rainy, and the gloom pitchy under the mats of foliage. Each dawn saw the attackers more worn-out and more 'trigger happy'. Until the pitiless strain had selected the toughest soldiers, three quarters of the wounded who

273

streamed back to the beachhead had no visible mark upon them. They were wounded in brain – shocked into uselessness by terror of the night. Many a man who would have willingly charged a machine-gun nest single handed by day wept with fear when the shadows grew long and he knew he must try to live through another night.

The galling part of it was the contemptuous confidence with which a Fijian scout detachment led by New Zealand officers wandered at will through the enemy lines after dark. They were as superior to the Japanese in the bush as the Japanese were superior to the American rank and file.

It was Isurava all over again – except that this time our lines of communication were 8 miles long, not 80. What tipped the balance our way were scores of dive bombers and a greater concentration of artillery than had ever before been used against the Japanese in the Pacific.

When I came back to the command post after my first visit to the regiment on the inland flank, I was haunted by memory – not of the dead scattered in the undergrowth in their positions of grotesque indignity, nor of the stench and bloody filth of smashed Japanese redoubts, but by memory of the living into whose features were stamped the jungle's brand of horror.

At the command post they said the Japanese were preventing a junction of the regiment advancing westward against Munda Point on the inland flank and the regiment advancing parallel with it up the coast toward Lambeti plantation. The situation, however, was being met. Pressure on the Japs' coastal flank was being increased. New beachheads were being established down the coast nearer the front and the heavy artillery was slowly but surely crushing enemy resistance. Tanks had been landed and would go into action tomorrow. That would clinch it!

I thought: What if the Japanese have deployed forces inland and stage a counterattack from the bush upon the exposed flank of these troops in their present condition? What good will tanks and artillery be then? There won't be any regiment left.

274

The Japanese either did not have the strength to make that maneuver or they hadn't the sense. The best they did was send two or three companies around the exposed inland flank through jungle and begin harrying command posts and isolated detachments far in the rear of the main forces. Even so feeble a move was sufficient to hold up the progress of the attack three or four days.

The regimental command post was forced back 4,000 yards near Zanana. A retreat? The colonel said no – but all the same, touch had been temporarily lost with the inland flank. Things were not so good. We'd better move cautiously, or better still not move at all. Early that morning the water point on the Bariki River, which supplied the forward areas, had come under fire of a Japanese patrol. The next 24 hours, I thought, would tell quite a story . . . I wasn't looking forward to it.

CHAPTER 21

UNFINISHED STORY

SEVENTEEN days after the Zanana landing the Japanese began their feeble infiltrating counterattack. The afternoon was quiet. I had been up the line to visit the northern flank and came back to the regimental command post for a rest. I killed time making a typewriter table out of green canes and split lawyer vine, and gathering armfuls of dry pandanus leaves to bind together the sloppy, red-brown mud on the floor of the tent.

At four o'clock I finished lashing the last crosspiece on the table top and was squatting on my heels thinking about nothing in particular, when there was a sudden prolonged burst of machine-gun fire from a new direction – the hitherto quiet jungle to the northwest. It sounded close – only a couple of thousand yards away.

A patrol went out to investigate immediately – a dozen weary youngsters with lines of tension creased about the corners of their eyes. They returned in 50 minutes at the double. The sergeant in charge reported that the camp of medics at the old command post site near the Bariki River had been attacked by a patrol of Japanese, 200 strong.

It looked bad – both for them and for us. The Japanese had come from the direction of the unpatrolled bush inland. We had fewer than 70 men to defend the camp.

Supper that night was frankfurters and sauerkraut, I remember. By the time I had finished eating, the defense platoon had put the final touches on a perimeter of shallow foxholes. A machine-gun and Browning automatic rifle pit was dug only five yards from the pegs of my tent. Sunset was quiet and twilight brief. The little wind had dropped.

The big guns were blasting again and the shells whooshed over in flocks of five and six. They burst against the Jap pill-boxes behind Lambeti.

When darkness came the bombardment stopped. I sat on a cot by the edge of a foxhole, listening to the sounds of the jungle waking up for the night. I had been listening to jungle noises for a long time, but this night they seemed to be more and stranger than I had ever heard before. There was the squeal of flying foxes, the harsh cry of hunting owls, the far-off thunder of frogs in a swamp, the scraping of crickets, an insect that sounded like someone softly beating an empty can with a rotten stick.

Attack came suddenly – the nerve-shredding *brhhh-brhhh* of an automatic rifle a few yards away. Within seconds every machine gun on the perimeter opened up. One felt rather than heard the sound. It was like a multitude of tiny hammers upon the spine.

Five of us jumped into the foxhole together. Bullets ripped gashes of moonlight in the inky drape of the tent roof. A grenade exploded with jarring concussion.

Two men were burrowing into the rotten coral ahead of me. Two others crouched over my awkwardly twisted legs. It was agonizing, but to have made them move would have exposed the others or myself to the withering Japanese fire. The hole was too shallow and small for five. The bullets were whining only an inch or two overhead. After awhile I peered at my watch and said: 'Half-past seven.'

The man on my knees answered: 'Who the hell cares what the time is? It's my birthday.'

'Many happy returns. Happy birthday,' said the man lying across my ankles.

Silence. The firing was cut off.

The moon floated above the trees. The moon of New Georgia is very bright and in its light the forest was a stark, speckled black and white. The insect chorus diminished. The cry of the hunting birds was more abrupt and harsh. Then a new sound came out of the cold, white moonlight – the sound of Japanese voices, shrill and high toned.

I was surprised and affronted. They chattered, shouted to one another arrogantly, groaned, screamed, and broke sticks. For men who so often died from making a noise, the noise they made had almost an obscene quality to it. They sounded like apes with human tongues.

The first burst of cross fire from our guns had hit hard. They had withdrawn 100 yards into the thickets and made no fresh move for 30 minutes. It was the longest half hour I have lived. I wanted to get out of the hole and go quietly away into the bush, but I knew I would never get through the perimeter alive. There was nobody above ground but the Japs.

I thought they were setting up mortars as they so often did in these night attacks. And 90-millimeter mortar fire at 100 yards' range would be very deadly, even against men in far better, deeper foxholes than ours.

But the next move was not mortar fire. Even though the first bursts of our guns must have pinpointed our perimeter positions clearly, the enemy was still uncertain of our strength and disposition. They sent in close reconnaissance.

One Japanese hid himself in a gully about 30 yards out and began squalling ludicrously: 'Aid, aid, doc! Give aid to me. I am wounded!' He just screamed the words because he had been taught to scream them, parrot fashion. Their pitch was as blood chilling as the cry of an epileptic. A few nights before, the troops might have fired on him, and the muzzle flashes would have betrayed their position. Not now.

Apart from the noise made by the squalling 'tactician' in the deadfall, the stillness of the jungle now became deathly. The birds were quiet. Even the frog chorus seemed hushed. Inch by inch I lifted my head. One rustle, and a grenade might have been tossed at me out of a bush, but I couldn't stand the blindness any more. I peered over the parapet.

In a little patch of moonlight about 15 yards away a Japanese soldier was standing upright, as still as a statue. I could see the shapeless folds of his uniform, the rifle he held, the glint of the bayonet, the peaked, shoddy cloth cap on his head. I saw him and perhaps twenty other men saw him – but no one fired. We knew he stood there deliberately inviting death, for a reason.

Somewhere behind him were two or three of his comrades with grenades ready. If anyone had fired they would have lobbed the grenades at the flash. Four or five Americans might have died in exchange for one Japanese life.

I would have liked the courage to keep watching the human bait while he waited for honorable death, but I lacked it. Inch by inch I put my head down.

There was a soft, metallic click. The man lying across my knees cocked his pistol. I twisted my mouth against his ear and breathed: 'Don't shoot! Grenades!'

He whispered back: 'Only if he jumps into the hole. They've been doing that lately.' But he didn't jump in.

The posts on the jeep track opened up furiously for 30 seconds. This time the screams were genuine. Afterwards the man who had been screeching 'Aid, aid!' withdrew to a greater distance and began imitating the cry of a stabbed man, calling after each shriek: 'Christ, he's got me in the guts. I'm stabbed! Water, water!'

He kept this up for half an hour at 30- or 40-second intervals. Then he crept in close again and began calling: 'Buddy, are you there? Please, please answer me!'

The main body of the enemy, still 100 yards away, broke out chattering anew. They had suffered sobering losses. They abandoned close attack and put snipers in trees. Every few seconds there would be a sharp whack and a bullet would come singing out of the thickets. One or two Japanese, working alone, edged up and threw grenades blindly. Two bounded off the earth at the ends of our foxhole and exploded, but no one was even scratched.

The war was going on elsewhere, too. From time to time our heavies would fire a salvo at Lambeti or Munda, but the noise was so normal by now that one scarcely remarked about it. Just after 11 o'clock, however, one of these spasmodic bombardments grew particularly noisy, and I heard shells that screamed in a different pitch. Instead of passing high and to the left, they were directly overhead and burst in the bush 200 yards away, northwest.

Four more followed, each closer. The last fell so near us that the sides and bottom of the foxhole bounced and shivered, and pieces of coral showered down on our twitching bodies.

The next explosion was to the southeast. I thought: Well, this finishes it! The Japs have got a three-inch in action, and sooner or later they'll hit the button.

An army of coconut crabs, disturbed by the concussions, started to move through camp. Four or five of the big ugly brutes came slithering and clicking into the hole and crawled over us.

Suddenly I realized that the shells were not Japanese at all; they were American! Somewhere, four or five miles away, a battery commander had decided to take the risk of supporting us. Firing blind, by map alone, the guns were putting down a box barrage on three sides of the command post to prevent the Japanese from bringing mortars close enough to bombard accurately.

Map firing by night in the jungle without visual observation of fire is a job for a virtuoso. One trivial error of calculation, and the guns would have done the job the Japs so far had failed to do – blown the whole camp area to glory.

No error occurred. It was a gunners' masterpiece. The spray of shrapnel drove the enemy from his encirclement in the open. For six hours the guns dropped a curtain of high explosive about us. Never once was a burst farther than 200 yards from the perimeter and only twice was one closer than 20 yards. In a swathe 200 yards deep the leaves of the vines and trees were wilted by blast or shredded by metal. It was a long time, six hours . . . burrowing deeper listening to them whistle . . . wondering about the next. A very long time.

When the light came the shelling ceased. A native runner brought through the lines a message that reinforcements were on their way from Zanana, which had also been attacked.

I waited until the last snipers were likely to have slid down from their trees, then crawled stiffly out and sat on the edge of a cot.

No one talked much. The man who had had a birthday borrowed my razor and solemnly shaved with half a cup of water.

from a canteen and a meat can for a mirror.

I went out into the brush. The defenders were coming slowly out of their holes. A patrol was dispatched to look for signs of the enemy. I found the colonel brushing his thinning hair before a steel mirror set on a tent pole.

'Good morning, Colonel,' I said. 'Have a good night?'

He grinned politely.

'What's the score?'

'Thirty Japs – so far. There are nine just down the road. Little suckers walked up it as if they owned it.'

'Anybody hurt?'

'One killed. One shot through the legs.'

I went to the road. Five Japanese, mangled by machine-gun fire, were sprawled like flabby sacks in the mud ruts. Four others lay around the bole of a big tree. They were pale yellow, and the blood showed bright against their unearthly waxen skins. They must have been out in the jungle for a long time because they were dirty and their boots were moldy. Pathetic little beards were sprouting on their slack cheeks and lips. Their bellies were swollen with malaria.

For the first time I found myself looking on the dead without pity. For behind the bright morning, the sparkling morning, was the memory of an ape calling with the tongue of a man: *'Christ, he's got me in the guts! Water! Water!'*

After breakfast I went back to Zanana beachhead to find out what had happened there. Another strong patrol had penetrated within 100 yards of the boat pool, but the machine gunners had smashed the attack. Japanese bodies were strewn along the road. Out in the bush were the shelled remains of two small 'knee' mortars.

A detachment of sullen-faced Fijian scouts was awaiting orders to go out and locate the raiders. They were meditatively honing their bush knives.

The beachhead defense company, however, was busy upon its foxholes. More night attacks were expected and reinforcements had been summoned from Rendova. To counteract 'infiltration' and minimize the chance of 'mistakes' in the darkness, the little earthworks were so clotted together that in the defense area there was more foxhole than flat earth.

An air-raid alarm sounded. I got out quickly. The prospect of being caught by bombers on that jammed beachhead disagreed with my stomach.

I went along to the regimental aid post and watched the medics attending three wounded prisoners, and the intelligence officers questioning them. They were men of the 6th Division, the 'Emperor's Own'. They said they had been sent from Truk to avenge the fate of their comrades on Guadalcanal.

One Japanese, a major, had a terrible thigh wound from a shell splinter. He was middle-aged and fleshy as a wrestler. He lay on a litter with his brown, almond eyes expressionlessly watching the medics about their work. They poured two pints of yellow blood plasma into his veins.

Then he said something in his own language and the interpreter bent over him. His hand moved with a gesture of distaste over the clotted blood and slime on his belly. The interpreter straightened his back. 'He wants a hot bath,' he said dryly. 'Privileged class.' A couple of minutes later the major sighed deeply, smiled, and died.

I begged a lift in a Higgins boat to the new beachhead at Laiana which had been established several thousand yards west to shorten the supply line to the left, the coastward, flank. The tanks were operating from here. The Japanese had got two new batteries into action on Nusulavita Island off Munda Point. They were dividing attention between the American 105's on Roviana Island and the barge traffic up the coast. A hundred yards ahead of us a Higgins boat was hit and dissolved in a fountain of wreckage and spray. The shells plodded steadily back and forth across the channel. Later in the morning dive bombers were called to deal with them.

The forward elements at Laiana were only 600 yards from shore. This was eliminating the problem of land supply with a vengeance!

That day – and the next – I held that discretion was the better part of war corresponding, and avoided running the

282

gauntlet of heavy Jap mortar fire up to the front. Even at that, the battalion command post was not immune. It was politic to hold any casual conversation with the head well below ground.

The troops were steadying. In day fighting they were getting the measure of the enemy. One lad came back boasting that he had shot nine Japanese snipers 'like God damned parrots roosting in a tree.'

The tanks were inching forward and clearing the enemy out of the thickest country. They wallowed and crashed and snorted through the undergrowth at two miles an hour. Each tank operated independently with a screen of riflemen behind it to prevent the Japanese jumping out of their holes and using magnetic bombs. It was remarkable how cheered the soldiers were by the sight of a machine to help them.

The jungle was still so dense that it was impossible to spot a Jap position until it fired. Sometimes you could not spot it even after it had fired. The tanks waddled up and down, slow as tortoises, pinpointing the enemy nests by the direction from which the machine-gun bullets rattled on their armor plate. Surely no form of warfare could be less spectacular, less observable.

There was bush, noise, death. Nothing else – no rolling clouds of smoke, nor flashes from gun muzzles, nor running men, nor shouting. More than 10,000 soldiers, American and Jap, were locked in a death struggle in positions extending about 2,000 yards from flank to flank. Yet at the points of contact between the opposing forces one rarely saw six live men together at the same time. The jungle drowned the battle like an opaque green liquid.

Progress was slow. The Japanese had made use of every natural feature in planning their defense. Sometimes it took 36 hours to reduce a single position. Repeatedly the advance was held up by some small, stubborn enemy post, fighting without hope. The enemy was prepared to die to a man rather than yield a square yard of stinking jungle. When the positions were reduced, their stench of conglomerated human dung and filth was appalling.

The fighting spirit of the attacking Americans was being

drained by sheer fatigue. It was found increasingly difficult to keep the inland flank properly supplied, though the jeep track to it was less than eight miles long.

The regiment inland had again established contact with the coastwise spearhead after being cut off for two days, but its command posts and the jeep track were still harried by night raiders.

No hope of relief lay in marine raider columns arriving overland from Rice Anchorage. The Rice Anchorage force had quite enough trouble of its own. It was fighting desperately to cut the enemy's supply trail from Bairoko to Munda, and to reduce Bairoko itself. So far it had had little success. A patrol of native scouts went out to establish contact with it and estimate its situation.

Eventually, the failure of the right inland flank to make any progress at all held up the entire attack. The men were now exhausted and must be relieved. Their casualties from shock and nervous collapse exceeded their number of wounded.

The command could not whistle up reinforcements of properly trained and hardened jungle fighters. There were none. It had no units trained to stalk the Japanese positions at night. It could not, at this juncture, switch the whole plan of attack to a frontal assault across the Munda bar and thus reap the benefit of the tremendous artillery, air and naval preparation. The Japanese defense system of the airfield was now a hollow shell, but there was no way of taking advantage of this while its jungle perimeter remained intact.

But the command could – and did – whistle up more machines to get it out of the tough spot it was in. The dive bombers came over in hundreds. The tanks mounted flame throwers to scorch the Japanese out of their pits. To the horror of the unseen battle was added the cloying stink of roasted human flesh.

The Japanese must have known that in the end they would be overwhelmed by sheer weight of steel, but still they fought on. My mind repeated the words of the Japanese admiral: 'We are willing to sacrifice 10,000,000 men to win our war in the Pacific. How many men is America prepared to sacrifice?'

Here was that policy in grim practice. What matter if 10 Japanese died, so long as they took one American with them? That was a supportable rate of exchange.

A toll of Japanese dead, balanced against our own, will never prove anything. Here, in New Georgia, in what should have been the final phase of an operation planned long and carefully to demonstrate what could be achieved by superiority of war machinery and of strategic concepts, was proof that the human element cannot be eliminated from any formula for victory. Here in New Georgia was a situation that might recur endlessly throughout the Pacific.

Here on New Georgia the machine would win. But it wasn't going to win with very much margin. Would that slender margin be enough assurance of success when the time came to apply the Munda formula elsewhere?

I wondered if the 17 months I had spent in New Guinea and the islands of the South Pacific had, after all, denied me any sight of victory in the making. Perhaps grand strategy envisaged some totally different plan by which Japan could be struck in the heart – or some plan by which the cohesion of Japan's war machine could be destroyed in its entirety rather than piecemeal.

Perhaps. So it proved to be. But on that I then had no more right of conjecture than any old gentleman at home, with a map on his knees winning the war nightly. It was utterly beyond the field of my observation.

The foxholes were down to the coral. The white grit was scraped up and scattered over the earth. The leaves of the myrtles were flabby, shaking in a sluggish wind. The sun of morning laid its quiet weight upon the bodies of men sheltering.

An air fight was going on overhead. The fighters whined and whistled and tapped. One fell flaming, and tossed among the treetops little spills of burning metal. We crouched closer to earth.

The mortar bombs smacked on the ridgetop. The heavies pounded Lambeti. The machine guns fired in quick, nervous bursts. A dead man lay in a bush.

Battlefield.

Twenty-one days had passed since the Higgins boats charged East Beach at the start of a nine-day schedule of reconquest. Munda still held on.

By now I was very tired. I had been told about a Japanese patrol that had clubbed to death American wounded lying on litters in foxholes near the Bariki River. I had gone forward, interviewed survivors of the massacre, seen the mutilated, pathetic dead sprawled in the blood-stained leaf mold of the forest floor. I resolved to write about it – with every bloody, depraved, savage detail complete. I was going to write:

Every word of this story is true and I'm writing it to rouse hate. You can't fight this war without hate. If you don't hate enough, you're going to be beaten.

You can't fight this war without killing – and being killed.

You can't fight this war comfortably or complacently – neither here on New Georgia nor there at home.

If you were ever justified in your decision to begin fighting it, then nothing can ever justify your surrender.

You cannot bargain. If the defense of democracy and liberty and your own way of living is worth the sacrifice of the life of one man, then it is worth the sacrifice of the life of every man down to the very last.

Only such wholeness and singleness of purpose in the defense of a principle can give reason to what I have seen and heard on the battlefield before Munda.

But I did not write it – until now.

On July 21, I returned to Rendova and sought orders to return to Guadalcanal, as it was apparent the New Georgia campaign could not be concluded for many weeks and the character of the fighting could not substantially change. On the other hand, the war in the air and at sea was likely to fluctuate and might easily produce events of great importance.

The last I saw of New Georgia was a patrol of leopard-suited men wading through the muddy water along the Zanana foreshore. Each carried a tommy gun tucked under his arm. Each was mud streaked, sweat stained, soul weary.

In a winding double line the soldiers shuffled against a background of mangroves. Behind the jungle above them, the cone of Kolombangara's volcano stood up in the clear sky. Mountain and forest, swamp and sea – and men dressed to look like beasts of the wilderness . . .

In that moment of departure I experienced a flash of awareness. Somehow the impressions of 17 months were summarized in a brief minute.

At five o'clock that afternoon I boarded a tank landing ship with its nose on the beach at Bau. Ten minutes later the shipping in the harbour was attacked by a large group of Japanese dive bombers that had evaded the fighter patrol. Four men stood beside me in the wheelhouse. We listened to the guns and the whistle of falling bombs. A 500-pound bomb struck the ship aft. It penetrated several decks and exploded.

The four men are dead. I am now walking again.

Why those four men should have died and I live and walk, I do not know. But I know this. The living have the cause of the dead in trust. The cause of the dead was the defense of what they believed to be truth and justice and decency. There can be no end to the story until what they believed to be truth and justice and decency is secure in the world of the living.

THE END